THE WAKE OF WAR

THE WAKE OF WAR

Encounters with the People of Iraq and Afghanistan

ANNE NIVAT

translated from the French by Jane Marie Todd

BEACON PRESS
Boston

BEACON PRESS
25 Beacon Street
Boston, Massachusetts 02108-2892
www.beacon.org

Beacon Press books
are published under the auspices of
the Unitarian Universalist Association of Congregations.

08 07 06 05   8 7 6 5 4 3 2 1

This book is printed on acid-free paper that meets the uncoated paper
ANSI/NISO specifications for permanence as revised in 1992.

Text design by Patricia Duque Campos
Composition by Wilsted & Taylor Publishing Services

Library of Congress Cataloging-in-Publication Data

Nivat, Anne.
   [Lendemains de guerre. English]
   The wake of war : encounters with the people of iraq and afghanistan / Anne Nivat ; translated
from the French by Jane Marie Todd.
      p. cm.
   Includes bibliographical references.
   ISBN 0-8070-0240-2 (cloth : alk. paper)
   1. Afghanistan—History—2001– 2. Iraq—History—2003–   I. Todd, Jane Marie II. Title.

DS371.4.N5813 2005
956.7044'31–dc22   2005011586

First published in France under the title *Lendemains de guerre: en Afghanistan et en Irak* by Librairie
Arthème Fayard.

TO LUCILE, MY MOTHER,
who so loves nuance and detail

CONTENTS

PART II
In Afghanistan, after the U.S. Military Victory of December 2001

Introduction

On September 11, 2001, I found myself in the company of seventy-four passengers, most of them Americans, aboard a plane flying from Paris to New York. The aircraft, already too far out over the Atlantic to turn back, was diverted by international air authorities to Halifax, Nova Scotia. There we stayed for nearly fourteen hours, without anyone bothering to inform us of the catastrophe in New York and at the Pentagon. The locked doors and the stress, combined with the lack of an explanation, gave rise to countless rumors. When we finally learned the horror of the crashing planes and the collapsed towers—one of the passengers heard it from someone on his cell phone, which, miraculously, was still working—some of the women burst into tears, and most of the other passengers shook their heads or shrugged their shoulders, forced to believe the unbelievable. The whole world was watching the tragic images being transmitted in a running loop by every television channel. And there we were, locked in a metal cabin at a remote airport, waiting—in some sense, outside time.

"One thing's for sure, it's the work of the Palestinians," some decreed, rather too quickly. "Or else of Saddam Hussein," said others. I no longer remember whether the name Osama bin Laden came up in our aimless discussions. In any case, the United States had been attacked on its own soil, and that is how the American citizens aboard our plane felt. An oppressive silence gradually set in in our restricted space. Water and food had to be rationed until the Canadian authorities, obviously overwhelmed, could bring in fresh supplies.

The response to that terrible attack was not long in coming: the war in Afghanistan drove out the Taliban, fundamentalist extremists with no respect for human rights who had welcomed Osama bin Laden, the terrorist the United States vowed to eliminate. Less than a month later, the Taliban were no longer in power, but Osama bin Laden had fled for parts unknown. Four years have gone by, and the Saudi terrorist still has not been arrested.

On March 20, 2003, soon after the second Gulf war broke out, I found myself working as a reporter in the Tajik enclave of Vorukh, Kyrgyzstan, in the former Soviet regions of central Asia. I had just spent the night at the home of the mullah Abubakhiddin. The previous day, the grumpy old Tajik had given me a rather poor welcome, making me wait outside his door before finally allowing me in. A few hours later, he swore to me in Russian that the dirty war taking shape in Iraq had put him in a particularly bad mood. He railed against Westerners' incomprehension of Islam, the cause, in his view, of all the present ills on the planet. "When I read the Koran, I start to cry and tell myself: how is that possible?" he said with a sigh. "All that chaos, the barbarism in this corrupt world, the mutual lack of comprehension, the lack of kindness between people, the manifestations of envy among men that lead to acts of terror. . . . How are we going to get away from that?"

Why was he so affected by that new war? Because Abubakhiddin had spent eight years in Baghdad as an interpreter for a Russian company (he had learned Arabic in a local madrasa, a Koranic school) and could not resign himself to the sight of the bombs and lethal missiles whose trails of smoke he had contemplated all night on his television screen in his cob house. "The American invasion won't settle any of the problems; on the contrary, it will multiply them," he repeated constantly.

I tossed and turned for many hours at the old mullah's house, unable to fall asleep on my mattress on the floor, situated above a root cellar whose slightly rotten odor was making me ill. It was that night that I decided to go to Iraq and Afghanistan, once the major military maneuvers and the media circus were over. I had to make sure that those voices "from under the ruins" were heard—the words of the women and men who live there, whereas we journalists, humanitarian soldiers, merely pass through.

Afghanistan, fall 2001. Iraq, spring 2003. Two different countries but the same war, bearing a dual label: on one hand, the American and allied operation against "international terrorism" in reaction to the catastrophe of September 11, 2001; on the other hand, a crusade to "liberate" oppressed peoples. In the aftermath of the military actions, the operation against "international terrorism" is still awaiting its legitimation. As for the crusade, once it has been acknowledged that the real power of the Taliban in Afghanistan and of Saddam Hussein in Iraq has been taken away, the "liberation invasion" raises many questions. What were the men and women of Afghanistan and Iraq feeling in their everyday lives? Had they all suffered under their respective dictatorship? Did they feel relieved? Has the West, in its rush to impose its democracy and its values, in any way convinced them that these values are legitimate?

My wish to ask those questions of the parties most directly affected led me to go to the two countries following the military interventions, which, though easily won, have had long-term consequences that are hard to make sense of.

It is not so difficult to go out into the field, forgo any immediate income, take one's time, and travel by the existing modes of transportation. That is the best situation for sharing with the people of the country genuine and intense moments of trust.

For the most part, I went by bus: the bus system is still operational, even though the country (be it Iraq or Afghanistan) is in the grip of complete chaos and there is sporadic potable water or electricity. But I also sometimes took group taxis. Those two methods of getting around are as common in Afghanistan as they are in Iraq.

I spent twelve weeks at a stretch in each country, questioning hundreds of people who live there, who love their home, and who are trying to continue living despite the chaos that has reigned there since the military interventions. I lived among them, dressed like them (wearing a blue burka* in the Afghan countryside and a black *abaya* [a veil] in the Iraqi desert), and shared their homes and their meals (hospitality is a primordial characteristic the two societies share). In some sense, the interviews I conducted speak for themselves, and the variety of interlocutors my travels afforded me (from north to south in each country) culminated in an exposition of the human problems there by means other than political, economic, or sociological research. In the first place, I wanted to give a voice to those who do not have one; above all, however, I confined myself to listening to them with an open mind.

In the countryside and in remote villages, trust is still almost intact; the joy of entertaining a passing stranger is unequaled. Sometimes, however, especially in the capital cities, where all the residents are at odds with themselves and seem lost at the prospect of an uncertain future, it was fairly difficult to find acceptance for my way of working. Whenever I found myself dealing with an "official," his first question invariably was "What newspaper are you working for?" the implication being, "Whom do you represent?" and, of course, "Who is paying you?" I had to reply to one and all that I represented "nothing and no one." In the end, I almost always gave preference to nonofficials, whom I had only to ask a few preliminary and banal questions to initiate an authentic dialogue. And I almost always had the impression—as in the Chechen mountains, the steppes of the Pamirs, the central Asian valley of Fergana, the remote *qalas* of central Afghanistan, the suburbs of Peshawar, and the arid plains of the "Sunni triangle" in Iraq[1]—that people were speaking to me from the bottom of their hearts.

---

*The burka is a full veil that covers even the woman's face, leaving only a narrow and uncomfortable mesh peephole, whereas the chador is a veil concealing the entire body and hair but leaves the face uncovered.

PART I

In Iraq,
after the U.S. Military Victory of April 2003

I

THE PROSCENIUM

Feeling only half content, I sip a cup of tea in a cafeteria in the center of Diyarbakir, the capital of Turkish Kurdistan. The pale light, the cloudbursts, the concrete blocks of buildings from the 1970s: all that grayness hems me in and oppresses me. Behind the curtain of rain, I perceive a black basalt mosque, one of the oldest in Turkish territory, and a piece of the fortification that has surrounded the city like a prison for a century and a half. It's the longest structure of its kind after the Great Wall of China; the people of the country boast that it stretches four miles. The sparkling Tigris, which I'll find again in Iraq, is meandering a few feet below.

Murat is a young Turkish novelist married to a Kurdish woman, who has come to Diyarbakir "to live as a writer." According to him, though the Kurdish people of Turkey value their own identity, "they would not be prepared to lose Istanbul or Izmir for anything in the world." Murat, the son of Communist teachers from Izmir, considers the Chechnen independence fighter Shamil Basayev a hero. Murat believes the situation of the Kurds has improved since the arrest of Abdullah Ocalan, leader of the Kurdistan Workers' Party (PKK), and his "collaboration" with the authorities in Ankara. Nevertheless, their rights, especially regarding their language and culture, are not always recognized by the constitution. Mavi, his young wife, is a medical student. She spends hours lying on the living room couch devouring Turkish translations of Gilles Deleuze and Michel Foucault while Murat, seated at his computer, translates editorials from English-language newspapers for the leftist daily *Radikal.* They hope to return in a few

months to live in Istanbul, where Mavi will set up her pharmacy and
Murat will continue writing his novels.

To get from Diyarbakir to the Iraqi border, we must first drive for
dozens of miles along the border of Turkey and Syria. On the Turkish side, there are many observation posts. Planted in the ground every hundred yards, they overlook a fenced-off no-man's-land. On the
road, we pass dozens of enormous trucks from Iraq transporting heavy
loads of gasoline. Everything is gray and muddy. The villages we pass
through seem empty, ghostly. Dismal market stalls selling spare parts
for trucks alternate with the many tire repair shops. Hung by Kurdish
women on lines strung between two concrete blocks, the multicolored
laundry of large families strikes a happier note. On the south side of the
border road, the Syrian plain, mysterious and majestic, invites us into
the Middle Eastern universe. And before us, to the north, the snow-
covered peaks on the eastern edge of Turkey, along with those of the
Caucasus and northwest Iran, rise in a halo of snow.

On the border, several hundred heavy trucks, standing quietly in
three lines stretching for some six miles, wait to cross from Turkey to
Iraq. Once they have been resupplied with black gold, they'll come
back to Turkey to refine their cargo, then return to the land between
the two rivers to sell their precious liquid. Ever since U.S. bombs damaged refineries in northern Iraq, that lucrative activity has moved to
eastern Turkey.

We pass all the trucks and come to a charming Turkish border
guard, who expresses himself in perfect English ("I spent several years
in the United States," he has time to boast) and even speaks broken
French. Barely looking at my passport, he authorizes us to pass with a
broad gesture. But that's only the first in a long list of procedures. I
must now find my way through the complex maze of the customs for-
malities required by Turkish authorities. First there are the soldiers:
they search my bag from top to bottom, seem very interested in my
maps of Iraq, and finally ask me to leave my business card (it's better to
have one!). Then it's time for the secret service agents, who vaguely try
to conceal their function. Finally, I find myself before the passport police. Clearly, they've decided to prolong their coffee break. The officers

simply turn their backs to the mob of weary-looking travelers, who hold photocopies of their passports in their hands.

Relieved of these fussy procedures that have lasted a mere two and a half hours, I walk a few hundred yards along an empty road and find myself in front of a dilapidated building, where three veiled women, rapt, are watching a television screen blasting in Kurdish. I see by the lopsided plastic clock hanging on the wall that it is an hour later than on my watch. So I really am in Iraq, or rather, as attested by the unstamped sheet of paper inserted into my passport by a customs agent with a large mustache, I am in the autonomous territory of Iraqi Kurdistan.

2

En Route to Erbil

At the bus station next to customs, there is no trace of the young Kurdish student who was supposed to be waiting for me. I have to make a decision. I choose to take a taxi to Erbil, the administrative capital of autonomous Kurdistan. Taïger, a local driver, was formerly a teacher. We agree on a price for the trip: thirty-five dollars (Erbil is more than 125 miles away). For the four hours the trip takes, Taïger, while driving at top speed, takes pleasure in sharing with me a few details of his life. At forty, though barely five years older than I (I would have said he was fifteen), he is the father of eight children, five of them sons. His grandfather came from Turkey, but, he acknowledges, "at the time, the borders weren't the same." Kurdish is his native language, and he also speaks fluent Arabic and a little English. He hates Turkey (every time we go by a Turkish truck, he points it out to me with the greatest contempt), which is guilty of mistreating the Kurds and of scheming against Kurdistan's independence. But what is his view of things more generally? "The main problem with Iraq is that all its neighbors want to see harm come to it. For Turkey, it's because of the Kurdish question—but as soon as trade comes up, oddly enough, tensions ease. Iran, our rich neighbor, has been an enemy from time immemorial. Syria goes its own way in an effort to attract the good graces of the Americans. Kuwait, along with Saudi Arabia, claims to be fighting international terrorism but is not acting aboveboard. Here in the north, we are more or less left alone for the moment, but our independence is far from certain."

The only consolation for him is the autonomy agreement for the three Kurdish regions, obtained in 1992,[1] which considerably improved living conditions. Taïger proudly points out that for twelve years the language of instruction in the schools and at the university has been Kurdish, but he recognizes that the level has "fallen a great deal" since the 1970s, when Iraq was considered one of the most forward-looking countries in the Arab world in education.

The former teacher declares he loves his country, Iraq, but he feels Kurdish first and foremost.[2] He has not forgotten the hard, humiliating years of Saddam's intensive "Arabization" campaign in the north. "We Kurds," he insists, "demand nothing in particular; we do not want Baghdad or even Kirkuk, which everyone is already fighting for. But we want to be left to live in peace. The little countries are an annoyance to their powerful neighbors, everyone knows that! The notion of 'democracy' varies from country to country, and there's nothing more amusing for Iraqi Kurds than to observe Turkey's gesticulations as it tries to pass for a democratic state. Even the United States is a proponent of a dual policy: they're democrats at home but become maniacal imperialists wherever it serves their economic interests. No one knows exactly what's in store for Iraq, even less for the Kurds," he explains, clutching his steering wheel. "I'd give anything to leave this country and try my chances elsewhere, in Europe, for example, where I have a few cousins. But how can I get there without a passport?"

Taïger shows me some ruins on the right side of the asphalt road crossing a vast plain, still soaking wet from winter downpours: "It's my childhood home; Saddam razed the village and replaced it with another, built in the late 1980s by and for Arabs—soldiers, to be more precise. That's what the Arabization policy that the Baathist regime conducted meant at a concrete level." He falls silent, lost in his memories.

We stop for lunch in Mosul, a concrete megalopolis, where, all things considered, I do not feel so far away from our ultraurbanized Western societies. The Iraqi highway system is in excellent shape; I encounter nothing like the difficulties I will have getting around in Afghanistan. In the nearby shops, restaurants, and transportation services, men nonchalantly attend to their business (a waiter earns three hundred dollars a month, versus sixteen for a teacher, Taïger remarks).

Women in black chadors, rushing across the street, pull their children by the sleeve and try not to get splashed by the speeding vehicles. Life does not stop at prayer time as it will in Afghanistan.

At nightfall, I register at the Dim-Dim Hotel in Erbil, whose vast lobby is decorated with imitation gilt, a few faux-crystal ceiling lights, and floor lamps shaped like palm trees. I am not out of my element: this temple in bad taste reminds me of the aesthetic values of the Russian nouveaux riches. Globalization requires it! In my room, I will have to click my TV remote control for close to ten minutes to find a continuous news channel; the thirty or so stations on which my remote control seemed to be getting stuck spew pornographic programs in the European language of my choice.

3

A KURDISH FAMILY

Bilal is twenty-five years old and the eldest of eight children (five boys and three girls). Having studied English for four years, he supports his brothers, sisters, and parents, who live in Kura, one of the poor neighborhoods on the western periphery of Erbil, almost at the edge of the Assyrian neighborhood.[1] Against his father's advice, one of his younger brothers, Oumet, managed to find refuge in Cardiff, Wales, three years earlier. Ever since his brother began sending money home on a regular basis, Bilal, who is ashamed of his neighborhood, has intensely wanted to move to a more "respectable" section in the center of the city. His father takes no notice. But as an eldest son who earns his own living and shares his modest income with the other members of the household, Bilal has some say in the matter. That's why he's planted a "For Sale" sign outside the gate to the courtyard.

His father is sixty-seven years old, a former police officer whose mother tongue is Kurdish and who has nearly forgotten his Arabic for lack of practice. According to what Bilal has told me, his parents are unable to understand the television channels in classical Arabic, whereas for him Arabic is like a mother tongue. He is even proud of his knowledge of Arabic, a rare feat in Kurdish territory. There are only three rooms in the humble and dilapidated concrete house—four if you count the cob outbuilding next to the henhouse that Bilal's father insisted on building for himself in the backyard. On the pretext that he sleeps poorly, he stubbornly refuses to spend the night in materials that—though certainly more noble—are not natural. That extra room only adds to the humiliation Bilal feels at having parents who don't know how to live any differently from their ancestors.

But he has another good reason to move: there are constant electrical outages. This morning, the electricity was on from five o'clock to seven thirty; it will not come back until midnight. Bilal is particularly upset. Glued to the screen of his satellite television, he surfs his favorite Arabic channels every day for nearly three hours. These are Al-Jazeera[2] and Al-Arabiya, but also the BBC, Euronews, and Western sports channels. In addition, without electricity kerosene lamps are needed to stay warm in the winter. Most are manufactured in Iran and sell for 350 dinars (a few cents) at the market.

There is also no water at certain hours of the day, since the pump for the closest well operates with electricity. But an ingenious subterranean network built by the neighborhood community has remedied that, and, not far from the entrance and the toilet, water is spurting up, practically warm, from a faucet located at ground level in the yard.

Bilal's family moved here twenty years ago, when Bilal was five. He has not forgotten the war with Iran: "One summer night, while we were all sleeping in the garden [if you can call a garden that twelve-by-eighteen-foot rectangular space circumscribed by the yard, where a single tree grows], we were awakened by bombers flying very low. I can still see their convex bellies, their heavy bodies. We dived into a kind of trench that my father had dug with his pickax and used that as a shelter."

Erbil is huge and flat, as if it has been crushed by its citadel, whose thick stone walls block the view of the plain at about fifty yards. The city's major arteries are made of concrete, and in the "rich" neighborhoods two- and three-story structures stand unfinished. By contrast, all the houses of poor people, whose children play miniature soccer in the middle of the street, are on one level.

At the restaurant where I take Bilal, we find ourselves in the "family room," separated by a curtain from the main room, that is, from the men, as in Iran. As Bilal goes straight for the usual appetizers (olives, onions, soup, salads with lemon) brought by the waiters in small saucers, he tells me that he has never eaten hummus, the traditional Middle Eastern chickpea paste, an Arab dish par excellence. Though frequently served in Europe in Middle Eastern restaurants, it is unknown in Iraqi Kurdistan.

The streets and shops are peopled exclusively by men, and the young women my age are soberly dressed in long, full skirts and sometimes in loose trousers and tunics. Over their hair they have pulled a head scarf, casually knotted at the back of the neck, almost like in Chechnya (where it is more a formality than an obligation). By contrast, the older women are concealed under a black *abaya,* the long "Iranian-style" veil covering the body from head to toe, though not concealing the face. Under my dark head scarf, I do not feel observed as I will in Afghanistan, though I sometimes arouse curiosity when people hear me speak English.

At nightfall, the many checkpoints in the central city cause delays, as motorists are obliged to stop and wait in line to have their vehicles searched. Then suddenly, surging out of the darkness, come the handsome faces of Kurds in camouflage, their Kalashnikovs slung over their shoulders. They are the militia of Massoud Barzani's KDP (Kurdistan Democratic Party), which controls the region. As each driver approaches the checkpoint, he slows down and opens his window. The soldier leans in and gives the travelers the once-over, then signals the driver to go on. These checkpoints do not seem very convincing to me, but Bilal believes the militiamen can distinguish a terrorist from a respectable person. "If you're well dressed and look calm, you can't be transporting TNT to blow yourself up," he declares.

In the city center, which has huge traffic jams, since several streets adjacent to the seat of government were closed to traffic (they were the target of an attack in December 2003), the atmosphere is close to panicky. For several months, a French institute and many other nongovernment organizations have had their doors closed to the public after realizing that in the event of a suicide attack, the safety of visitors was not guaranteed.

Although he is rather ashamed of his father, Bilal is proud of his younger brother Oumet, who had no hesitation in going through Iran to get to Turkey, where he stayed locked in a hotel room for three months for fear of being arrested. Then he spent nearly eight months in Greece, including three in prison for "illegally crossing the border." After that, he went to Italy, where he was robbed of a thousand dollars,

and finally to France. He could have stayed in France, but he preferred
Great Britain. He shares his apartment with two Sudanese men and has
never complained about his new life. For Bilal, Oumet is a model of
courage and perseverance. The young man, who cannot afford a cell
phone, periodically goes to the post office and pays four dollars a minute
to be able to hear his admired brother's voice.

"They certainly got rid of one Saddam for us, but there are still two
left!" Bilal notes sarcastically, referring to the leaders of the KDP and
the PUK (Patriotic Union of Kurdistan). These two leaders remain
popular, but residents criticize them for getting rich illegally, and in
particular for pocketing the many dividends of the UN's Oil-for-Food
Program over the last ten years, as well as the enormous revenues in
customs duties from Turkey, Iran, and Syria, which their extended families divide between them. Deeply affected by the "civil war" of 1994–
1998, which followed the 1991 insurrection, Bilal, like a majority of
Kurds, ardently wants the two main parties of his country to finally establish a lasting peace and form a united government. Having two administrations on such a cramped piece of land makes little sense, and
the political enmity between the two leaders undermines the credibility of the Kurdish cause throughout the world.

Bilal would be tempted to believe in the promises the United States
made, especially Paul Bremer, who in 2003 was named the administrator by President George Bush. Bremer has loudly declared that the
recent events, especially the notable absence of an Iraqi state, ought to
make it easier for the Kurds to definitively create their own state. Bilal
has heard commentators, and also Iraqi politicians in the Governing
Council, cite "the autonomous democratic Kurdistan" as a shining example and call it a pocket of security in contrast to the rest of the country.[3] He is bursting with pride about that.

At the foot of the citadel, a few vendors sell laminated maps of "Greater
Kurdistan," which encompasses the geographic zones peopled by
Kurds in Syria, Iraq, Iran, and Turkey, as well as a few maps of Iraq. At
a sharp bend in a road, we notice people crowding around folding ta-

bles. Behind them streamers wave, bearing the words "If you want to participate in the future of Kurdistan, sign up here!" A few hours ago, the petition in question (its title is "For a Referendum on Kurdistan") was signed by all the ethnic groups of the country, as the young volunteer manning the stand excitedly announces. Some petitioners, not knowing how to sign their names—or perhaps wanting to emphasize their willingness to make sacrifices—simply pressed a blood-stained thumb on the page. For the young militant, Kurdistan's independence is a way for the country to differentiate itself from the Arabs while continuing to be part of Iraq. "For decades, the Kurds have struggled for their right to self-determination," he says with conviction. "Now that Saddam is no longer in power in Baghdad, we owe it to ourselves to determine our own future."

The organization committee for the Kurdistan referendum will claim it collected nearly two million signatures in the cities, towns, and villages of the region, only a few days after the document (the idea for which came from local universities and teachers) was taken around to all the large localities. It will be sent to important figures such as Kofi Annan, secretary-general of the UN, the high commissioner for human rights, and George W. Bush, as well as to the Kurdistan parliament and even members of the Iraqi Governing Council (IGC).

The referendum calls for allowing the Kurds to define the form their future relationship with the Iraqi state will take. Three possibilities might be offered to them: total independence as a sovereign state; an American-style federal system based on existing government structures (the option preferred by the Governing Council); or a geographic, not to say ethnic, federalism, which would turn Kurdistan territory into a single federal union (the option least favored by the United States).

This concept of "geographic federalism," which the Kurdish parliament agreed to back in 1992, sidestepped many problems that are now reappearing with the fall of Saddam Hussein. Take, for example, the city of Kirkuk. For historical and geographic reasons, the Kurds have always considered the oil-rich metropolis their own. Yet Kirkuk is located just outside the Kurdish administrative region, which encompasses the provinces of Erbil, Sulaimaniya, and Dohuk and has always been inhabited by large numbers of Turkomans, Arabs, and various Christian minorities. To complicate it all, the last years of the formidable "Arabization" campaign conducted by the dictatorial regime in Baghdad radically altered the demographic balance of the zone, swelling the number of Arab colonists and forcing the other ethnic groups to leave. How will the problem of Kirkuk's identity be settled?

If Bilal has finally agreed to have me interview his father, especially about his past as a *peshmerga* (a Kurdish independence fighter), it is because, fundamentally, he does not repudiate his deep Kurdish roots, even if his parents' way of life is difficult for him. He takes very seriously his role as interpreter as we talk, seated on the floor of his father's room, and even yields to my request to refrain from intervening. His restraint, however, does not stem from a lack of desire on his part!

"I was born in Hiran in 1935," the old Kurd recounts, "a village not far from Shaqlawa in the mountains north of Erbil, near the Turkish border. I left the village at twenty-nine, never having gone to school, since there was none. I would so much have loved to get an education, but my father refused to send us to school in the neighboring village, which was more than ten kilometers [six miles] away. He would have had to pay for transportation; and then, hands were needed at home. My father, a farmer and shepherd, died when I was ten years old. He had ten children and two different wives. I'm the seventh in the birth order. My elder brother was fifteen when he took charge of the household. At thirteen, I began to work as a shepherd. I also took care of the fruit orchard, especially the pomegranate trees, whose fleshy red berries we occasionally sold on the Erbil market. I learned Arabic during my military service in the Royal Guard from 1956 to 1958; the officers spoke only Arabic. Ours was a mounted guard, and I was responsible for two horses. It seemed to me that our ruler, Faisal II, was extremely popular and well respected.

"Next came Kassem,[4] a socialist. At the time, people didn't distinguish so much between Kurds and Arabs, and there were more Arabs in the north. With the return of Mullah Mustafa Barzani and the Soviet Union, things deteriorated and the war against the Kurds erupted.[5] In the meantime, I had returned to the village, where I resumed family farming activities. In 1970 I also joined the police force, thanks to the intervention of a friend who knew the local police chief. The conflict between the *peshmerga* and Iraqi law enforcement was at its peak, but I needed the salary because my first wife was very ill. I had barely joined the ranks of the police when our entire bureau deserted and joined the underground controlled by Mullah Mustafa Barzani. We didn't have Kalashnikovs yet, only old light weapons dating from the British period. Our supplies, though insufficient, came in regularly, but we lacked heavy weapons. Our struggle lasted until the Algiers accords, which sealed our defeat.[6] In the meantime, for lack of medicine my first wife had succumbed to her illness, and I remarried.

"Then began the exodus of the former 'freedom fighters' to Iran, despite the Shah's efforts to prevent us and the measures taken by the Baghdad government to get us to come back to Iraq. With my second wife and our two eldest children,* we went to a camp of Kurdish refugees in the mountains of northwestern Iran, near Ziveh.[7] We were so annoyed by these agreements that we threw our weapons into the river. That defeat sticks in our craw to this day.

"We spent six months in that camp in the company of more than a thousand other families, firmly convinced that when we returned to our country it would be to continue and finish our revolution. One day, the Iranian authorities in the camp, which was administered by the international Red Cross, asked me if I wanted to seek exile in the United States. At the time, that was still possible. I categorically refused, because my elderly mother was still alive in the village and I had to return there." (At this point in the story, I sense a twinge of regret in the father's voice and enormous disappointment on the part of Bilal, who surely would have liked to be born in the United States.) "Shortly thereafter, I received three alarming letters from my mother, and I made the decision to return home. We left in military trucks chartered by the Iraqi government.

---

*An elder brother of Bilal's, who was born in 1971 and died in a work-site accident in 1995; and his elder sister, now married.

"I had been naive to believe that everything would come off without a hitch. Hardly had I set foot on Iraqi soil than I was exiled to the south, not far from the border with Saudi Arabia, where I remained for nearly a year, unable to get news to my family. The Baathists, who had taken power, exiled all Kurds for fear they'd continue their revolution. My wife stayed in Erbil with our two children. In Baghdad we were exhibited like livestock before a public that mocked us with applause. We barely avoided being lynched. Then we were transferred to Diwaniyah (in the south). Our torturers called us traitors. They wanted to know how many Iraqi soldiers we had killed and where the weapons came from. In the end, I was placed under house arrest with nine other former fighters (four from Erbil and six from Sulaimaniya) in the town of Ash Shabakah, in the middle of the desert.

"Even as a minority, even in their hands, I felt the Arabs feared the Kurds, and that made me proud. Not knowing what else to do with us, they recruited us as police officers. In fact, that was the best way to keep an eye on us, in that oasis rising from the desert, where it was impossible to flee without being immediately spotted on the only road linking us to An Najaf, the chief town of the province. I thought I'd never see my wife again. Every day I was afraid it would be my last. In addition, three months had gone by and we still hadn't been paid our salary. I was elected representative of my fellow sufferers. I went to talk to our boss, who laughed in my face and advised us to go ask for that salary from 'Mullah Mustafa'! After we'd made that demand, they took away our weapons, believing we might be dangerous."

After a few months, the ten exiled men were finally allowed to return home. Bilal's father jumped on a bus heading north. On January 12, 1978, he returned to Erbil, and family life resumed. During the decade-long war against Iran, he did not fight but instead worked in construction. After the proclamation of Kurdish autonomy, and three months away from a well-deserved retirement, he was reinstated in the police force, like most of the former *peshmerga*.

The old man remembers with emotion the visit by Danielle Mitterrand, the wife of the late French president François Mitterrand, who is considered in the region the "mother of all Kurds," one of the few personalities in the Western world to have taken up the cause of the people. Today he's sorry he fought so hard and gave so much to the Kurdish cause "for nothing." "I'm still proud to be a Kurd, and I feel freer today than I did fifteen years ago, but I know that the idea of a federal Iraqi state or of some sort of independence for Kurdistan is rather illusory. We've already lost so many opportunities to organize ourselves into an independent state!"

The end of Saddam's regime and the unsettled period that has followed are of no value to the former police officer. "For us, Saddam Hussein was worse than Hitler, who did not use chemical weapons on the Jews of Germany [he does not mention gas chambers]. If the United States is the policeman of the world, as is claimed, why don't they act definitively on our behalf? They helped us liberate ourselves from Saddam; they must now come to our aid to establish the border between us and the Arabs.[8] If we had our own borders as a sovereign state, we'd be more respected by Turkey, Syria, and Iran. I don't expect total and immediate independence, but we need to set in place a system, federal or not, that guarantees our intangible right not to depend on Baghdad." His language is even tinged with xenophobia when he champions, as a first solution, the repatriation of the Kurds established in southern Iraq "to here in the north" and the expulsion of "all Arabs who are in our territory." And though he is aware of the catastrophe that a potential conflict with U.S. forces would produce, he doesn't hesitate to envision a "cooling" of their relationship if the Kurds perceive that their "ally" does not support them as much as they would like.

The ice is definitely broken between Bilal and me, and the young man, though timid, confides in me how painful the burdensome customs associated with marriage are for him. The ceremony in itself costs the fiancé's family a great deal, of course, but there is something else entirely: Bilal dreams of marrying for love. He doesn't want his parents to choose his future wife and has even made his choice, a neighbor's daughter, with whom he is secretly in love. She is twenty-one, and they met seven years ago, on the vacant lot used as a playing field by the neighborhood children. But because of these "stupid" customs, it turns

out she is betrothed to one of her cousins, considered a "catch," and he
cannot even speak to her openly anymore, since her parents forbid it.

He could ask them for his beloved's hand and raise his level of education, which would allow him to work with foreigners, hence to earn
money in dollars. But they would refuse him all the same. The girls he
has met thus far at the university were "too overbearing," or he was
ashamed to bring them to this house he hates, on the outskirts of the
city, and to introduce them to his parents.

Bilal is at his wit's end.

After "greater *Īd,*" the Feast of Sacrifice, which he will spend with
his family, Bilal intends to go to Mosul[9] to get on a list of potential
translators being recruited by the U.S. Army. The monthly salary of
five hundred dollars, a significant sum, which his family needs, tempts
him, but his parents—along with his brother who has settled in Great
Britain—refuse to let him go. They argue that as the eldest son, his
place is at home, and that working for the U.S. Army could prove dangerous. Not particularly reckless, Bilal has also explained to me that if
it meant patrolling with soldiers in armored vehicles and sharing their
military life, he would not be interested—because of the danger, of
course, but especially because Bilal profoundly distrusts those ignorant
soldiers who never miss an opportunity to express their contempt for
the people of the country. And that, the fragile but proud Bilal could
not bear.

Even though he has a college degree, Bilal has never left autonomous
Kurdistan and has never even been to Baghdad. He is full of received
notions about the famous "Sunni triangle," where he enjoins me not to
go. Conversely, his mother, illiterate but cunning, assures me that if I
cover myself with an *abaya* I'll be safe there.

4

A YOUNG LEADER

Khaffour Mahmouri is a thirty-five-year-old historian and the author of seven books, including a historical work published in Erbil in 2001 on "the risks and consequences of Arabization in Kurdistan from the eighth century to the present." Born in a village near Mahmour at the far edge of Erbil Province, he lived there until 1988, when agents of the dreaded Mukhabarat (Iraqi secret service) arrested him. He was eighteen years old at the time, a young journalist advocating Kurdish independence. Five months later, when he got out of prison, he became a contributor to the official newspaper of Massoud Barzani's Kurdistan Democratic Party. On March 21, 1991, the fierce anti-Kurdish repression that followed the Shiite intifada led him to create his own party, the Kurdistan National Democratic Union (KNDU), with ties to the influential KDP.

On January 13, 2001, he launched the Committee to End Arabization, whose aim was to denounce the spoliation brought about by that unjust practice. At present he wants to organize a conference by assembling researchers and university professors of various persuasions, including Arabs and Kurds of the diaspora, to prevent potential "Arab chauvinists" from coming to power in Baghdad and perpetuating Arabization.

"I recently talked with one of the political advisers of the Iraqi Governing Council[1]—set in place by the United States—whom we had asked for help in reclaiming a number of properties. They promised to start looking into the problem, but I don't see any help forthcoming. The Americans are swamped by our demands. We have come to understand they won't help us, since they refuse to get involved in Iraqi internecine quarrels. According to them, the Arabs must stay where they are, since Iraq belongs to 'all Iraqis,' it's our common homeland. I had to make them understand that without their help we would have to find a solution on our own."

The Arabization policy that Saddam Hussein and his government conducted for more than thirty years, with the aim of changing the demographic balance of the oil-rich regions of the country in favor of the Arabs, comprised two parts. First, the Baath Party deported Kurds en masse and replaced them with Arabs. Second, the central government of Baghdad distributed lands in the northern part of the country to Arabs, to entice them to settle there. As a result of the first initiative, entire villages were destroyed.[2] The rebuilt villages were then given Arab names. Until the 2003 war, the Kurds who had been forced to leave their lands could not return to their villages. Now several tens of thousands of them want to move back to their traditional territories. It has reached the point where the humanitarian agencies and nongovernment organizations specializing in population movements are overwhelmed.

The reclamation of lands is therefore the number-one problem. The first step may be to open offices in various cities of Kurdistan where reclamation request forms would be distributed. After an analysis of the applications, determinations would be made by an investigatory committee, but every plaintiff would have to provide proof of ownership. In cases that cannot not be resolved satisfactorily, financial compensation ought to be provided. Aid to rebuild villages is still the source of endless debates, beginning with the many controversies surrounding the "green line" that separated the territory administered by Saddam's regime and that of the Kurdistan regional government (KRG).

Take the example of Mahmour. An hour's drive south of Erbil and Mosul, Mahmour District is part of the Erbil governorate controlled by the KRG since 1991, but the city of Mahmour is located south of that green line. According to the coalition provisional authority (CPA) controlled by the U.S. administration, the city of Mahmour is thus a dependency of Mosul and Nineveh Provinces. Nevertheless, the Kurdish government based in Erbil has never considered the green line anything other than a figment of Saddam Hussein's imagination, hence devoid of any legal value, and it countered that the city has always been its responsibility, since its populations are Kurdish. It therefore offers its help.

The coalition provisional authority has replied that such aid ought to be lavished on "internally displaced persons" (IDP), that is, those inside the borders of the autonomous Kurdish governorate, and has called a halt to these charitable intentions. It is particularly adamant about respecting the administrative borders that were valid when it occupied the country. It embraces the status quo ante and has shifted the responsibility for abolishing the famous green line—hence for creating new administrative borders—to the new Iraqi government that is supposed to be set up after the 2005 elections.

Nevertheless, the authorities in place in Baghdad agree that the situation is complex. The governorate of Nineveh has neither the same experience nor the same resources as the autonomous Kurdish government for addressing the problem of displaced persons. That view is confirmed by humanitarian organizations, which agree that sections of the Nineveh goverornate peopled by Kurds were located inside the green line. Then why has Baghdad adopted a wait-and-see policy? Because, in the absence of an elected government, the coalition authorities refuse to settle definitively this eminently political problem.

Khaffour Mahmouri had a very difficult year in 2001. The deportation of Kurds and their replacement by Arabs, accompanied by changes in the names of villages, was at its most intense then, and Kurdish newborns were often even given Arab first names. But during the first weeks of May 2003, Mahmour once again became 100 percent Kurdish. "Even though material conditions are precarious, the settlements have to be rebuilt and people have to find work again. Even though we have to start over from scratch, the Kurdish populations are happy to reclaim their lands, and I will defend them politically," declares Khaffour, who is constantly crisscrossing the district trying to work out villagers' grievances.

He regrets that he is one of the few on the Kurdish political scene who are truly concerned with this painful question, "since the two major parties, too worried about losing the many advantages they've acquired, are blinded by their exclusively pro-American policy." Khaffour does not believe in a federation. In any case, he says, it will be "annexed by Iraq." For him, as for most of my Kurdish interlocutors, all that matters is the right to full and inviolable Kurdish independence. "If they do not recognize it, we will seize it," he declares, not losing an opportunity to remind me that the Kurdish people have never attacked first but have always defended themselves. "If we do not acquire our independence, the Near East as a whole will find no peace," he concludes provocatively.

We leave for Mahmour District. The houses in the towns we pass through—flat, the color of ocher, and virtually without apertures—blend into the landscape. The only vertical elements in this horizontal universe are the many television antennae sticking straight up from the flat roofs, along with, here and there, a few ugly and almost incongruous water towers. The sole bright spots on the roadside are the multicolored carpets drying on the low walls of houses after spring cleaning.

In Dibaga (a town of one thousand residents), a few miles outside the zone controlled by the Kurdish government, the concrete street stalls along the only access road are in a sad state. If we are to believe the stories of people from the area, they were intentionally looted in April 2003 by fleeing Arabs. The school has reopened, however, and students are taught in Kurdish. We enter a two-room house in which two Kurdish families (twenty-three people) have been living since the end of April. They are rather impressed by the delegation that has come from the city, especially by the presence of Khaffour, who looks very modern in his suit and tie. The women crowd into the kitchen while the two men of the house, both with mustaches, have us sit on a synthetic carpet; it is so thin that we can feel the cold of the concrete under it. So long as neither of them has finished building his house, the two men say, they will stay in this uncomfortable little place. They are happy to be back in their village after spending fifteen years waiting for this moment and living in a tent at a refugee camp not far from Erbil. We are brought glasses of fresh water on a tray, as well as gas heaters. Outside, two cocks are noisily squabbling.

The two men of the house say that when they arrived, they had trouble recognizing their village, since most of the houses, destroyed when they left in 1988, had been rebuilt, then destroyed again by Arab colonists after being systematically looted. Everything had disappeared, including doors and windows, along with their frames. The men's recriminations are practical in nature: they want water, electricity, and road and pipeline repairs. They have very little to say about U.S. soldiers who, on that sun-scorched plain, simply pass by in their tanks: "We don't know what they're up to. They never stop to talk to us."

On the road to Mahmour, we stop in front of a group of new prefabricated houses, all alike, rising up from nowhere. Villagers soon come running, followed by their sheep. An old man addresses us in a tremulous voice: "In 1987 bulldozers completely razed our village, which was standing right here. We were deported in a military convoy without warning, unable to take any personal effects with us." He asks us to follow him onto a hill, whose grass-covered mounds bear witness to buried ruins. He holds out his emaciated hand: "The school was right there, the mosque, there, and my house was over there." The others listen reverently. Some lower their heads, distressed. "And now," the old man continues, "a foreign nongovernment organization has decided to rebuild our hamlet down there.[3] We're moving down the hill. But look at those houses built by Australian engineers! They'd have done better to ask for our help; we're experts in construction. . . . If I kick the houses, they'll collapse like a house of cards!" he exclaims, provoking embarrassed laughter among the young people in attendance. I'm invited to enter a house. I do in fact observe that the walls are askew and the window mounts crooked. The foreign humanitarian aid has terribly disappointed the people around me.

The arrival of the water delivery truck puts an end to our discussion, and the crowd immediately breaks up.

On the other side of the road from "Australian Village Hill," as the people here have already dubbed the houses, is the hamlet of Gawara (in Kurdish), formerly Tel-el-Ayad (Arabic), which consists of fewer than ten cob houses. We are welcomed by women in rags, almost all of them smoking cigarettes, which astonishes me. They don't even put them out when we arrive. "We smoke because we have worries," one of the oldest ones says simply. I can believe it. It's the quiet time of the afternoon, and they're waiting for their men to come home. Some of the men work as day laborers in the nearby gypsum quarries. The less fortunate ones whitewash the exterior of houses that are under construction. Here, too, the newly returned Kurdish families complain about their living conditions. In this village built by Arabs, the houses are spaced apart but have no yards, which goes counter to traditional Kurdish settlements. Having to accommodate themselves to these "colonist" houses leaves a bitter taste in their mouths.

As we enter Mahmour (population forty-five thousand), a color photograph of a shaggy-haired, wild-looking Saddam Hussein, taken when he was arrested by the Americans, has been Scotch-taped to the checkpoint booth. We have lunch at Khaffour's mother's house, and then visit the son of the village's founder, old Hawar, born in 1920. The son and his wife welcome us into their living room. The two old people are sunk deep into a couch, wearing typically Kurdish outfits. He has baggy pants belted with a scarf high at the waist, she a long dress.

"I've never left this village, except when the Iraqi authorities forced me to in 1963," the patriarch recounts, his shiny blue eyes barely open. "At the time, the Arabs were more powerful than we were, they'd been given tractors, and they were well organized." I note that a man in an impeccably ironed white shirt who is serving us carries a pistol in his belt. "Now the Arabs have gone back south, and the squabbles incited by Saddam can finally end, even if coexistence remains difficult," he predicts. His father had nineteen wives. One of them, his mother, was an Arab, "because you really had to be on good terms with them," he explains without elaborating.

Apart from a few hills looking like land waves frozen in midmotion—they are tells bursting with archaeological treasures—there are green expanses, sometimes grazed bare by countless flocks of sheep. Not so long ago, the huge concrete billboards with iron frames at the entrance of every village and at every important intersection displayed the painted image of Saddam Hussein. Now they stand gray and empty, symbolizing the uncertainty of Iraq's future. Sometimes one of these billboards boasts a portrait of Massoud Barzani, the strongman in the region. A ribbon of sequins, set ablaze by the oblique rays of the late afternoon sun, shimmers in the distance: it's the vast Tigris arriving from Turkey and meandering nonchalantly toward Baghdad. We travel to the edge of the "protected zone," that is, autonomous Kurdistan. Khaffour has chosen to take precautions: two carfuls of armed men escort us.

The young historian does not resist the temptation to show me what remains of his native village, located on a promontory facing the river. Of the rows of clay houses destroyed in 1984, only a few irregular clods of dirt remain, along with the cemetery, which we reach by foot. Most of the tombstones were broken into several pieces and have been reassembled only recently. Khaffour, his palms open, silently meditates in front of the sepulchres of his father, his two brothers, and his uncle, all killed by Saddam. "For years we were not allowed to come here and honor our dead, whereas they"—he points his finger accusingly at the nearby Arab village—"had every opportunity to graze their flocks and do their farming on our lands!" After the liberation, Khaffour and his men visited the sheikh and told him that "all lands were to be returned."

To prove to me that he's on good terms with this sheikh, Khaffour resolutely takes me to visit him. On our arrival, all the men who were taking advantage of the last rays of sunshine on their doorsteps converge toward the village chief's *diwaniya* (a long rectangular room for houseguests). Eager young boys bring cushions for our backs. When Mohammad El-Kadouri begins to speak, we hear only the clicking of beads, fingered mechanically by some thirty men hanging on his every word. My Kurdish companions have immediately—and it seems, automatically—switched to Arabic.

"The land was offered to us by the government fifteen years ago. Now we've returned it to its former owners, who made us do it," the sheikh says slowly. "But we must not be blamed for destroying the cemetery. That's the handiwork of barbarians who go from village to village spreading terror. We don't know who they are."

New people are constantly coming into the room, and, in accordance with local rules of decorum, we must stand up each time and welcome them, giving our best wishes and exchanging the long conventional greetings used among Arabs. The men shake hands and kiss twice; sometimes they even embrace. Khaffour is very much at ease and follows suit.

Finally, the conversation moves to a different topic. Someone wonders whether the fall of Saddam Hussein's regime can really change anything. Everyone is eager to express a view on the subject, and the initial solemnity becomes a joyful brouhaha, with everybody competing to see who can shout the loudest. Someone explains that his house in Mahmour is "occupied" by a Kurd who keeps him from selling it. Another constantly repeats that "under Saddam, at least we were safe." "Speak for yourselves, Arabs!" retorts a Kurd in our group. Naturally, they all talk past one another, but they do talk.

At a final stop in another Arab village, we meet Hamid Majd Ahmad, a former Iraqi soldier enlisted in Saddam Hussein's Republican Guard for the previous fifteen years; yet he is still Khaffour's friend. He too is dissatisfied. Idled by the "liberation," he wants to capitalize on his military experience and degrees to get hired by the Erbil police force, and for that he needs the help of the Kurdish Khaffour. "Kurdistan has lived as a democracy for ten years, and they'll accept an Arab police officer, don't you think?" he asks with a burst of laughter. Then, suddenly nostalgic, he tells the story of his last days of professional life in the service of the head of state: "We suspected that war was going to break out, and our morale was at its lowest point. Saddam had sent us to Kirkuk with the order to fight. That's because for the approximately five thousand men in the Guard, war was our reason for living and we had to be ready to sacrifice ourselves in any circumstance!"

His elderly mother joins us, cup of tea in one hand and cigarette in the other.

"Oddly enough," he continues, "at the critical moment, we received no order from Baghdad, and so we didn't fight. We were finally asked to withdraw to Babel, south of the capital. It took us a day to get there with all the U.S. bombing. As poor foot soldiers, we couldn't do anything against the all-powerful enemy air force. . . . When it was all over, which is to say, very quickly, we threw our uniforms away and went home, tired, dirty, and depressed."

That was the sad outcome of his life in a "gilded cage," as Hamid himself calls those fifteen years. He is intent on understating the conflicts between Kurds and Arabs: "How can we Kurds and Arabs envision separate futures? The tensions were created artificially by Saddam Hussein. This is an area where the Kurds are in the majority. As an Arab, I support their efforts to live autonomously among themselves."

Khaffour is not unhappy with these "politically correct" words and gives an appropriate smile. For the coming municipal elections in Mahmour, he has plans to put a few Arabs on his party's slate. Hamid Majd Ahmad will no doubt be one of them.

We return to town and have dinner at Washington Restaurant. Located in the center of the city, it has enormous glass walls lit by neon and multicolored blinking lights, which are very fashionable in Iraq. Between two mouthfuls of tabbouleh, Khaffour sums up what we have learned today with a peremptory judgment that astonishes me: "The start of that Arabization policy in our region coincided with the arrival of Islam. The Arabs are barbarians by nature; their culture is nothing but thievery, looting, and killing!"

Reconciliation does not seem imminent.

5

THE MAJOR HOLIDAYS

I depart Erbil for Sulaimaniya with twenty-three-year-old Rawand. He
is the eldest son of Dr. Shoukrya, a historian of Kurdish culture and
folklore and professor at Salahaddin University in Erbil. I made her ac-
quaintance there because she speaks Russian. For two hours our taxi
crosses a uniformly flat landscape, its monotony interrupted from time
to time by enormous buildings, former military garrisons for the Iraqi
army, which were riddled with holes by the U.S. Air Force. The road is
very good. Many taxis and buses make their way along the road on the
eve of the Feast of Sacrifice, the most important religious holiday, which
coincides with the end of the great pilgrimage, when pilgrims immolate an animal in memory of the sacrifice of Abraham. For four days,
people will be at home with their families, feasting and wishing one
another well.

A cirque finally appears in the mountains, and I distinctly perceive
the white houses of Sulaimaniya (built, it is said, by Süleyman the Magnificent), located on a knoll three thousand feet in altitude.

The hospitable home belonging to Dr. Shoukrya's parents is in the
mahalla chovakh bakh (Kurdish for "neighborhood of the four gardens"),
where Dr. Shoukrya's four sisters and one of her brothers reside. The
brother is a businessman who spent more than twenty years in Russia
and two in Sweden. None of the sisters is married. They have devoted
their lives to raising the children of a fifth sister, who died of cancer in
Syria (she had been transported there illegally for treatment). Before
leaving Erbil, Dr. Shoukrya solemnly showed me the "book of tears"
compiled and published in honor of her deceased sister, as Kurdish tradition dictates.

The concrete building stands on slightly higher ground than the peaceful street it occupies parallel to the city's central thoroughfare. It is large, consisting of at least ten rooms but only a single story. Like most of the houses around it, it has a small interior courtyard covered with grass. From the window of the living room I glimpse a rusted garden swing on the lawn. The whole family is gathered in the living room. It is rather cold. The auxiliary electric heater also serves as a hot plate, keeping water for tea at a constant temperature. Young and old alike are sprawled on the couches—only a few are sitting directly on the floor—and watch the television, which is on constantly. The whole family's attention is focused on the set. The cousins fight over the remote control while their aunts insist on turning up the sound whenever the news comes on, that is, about once every hour. Like in most Kurdish homes, Dr. Shoukrya's family acquired a satellite hookup as soon as they could, in 1991, which allows them to receive more than three hundred channels in some thirty languages at minimal cost. A standard dish costs forty dollars, and a decoder ninety.[1]

On the news we learn that on the eve of the last day of the pilgrimage, security measures have been tightened in the chief European airports, leading to delays and inconvenience for passengers. Everyone here is both excited and anxious about the coming holiday. In fact, the eldest sister, Aïsha, will remain at the kitchen stove until tomorrow.

On the morning of the first day of *Īd-al-adhā* (the Arabic equivalent of "Feast of Sacrifice"), after devouring a hearty holiday breakfast— mounds of rice accompanied by meat—the families gather for a ritual at their loved ones' graves. Every Muslim with enough money is also supposed to sacrifice an animal, usually a sheep. Part of the offering will be consumed by the one making it, and the leftovers will be distributed among friends and family. My hosts do not immolate an animal, but they will go to the cemetery.

In the latter part of the day, members of the household divide into groups; some go out to pay visits and others remain at home to welcome guests. Everyone who comes by receives a square of chocolate or other candy, and the children take advantage of the situation to ask for a little pocket money from their parents. Throughout the day, people

will gulp down liters of black tea, served in *piala*—little handleless
glasses placed on a saucer and filled to the brim. On this day of sacrifice, there is an attitude of contrition and remembrance. KURDsat,[2]
the local television station, broadcasts in a continuous loop the archival
film *Bloody Friday* (March 1988), the chemical massacre of the Kurds
by the Iraqi regime in Halabja. These alternate with close-ups of beautiful Kurdish faces against a background of nationalist songs.

The main cemeteries of Sulaimaniya stand adjacent to each other at
the top of a hill. I take the bus there with Bahar, one of my hostesses,
and we finish the journey on foot. The crowd is dense, and there is total cacophony. Taxis go by, dropping off visitors; cigarette and incense
hawkers shout out loud; Land Rovers and the latest BMWs gun their
motors, adding to the confusion. The sobs of women kneeling at the
gravesites reach us in waves, along with the monotonous chanting of
suras by the mullahs. The cemetery is huge. We struggle along through
a maze of sepulchres covered with gravel and sometimes decorated with
a succulent plant. Some women stumble and break their heels, and others lose their veils and then immediately replace them. Several sit down
on stone stools planted on the ground near the graves and begin to pray,
often noisily. They deposit sticks of incense on the sepulchres and wait
for a cleric to come by and pronounce a few holy words.

For a long time we follow a mullah in a white turban who moves
from grave to grave, melodiously singing a few verses from the Koran
in exchange for hard cash. He always does the honors in the same way:
he crouches behind the grave and, cupping his hand around his mouth,
directs his chant toward the tombstone. Some women devotedly visit
the burial vault of a locally venerated holy man, where they pray for a
few minutes before returning to "their" grave.

We return home on foot through filthy deserted streets with many
closed shops. The city has broad avenues, and on this holiday they are
crisscrossed by desperately empty white-and-yellow taxis. The Sulaimaniya Palace, a huge business hotel with green-tinted windows, dominates the municipal park below. Inside the hotel, businessmen tap
impatiently on the keypads of their cell phones;[3] in the park, a hand-

ful of street photographers, cameras slung over their shoulders, pace
while resolutely waiting for clients. Most of the women on the street
are wearing jeans and no head scarf, which gives the city a Western feel.

At home, the living room has filled with guests. They sit for twenty
minutes or so—some lean against the couch on the floor—and then
leave. The four sisters, loaded down with trays of coffee and cookies,
shuttle back and forth between the living room and the kitchen. One
of the visitors is the singer Diary Qaradakhy, a thirty-nine-year-old rising star on the Kurdish musical scene. "In my opinion," he says, "there
is no immediate solution to the Kurdish problem. The truth is that half
our population does not understand what federalism means. What the
Kurdish and Arab peoples have is something like a marriage: it won't
work if it's forced on them. Saddam Hussein instilled a hatred of us in
the Arabs, and the uneducated Kurds hate the Arabs in turn. We must
tolerate each other, but it's not easy." He's a realist and recognizes the
"superiority" of Arab culture in music: "It's not at all surprising that
we Kurds listen to and appreciate their music . . . whereas they don't
know ours at all."

By midday, the awful news of the double attack perpetrated in Erbil is
being broadcast by the international channels.[4] Journalists immediately start calling the holiday the "Kurdish September 11." The images
of carnage—buildings blown up, blood-splattered debris, a terror-
stricken populace—repeat in a continuous loop without commentary,
alternating with images of the planes crashing into the Twin Towers of
the World Trade Center in New York on September 11, 2001. The family with whom I'm staying prefers the two Kurdish channels available
by satellite, even though they know that the journalists' professional
standards are sometimes not as high as those on the internationally
broadcast Western channels. They don't watch Al-Jazeera, not because
it broadcasts in Arabic, which they all understand in any case, but because it is considered too biased in favor of the former regime of Saddam Hussein, hence too anti-American.

Rawand's family is overcome with sorrow. None of them can believe
their eyes. The journalists on KURDsat are wearing black armbands.

"These events must unite us against terror," they keep repeating. Political figures from the region's two largest parties, the targets of the
terrorist act, drop by the studios one by one to express their sorrow. One
of Rawand's young cousins is nearly hysterical and declares straight out
that in view of the act of barbarism, "all the mosques must be destroyed
and all who go to them arrested." We learn that the individuals who
committed the double suicide attack had dressed up as mullahs, concealing the explosives at their waist under their full robes. "They should
be thrown into six-by-six [eighteen-by-eighteen-foot] cells equipped
with ten radiators turned on as high as they'll go, to show them what
hell on earth is like!" the cousin continues in an agitated state. An
interview with an apprentice terrorist who was his own age (seventeen), broadcast several weeks earlier on the same television channel,
distressed and outraged the young man. The terrorist, arrested just before committing his act, stammered that he didn't have enough money
to feed himself and that members of Ansar al-Islam, a radical Islamic
movement of Afghanistan war veterans (based in the mountains of
northeastern Kurdistan), promised him that if he went through with
it, he would go "straight to paradise," where he could "eat his fill."

Is that young man in prison today? "No, the police executed him,"
replies Rawand's cousin with satisfaction, insisting, "they should kill
them all," including those who have not yet committed a crime but
who might be preparing to commit one. "How can you let someone
with evil thoughts live?" he exclaims naively. I remark that these ar-
rests and executions without trial are hardly "democratic," even though
Kurdistan claims it is proud to be a democracy. It's no use; he doesn't
back down.

Rawand's remarks are more moderate. He notes that under Saddam,
violence "had become the norm, so no one's shocked by it anymore."
He adds timidly that the attack is proof that the many checkpoints on
roads inside Erbil are useless. In that case, how can terrorism be fought?
Rawand, born in 1981, points out that he has lived his whole life in
wartime: first the conflict with Iran, then the two Gulf wars, and now
the permanent threat of terrorism, which particularly grieves him. He
demands his share of happiness and a life without worry, comparable to

that of young men his age in the West, whose lives, he believes, are easy and carefree.

His greatest desire is to obtain a passport (not an easy task for a citizen of autonomous Kurdistan) and to visit his large family, who live in exile in various European countries (Spain, Great Britain, Sweden, and Holland). He is not at all tempted by the notion of exile. He doesn't want to go to Europe, he says, except for "picnics," rest, and relaxation. "I'd like to see and experience everything I'll never be able to do here, things they show on television." Rawand is especially preoccupied with the possibility of having a sexual experience before marriage, something he declares impossible in his country. "In the West," he tells me, "you're saturated with sex, which even causes certain problems between couples. You see that in the movies. But here we're starved for sex," he admits with a laugh, "and that changes everything!"

According to Rawand, Erbil is not a city where it's easy to meet girls, "much less speak to them freely." Its residents are too conservative. A few days earlier, to celebrate the end of the university trimester, he managed to purchase a few beers and a bottle of whiskey, but he was forced to drink them on the sly with two friends in a residence for provincial students, the only place in the city where it's possible to listen to music in peace while singing and drinking. As for movie theaters, he tells me, they've been open to everyone (except women) since 1991, but they show nothing but pornography. Porn films are part of a very lucrative video market, and more recently satellite television has entered the picture. Hence some of his friends "earn a great deal of money" recording on DVD all the pornographic films broadcast over the pay channels, then rent them for the modest sum of a dollar a day. It's also possible to buy a DVD for three dollars, but rentals attract more clients "in need of sex."

Rawand greatly prefers Sulaimaniya to Erbil and considers it more modern. Many liquor stores are open on the central floodlit avenue, as well as restaurants where women and men mingle. The young man, dressed in tight jeans and a leather jacket, has soft jet-black hair and a beardless face. In his wallet he keeps a photo, folded in four, not of a fiancée but of a Turkish friend from Ankara. He met the young man a few months ago in Erbil, where the Turkish friend had supposedly gone "on business." Rawand doesn't really know what kind, but that doesn't interest him. The important thing is that they're friends. The two boys call each other regularly, and as a result Rawand now dreams of studying in Istanbul.

His plan is to come back to Iraq more mature, to marry, and to work in his field as a geologist with a local oil company, even though there are few job offers in that sector. "I'll have to be patient. The way to a better life in Kurdistan doesn't rest solely with the establishment of a federation; we need to live in a more stable country."

Although he speaks Arabic fluently, he seems to have no desire to visit the Arab countries neighboring Iraq, whether in the Near East, the Persian Gulf, or North Africa. The only exception is Egypt, "where the girls—the singers on television—are magnificent." Rawand tells me confidentially that he does not "believe" in Muhammad the prophet, that he never goes to the mosque and has no intention of taking a pilgrimage to Mecca. That's surely a result of his upbringing. His mother is an atheist, though his father and two younger sisters are observant. Of the five pillars of Islam, he admits to practicing only the *zakat,* the tithing of a certain percentage of his property. And he adds: "You don't need to be a Muslim to help your neighbor!"

As for his English, he learned more from watching American films and playing computer games than he did at school, where standards are low. Taking advantage of the U.S. troops stationed in his country, Rawand, who is sociable by nature, has made an effort to strike up conversations with U.S. soldiers anytime he can, "just to practice." He even managed to get himself hired for a few months as a cashier at an on-base Internet café. He talks of that experience now with a certain irony: "I was curious to see how ordinary U.S. soldiers treated the Iraqis. They're obviously afraid of them. It's like they think every one of us is a potential enemy. I felt it was hard for them to trust us, and they rarely opened up, even to me. I did get to be on what could be called friendly terms with some of them, though."

But when Rawand wanted to learn the number of soldiers on the base, purely as a matter of curiosity, he was taken to task. "I was in the Internet room of the 101st Airport Division. It's open twenty-four hours a day and was always full. I wanted to figure out when I could have a few minutes' rest, and I made the mistake of asking one of the soldiers how many were on the base, because I was sick of working like a dog! 'Three million,' he replied, which seemed bizarre to me, and of course I didn't believe him. Ten minutes later, an NCO came by and asked me to follow him. When he had me alone in an office, he asked me if it was true I had tried to find out how many soldiers there were. I said yes, calmly explaining why I was curious. The American soldier informed me in all seriousness that I could be arrested for asking that question. I was flabbergasted. When he saw how astonished I was, he calmed down and told me that it was all right just once, because it was only my second day. So he forgave me after I apologized but warned me that in the future I should never ask a soldier for information about other soldiers, their activities, or their ranks." How to explain such behavior? "It's fear, real, tangible fear," Rawand repeats. "When I was working with them, they were fired on every night!"

When I ask whether he feels primarily Kurdish or Iraqi, the young man makes this reply, as his cousin looks on in anger: "I'm Iraqi in the first place, then Kurdish. When someone asks me where I come from, I'm compelled to acknowledge that I'm Iraqi, since Kurdistan does not exist as an international political entity. When it does—*insh Allah*— I'll declare myself Kurdish."

Rawand is an optimist and hopes that Arabs and Kurds will manage to live together, "because we've coexisted for a long time, even though some now denounce the evils of 'Arabization.' Since the end of the war, all these processes have depended on the United States, which has become responsible for how the occupation of Iraq unfolds. But they're certainly going to cut back the number of troops in the future. They'll just set up a few permanent bases, as in Germany or Kuwait, for example. In short, I don't see what the problem is."

In the evening, I meet Sherzad Hassan in a hotel lobby. He is fifty-two years old and a sociologist and novelist—a "freelance writer," as he defines himself. He returned to Kurdistan after spending nearly a year in

Finland. The author of seven novels, he has also translated various literary and sociological works from English. In the last five years, he participated in setting up UNESCO's educational programs, but since the "liberation" of the country, the international general assistance fund that funneled large quantities of money into Kurdistan through UN agencies has been considerably reduced.

Sherzad takes time to reflect on his role as a writer and the lack of openness in contemporary Iraqi society. A great connoisseur of the sacred texts of Islam, which he studied for twelve years alongside his other fields of interest, he is also excited by Marx and Dostoyevsky, whom he has read in Arabic translation. He demands the right to ask questions, even though Iraqi society is not accustomed to that. "I came to realize that Islamic societies do not question things, that irresolution and doubt have no place in them. They are societies of certainties," says the former English professor. Hence, as a result of taking on taboo religious subjects in his novels, he has been arguing for several months with Islamists shocked by his writings.

When he comes to the political problem of Iraq as a united nation, Sherzad is categorical: "Iraq as a single indivisible nation does not exist. It's pointless to try to piece together the fragments of our old country using the old glue; it won't work! There are too many problems among the different ethnic groups, and it seems very unlikely to me that Sunni clerics and Shiite clerics can ever get along!" he observes. "We Kurds have been away from Baghdad for too long now. The Treaty of Lausanne crucified our people. The rift has grown over time and has become unbridgeable." The prospect of a trip to Baghdad, the first in eight years, appeals to him, but his wife believes it would be too dangerous (his Arab friend, the current minister of culture and information in Iraq, confirms this). "Too bad; I really would have liked to browse the book market on Mutanabi Street again and buy books in English that aren't found here in Kurdistan," Sherzad laments.[5]

The idea of installing a democracy after twenty-five years of Baathist dictatorship seems folly to him: "Suspicion prevents peaceful relationships. Tolerance is difficult, and our society is not at peace. To coexist successfully and peacefully with the Other who is not—not yet?—acting against you, but whose attitude is something less than friendly, is a real challenge. For example, the Shiite groups in the south reject the very notion of federalism without understanding properly what it corresponds to, and all the neighboring Arab countries consider Iraq the advance guard of a front mounted against Turkey and Iran. But a democratic society develops and prospers in the rich soil of a 'civilized' civil society. In Afghanistan, it's clear that the society that produced the Taliban cannot suddenly begin to live 'democratically' under a new regime. Well, the same is true in Iraq. You mustn't demand too much of us."

But on the whole, Sherzad is skeptical about the intrinsic value of democracy: "As the philosopher Noam Chomsky suspected, America has a virtual democracy. The pluralism of the media further simplifies the task of propaganda, making control of the masses easier. Even in liberal Western societies, real democracy is limited. Once you're elected, you can do anything at all. In those countries, elections have been turned into alluring spectacles, but when you return to reality, corruption, weakness, and disappointment prevail."

What to do, given so much pessimism? How to go on living? "That's the real tragedy we're dealing with," Sherzad replies calmly, taking a sip from his glass of warm milk. "Even if Kurdistan became truly independent, it wouldn't be an exception. There'd still be abominable prisons, many violations of human rights. Most people think we still have to live 'waiting for Godot'!" Sherzad admires Samuel Beckett, as well as James Joyce and D. H. Lawrence, who were part of his department's curriculum in the 1970s. "Arabs and Iraqi Kurds are waiting for Godot, who will certainly arrive to save us, since there's no other solution, or so we think!" he explains calmly. "But Godot won't come because Godot doesn't exist, and the United States is not Godot. Yet many want to believe in his existence. The idea of a savior goes back to caveman days. Later on, people believed in Zarathustra, the prophet Muhammad, or Mahdī.[6] People expect these prophets to materialize in one form or another and sweep away all the incomprehensible things happening in the Islamic world. Everyone lives with illusions, since no one can live without hope. The role of politicians, our own included, is to maintain that hope by lying to us. . . . After eleven years of autonomy, the level of corruption in our two parties is unparalleled. The 'pure' mountain fighters have long since disappeared. In our democracies, nothing's easier than to become an 'enemy of the people'!"

Yet it is concern for that imperfect people that has definitively shaped Sherzad's life:

"In 1994, when I was teaching secondary school, I sold my bed to provide for my family's needs. Since living conditions were not improving, we emigrated to Finland, but it didn't feel right there. We declined to become Finnish citizens and came home. We were living in comfort and safety there, but I felt useless. As a writer, my place is here. I'm not particularly patriotic, but it's only in this complex territory that I really feel I'm alive. Here, at least, I see the people suffer, I suffer with them, and I write about what I see."

6

A TURKOMAN FAMILY

The Turkomans represent the third largest ethnic group in Iraq, after the Arabs and the Kurds. They speak Turkoman, which is a Turkic language. They have a close relationship with Turkey and traditionally live in the central and northern regions of Iraq. Originally from central Asia, they settled Iraq thousands of years ago during a long migration. They grew in number under the Abbasid caliphate, and then took root in the region of Kirkuk and Mosul, as well as in the northwest. Their exact number is unknown. According to the last census, conducted by the British in 1957, the Turkomans numbered 590,000 out of a total population of 6 million, which would be the equivalent of 2 million today.

The family of Arshad Al-Hirmizi[1] is very observant. Everyone stops his or her daily activities for a few minutes during the five prescribed prayers, and the women pull on long white head scarves to pray. When they open the door to a stranger, they cover themselves with a hood-and-scarf combination that is very common in the countries of the Persian Gulf (Arshad's wife, Seefa, brought a few of them back from Saudi Arabia for her sister-in-law) and conceals their hair, neck, and bustline. The electricity is often out. A fuel oil heater has been installed in the living room and another in the dining room in an attempt to warm the vast rooms. For years the family lived without windowpanes, but new glass was recently installed, a gift from the local government after the fall of Saddam.

Nidret, a forty-year-old English professor, is Arshad's sister-in-law.

She is passionate and has a great deal to tell me about her teaching experience during a period when everything has been turned upside down: "For the time being, there hasn't really been much change in the curriculum since the end of that abominable regime. Of course, the slogans glorifying Saddam have been eliminated, and we just received new English manuals without Saddam's official photo on the flyleaf. For the other manuals, we had the children remove the photos, and they grimly tore them up, but without really realizing the meaning of their gestures. As in the other primary and secondary schools in Iraq, we used to spend several hours every Thursday morning assembled in the schoolyard singing to the glory of 'our beloved leader.' Now the children are witness to our sudden hatred for Saddam, taboo feelings we had always concealed. They have trouble understanding why the songs are banned. They'd been accustomed to them since they were in day care. I still catch my three-year-old daughter often humming those propagandistic refrains. The melody has gotten stuck in her head, which was the whole point. From their earliest years, children had to be brainwashed. At day-care centers, they're now made to chant verses from the Koran; I don't know if that's any better. . . . Only the *watanya* [nationality class] was eliminated from the curriculum.[2] It was replaced by history and geography. And let me add, at a more down-to-earth level, that the teacher's chair I sit on, composed of four concrete blocks piled one on top of the other, has not been replaced, and the students still shiver from the cold."

Nevertheless, more than seventy million new textbooks were printed in Jordan and Iraq under the aegis of UNESCO's and UNICEF's education programs, just in time for the beginning of the first post-Saddam school year. The Baathist ideology was eliminated, but the complete recasting of the curriculum for various ideological subjects, especially history and geography, will take time. The primary-school manuals will include lessons on human rights (the history and operation of various international institutions and documents such as the International Court of Human Rights, the Universal Declaration of the Rights of Man, and the Geneva Convention, little known by Iraqis). They will also deal with the danger of land mines. Schoolchildren will be taught to identify the different types of mines and how to react if one of the deadly devices explodes.

Nearly 12,000 of the 365,000 teachers in the country were dismissed because they were members of the Baath Party, which they were once strongly advised to join. Nidret, who did not belong to the party, still teaches, despite difficulties. The salaries of those who were not suspended increased a great deal (hers went from $5 a month to $250, only slightly less than what university professors earn), and UNICEF is training 2,000 teachers a month in new pedagogical theories and methods.

Nidret admits her uncertainty and fear in this unprecedented political situation: "I'm afraid we'll go on suffering, in a different way no doubt, not necessarily because of the Arabs but because of the other ethnic communities [without saying so, Nidret is targeting the Kurdish community]. I dread the dissolution of Iraq as an entity. That's because we Turkomans want to be part of Iraq, and in no case part of a part [that is, of Kurdistan]. We're in favor of a single government for our country, with a president at its head . . . and if he's a Shiite, we'll accept him! As a matter of fact, we have Shiite Turkoman friends with whom we're on excellent terms. Personally, I'm in favor of a return of the king, Sherif Ali Ben Al-Hussein.[3] A monarch always stands above divisions. We'd be a constitutional monarchy, like Great Britain. I'm nostalgic for the time of peace and tranquillity under the Hashemite monarchy, which my Turkoman grandparents told me a lot about. But if the state were to become federal, we'd constitute one of the federated parties. Iraq is like one big family, and the Turkomans want to be part of it. But I'm very afraid that in the end the federation will only divide us. . . .

"I'm also afraid of the increasing security problems. The double suicide attack perpetrated in Erbil is undoubtedly part of the settling of accounts between the fundamentalist Ansar Party and the two Kurdish parties. Those terrorists are hurting the image of Islam, which is a religion of peace. Vicious rumors have it that the Americans themselves organize those acts of terror to justify their presence. At least under Saddam, we weren't afraid to go to the market. Today we feel completely unsafe."

At school as well, the climate is poisonous: "When I made the mistake of telling my students that we were not yet accustomed to democracy, they immediately reported it to the new principal, who summoned me to her office. I was not supposed to talk that way to the children. We have to pretend we know what democracy is, to show how happy we are about what's happening to our country! Another time, I explained to the students that it was wrong and immoral that the looters in the city have not been arrested; I never mentioned that most of them were Kurds. But once again, Kurdish students complained to the principal, claiming they had been singled out. The truth is, we're all still paralyzed by fear."

Because she is a Turkoman (part of an ethnic minority) and was not a member of the Baath Party (that is, she did not embrace the majority opinion), Nidret's position at her neighborhood school was always vulnerable, not to mention the fact that she refused to change her nationality. She and her husband, for example, were never able to buy property in Kirkuk, since that privilege was reserved for the Arabs.[4] "The administrative pressure compelling us to become Arabs got stronger in the last years," Nidret remembers. "Yet we were perfectly aware that even if we'd given in, we'd never have been considered anything but 'Arabs on paper.' "

The U.S. occupation throws her into complete confusion. In the first place, there's her exasperation with all the electrical outages caused by power stations damaged by the U.S. military during the two wars. The military is doing nothing to repair them. But she also accuses the United States of being overly aggressive: "People say that during raids, [the soldiers] make everyone in the household go out into the street so they can work more easily. Most of the time, they steal jewelry and savings and no one can raise the slightest objection. If they behaved differently, there wouldn't be so much resistance. People thought they'd be able to perform miracles, and it's finally dawning on us that that's not the case."

Nidret's husband, Adb, an engineer at Northern Oil Company for more than thirty years,[5] points out that of the twenty thousand or so employees in the company that was taken over by an American civilian, only three hundred were dismissed. Even though Adb is a Turkoman, has never been a member of the Baath Party, and refused to Arabize his name, he managed to remain with the company over the years, a real feat.

The goal of Arabization, pursued by the Baath Party over the last three decades, was to establish the dominance of Arabs over the other communities—especially Turkomans and Kurds. Under Saddam, pressure continued to be exerted on Turkoman, Kurdish, and Assyrian families to leave the city and settle elsewhere, including in the inhospitable regions of southern Iraq. As for the cultural rights the Turkomans enjoyed—limited, to be sure—such as being taught in Turkish in primary school and having newspapers and local radio stations in Turkish, these were eliminated in 1972.

Fifty-five-year-old Arshad was born in Kirkuk to a Turkoman father and mother. He left Iraq in 1980 at the start of the war with Iran and settled in the Persian Gulf. He is currently the head of a hospital-equipment business in Saudi Arabia. He finally came back for the Feast of Sacrifice this year, after being away for twenty-three years.

What he discovers both excites and scandalizes him, particularly the enormous scope of infrastructural damage and above all the low level of Iraqi consciousness, a clear consequence of the way his compatriots have been kept in isolation. Arshad recounts that one of his friends, a lawyer, also from Kirkuk, has lived in Dubai, United Arab Emirates, for twenty-seven years. When he returned to Iraq, the country he rediscovered seemed so poor and foreign that he felt as though he'd landed on another planet. His city looked like a huge wasteland. At the cemetery where he went to meditate on his mother's grave, he was moved to pity by the face of a ragged child and offered him a little money, but the boy refused it. "These people have nothing left but their pride," Arshad's friend said sadly.

A key city in the former Ottoman *vilayet* of Mosul, Kirkuk,[6] the fourth largest city in Iraq, is the envy of all. At the start of the U.S. invasion, in a gesture of brotherhood toward its Turkoman neighbors in the region,[7] Turkey warned that it would not tolerate the Kurdish *peshmerga* besieging it in too visible a manner.[8] But the Kurds did everything they could to stay there. In the view of the Kurdish political parties, Kirkuk historically belongs to Iraqi Kurdistan, despite the fact that the Kurdish population there has been reduced by the Arabization policy. For these refugees, the Kurdish parties demand the imprescriptible right to return and settle there. After nearly eighty years of struggle against the different regimes in power in Baghdad, they believe they have earned Kirkuk. Jalal Talabani, head of the PUK, even compared that aspiration to the Palestinians' plans for Jerusalem. But the Turkomans categorically refuse to become part of any "Kurdistan," even if it is Iraqi. They claim a "historical" right to the city, alleging they were the first to settle the area. The coalition authorities, extremely cautious on this matter, confine themselves to pointing out that the municipal council of Kirkuk is composed of Arabs, Kurds, Turkomans, and Assyrians, with two members per community.

Arshad is particularly preoccupied with the fate of the Turkoman community in Iraq since the fall of Saddam's regime. He passionately defends it in his publications abroad, through the international colloquiums he organizes and his cultural foundation based in Istanbul, and he closely follows the fight over Kirkuk. "Kirkuk is a mix of different ethnic groups, but the largest ethnic component has always been Turkoman. We constituted nearly 90 percent of the population until the 1950s and 1960s. But when the oil companies started hiring unskilled foreign labor, it was Kurds who settled in the outlying areas," he explains.

He gives his version of what happened when the city was liberated on April 10, 2003, after the Americans arrived in Baghdad: "Despite the promises by U.S. soldiers, Jalal Talabani's Kurdish militias and a few of Massoud Barzani's troops—the former from Sulaimaniya, the latter from Erbil—came along and invaded the city. They seized the main government buildings and lost no time burning down the administrative archives, especially the cadastre and the records office. Their goal was to conceal the city's real ethnic composition. Everything that could be looted was, right in front of the U.S. soldiers, who observed that plunder with complete indifference. Only the governments of Turkey, Iran, and even Saudi Arabia denounced what they rightly called 'ethnic cleansing.' 'Kurdization' had already replaced Arabization. The Americans were embarrassed and finally promised that the *peshmerga* would leave Kirkuk within twenty-four hours. The Kurdish militias pretended to obey, then returned in civilian clothes bent on the same tasks. They put up signposts in Kurdish everywhere and even replaced the street names with Kurdish designations!"

"We're outraged at the lack of fair play among the Americans," he continues. "They'd barely arrived when they imposed a Kurdish governor on Kirkuk. That may be a kind of revenge for Turkey's refusal to get involved in the war![9] They certainly wanted to punish the Turkomans because we didn't collaborate the way they wanted. As for the Governing Council with its twenty-five members, it claims to be representative, but it's not. We have only a single member, a woman with no political weight, whereas the Kurds have five. It's a disgrace! Not only do the Americans decide in our place, but they don't give a damn about the internal political situation of our country. Before they go, they'll set up bases and establish a government that will be loyal to them. We're grateful that they rid us of Saddam Hussein's regime, even though everyone knows he hadn't had weapons of mass destruction in ages, but now we don't want anything more from them!"

Arshad is convinced that the way the 2005 general elections are organized will work in favor of the Turkoman population, whose true weight in Kirkuk will finally be recognized. The fragile ethnic balance of the city is to be preserved, according to strict humanitarian rules and thanks to ad hoc commissions. "We Turkomans accept the Arabs, who arrived twenty-five years ago and whose children were born here," he says. "We don't proclaim Kirkuk a Turkoman country, but we don't tolerate it being called a Kurdish country either. We want Kirkuk to remain Iraqi. By the way, that shows we have nothing against the Arabs!"

To confirm his assertions, Arshad arranges a meeting with Dr. Sadettin Ergec, head of the Turkoman Council, which has represented the Turkomans in Iraq since the "liberation." Thanks to that council, a local television channel and a radio station broadcasting in Turkish, as well as a few trade unions, appeared shortly after the Saddam regime was overthrown. The council defends the rights of the community but rules out any use of force. Needless to say, there is great exasperation in the face of Kurdish "provocations."

Atop the house surrounded by fruit trees, two banners are flying: the Iraqi flag and the Turkoman flag, a white star and a crescent moon against a sky-blue background. "We had to act fast after the fall of Saddam's regime. Otherwise the power vacuum would have been filled by the Kurds who'd occupied our city. But we fight democratically and peacefully," explains Ergec. He is referring to a demonstration on December 31, 2003, by several thousand Turkomans and Arabs on the central square of Kirkuk. Demonstrators were heading for the office of the new provincial governor, a Kurd. The *peshmerga* responsible for protecting him reportedly fired on them, and three people are said to have died.[10]

"We have been extremely confused by what has happened since the 'liberation.' We thought no one could be worse than Saddam Hussein, and we were wrong. The Kurds behave just like the dictator who oppressed them. Let's be clear: this city is at the center of our historical territory; no one will drive us out, and no one will prevent the Turkomans from expressing their discontent. If the Kurds intend to deprive us of the petroleum from the rich subsoil to increase their importance on the world scene and to force recognition from the international community, well, they won't succeed! We thought that the shared suffering in our past connected us to the Kurdish people, but the Kurds have turned out to be unjust and aggressive. We have nothing against the ones who've lived in Kirkuk for more than ten years, but we're upset by the intruders who've been knocking on our doors since the 'liberation,' supposedly to reclaim their possessions. They're being manipulated by Kurdish leaders, who are pursuing their terrible political schemes."

Like all Iraqi metropolises, there is nothing aesthetically pleasing about Kirkuk, "the city of black gold." Concrete cubes stand next to one-story cob houses whose outer walls are a slightly warmer color of ocher. Arshad explains that the absence of architectural harmony in Iraq can be attributed to a complete lack of education in taste going back decades. In the 1920s, he assures me, Kirkuk was a stone and alabaster city painted white. I observe that the scaffolding on work sites is made entirely of wood, as in Kabul. Pressed tightly together, these pieces of wood look like large matchsticks, giving the construction they shore up a strange look of fragility.

On an imposing hill, with the Khasa River meandering lazily below us, I make out the citadel where a former Turkish general once refused to raise the Iraqi flag, even after the treaty handing the city over to Iraq had been signed.[11] Although destroyed by Saddam in 1994 and looted from top to bottom, it is still impressive. We are strolling among the few houses hidden behind immaculate white walls, whose small courts open onto a maze of recently built rooms that have escaped destruction. Arshad's state-of-the-art movie camera attracts kids playing among the stones. The residences in the Christian quarter, like the one that once belonged to Toma Hindi, patriarch of one of the 150 Chaldean families who lived in the citadel in the 1920s, are the best preserved. Hindi's home is an elegant building dating from the eighteenth century, with colonnades and reception rooms overlooking the bazaar.

The oldest building in Kirkuk, built by Seljuk Turks in the twelfth century and topped with a high turquoise minaret, is the tomb of the prophet Daniel, ruler of Babylon when the region was controlled by Nebuchadnezzar.[12] It's a vast, austere room that receives many visitors. Two veiled women are meditating there as I go by. They have removed their shoes at the entrance and walked barefoot on the cold ground. Next to the tomb are the remains of an Ottoman cemetery where the families of the local elite chose to bury their loved ones, not far from the holy man.

As we come around a ruin, we catch looters at work. They are Kurds and don't even try to hide, addressing one another in their own language in front of us. The five confederates, dressed in the traditional trousers of their community, are in search of pieces of scrap iron or shards of pottery decorated with verses from the Koran, which are easy to sell. The three Turkoman children who have decided to escort us are lively and cheerful. When Arshad wants to give them candy, the first refuses, and then the second as well; finally, when the third one pockets it, the other two make fun of him, calling him "Kurd!" They have no Kurdish pals, they tell us, because they live in an exclusively Turkoman neighborhood. At school they are also among themselves. Are contacts between communities carefully avoided perhaps?

Finally, we visit Ata Tarzibashi, the senior lawyer of Kirkuk. He is a Turkoman and a famous author, having written nine books on Iraqi Turkoman literature and poetry. Arshad has come to express his good wishes for the Feast of Sacrifice. He too is not at a loss to criticize the current situation: "We have gained more freedom of expression, but we've lost the assurance of a more or less predictable future. We'll have to get used to that lack of security. I don't see any future for a country occupied by foreign powers that purposely turn communities against one another. The British occupation had nothing like the severity we see in the Americans. The British paid more heed to the people. The proof is that they brought Faisal's grandson back to the country! Whether the Americans stay or go, I see nothing but problems. We're at an impasse."

We listen to him as we sip our coffee when two of his former students, a Kurd and an Assyrian, come in and sit down beside us. They are members of the local government council set in place by the Americans. They too came to give their best wishers for *Īd*. Right away, a lively discussion ensues, with each party remaining polite but firm in his position. The Assyrian, a very dynamic shopkeeper in suit and tie, is particularly struck by the lack of real authority on the local council. It has no budget; the population presents its problems, but no one is able to solve them. The Kurd, conversely, points out the injustices endured by his community, which has lost its attitude of tolerance. During the discussion, he mentions the first Iraqi constitution of 1925. According to him, it stipulated that Iraq was composed primarily of Arabs and Kurds. Arshad is indignant and replies that no, on the contrary, the constitution was known for not discriminating on the basis of ethnic origin, religion, or language. All Iraqis were equal before the law. It was the constitutions of 1958, then of 1970, that identified the two peoples, "Kurdish" and "Arab," and gave them a prominent place. "For us," notes Arshad, "the constitution of 1925 was better than all that followed it, even if it did defend a monarchical system!"

While we share our last breakfast, nicely set out on the table in the dining room, which is separated from the living room by a charming Japanese sliding door, Nidret draws me into one last passionate discussion of Iraq. The young teacher is categorical. "The new enemies are the Americans," she declares, opening her chestnut brown eyes wide and energetically shaking her head of short-cropped black hair. "They indecently supported Saddam until the invasion of Kuwait. Before that, they intentionally incited him to start the war against Iran to weaken us. Saddam was an abomination, but now we're under occupation by individuals who obviously don't understand us. Is that any better?"

7

En Route to Baghdad

There's a crowd at the stand of taxis headed for Baghdad. Arshad insists on offering me the two front seats in the communal taxi so that I'll be more at ease.* I'm on the driver's right, with three silent men in the back seat. We set off aboard the ancient sky-blue Chevrolet. After about twelve miles, we stop at a checkpoint before entering Saladin Province. An Iraqi police officer asks to examine the passports of the men in the car. He doesn't even look at me, much less speak to me.

Behind me I hear a flurry of activity. The men show their passports, except the one seated in the middle, who seems frail and distraught. The tension escalates. Suddenly, the officer opens the doors and brutally drags the man out of the vehicle. While he cuffs the man's hands behind his back, the car is searched—rather superficially, since no one even asks me to leave my seat. I realize that the man without papers is a Kurd, whereas the other two passengers and the driver are Turkomans, and the officer of the law is an Arab. The Kurd disappears into an Iraqi police jeep that speeds off in a cloud of dust. We leave immediately. The incident is closed.

On the straight road heading south through Tuz Khormatu and Bakuba, we run into a few rare U.S. military columns, the first I've come across. Since the security situation was better in autonomous Kurdistan, their presence there was discreet. The cars and the passengers are checked

---

*In Iraqi communal taxis, five seats are always available, whatever the type of vehicle: three in the back seat and two in the front, even though being crammed together is uncomfortable and dangerous.

every time we enter or leave a large urban area or province. Government workers in dark blue uniforms, sporting armbands reading "IP" (Iraqi police), do the honors.

On either side of the asphalt, bands of kids are offering gasoline, which they procure at the service station and resell at a slightly higher price. That way, the motorists won't have to stand in line. As I was leaving Kirkuk, I saw another business of this kind, but that was much more spectacular: duty-free cars on giant trailer trucks were being sold in the middle of the street. They generally came from Kuwait in crates from Dubai, United Arab Emirates, and easily crossed what has become a porous Iraqi border. Most of the Iraqis I'll meet during my journey will recently have acquired a used car for two or three thousand dollars. It is such bargains (I will observe the same phenomenon in Afghanistan) that have led to the tenfold increase in road traffic in the major cities, especially Baghdad.

On the outskirts of the cities we pass through, the black outer walls of new houses, or of houses under construction (covered with tar to protect against the cold and the inclement weather), give the concrete blocks a mournful look. The area around them is bare, devoid of vegetation. Sometimes a mule with a packsaddle, accompanied by a shepherd in a beret, leads a dense flock of sheep, and the massive wave encroaching on the road can slow traffic for a long time. At an intersection where street repairs are being made, a few shepherds have stopped to observe the laborers running their noisy cement mixers. Then they resume their peaceful walk beside the line of telephone poles stretching endlessly over the plain. The cob villages resemble those I will encounter in Afghanistan, but the walls enclosing their courtyards are very low, almost nonexistent, compared to Afghan walls.

We drive fast on these thoroughfares, which were not damaged in the last war. Nothing is forbidden here. Our driver systematically passes every vehicle ahead of him, indifferent to the flashing headlights of cars coming toward us, which he sometimes grazes as he rushes past. Japanese Hino trucks, very common on Afghan and Pakistani roads—where they are lavishly decorated—are valued just as highly by Iraqi drivers, but they do not sport any ornamentation here.

A few tells rise up in the distance. To the south, the landscape changes. It seems to be getting pinker, softer. I notice date palms heavy with fruit, swings hanging beneath them. The sky suddenly turns threatening: then, a refreshing downpour. Dark shadows draped in *ab-baya* quicken their pace to outrun the storm. The Iraqi flag is waving everywhere, as if I had just crossed into another country, as if I had only just entered Iraq.

8

BAGHDAD

Baghdad—"Gift of God" in Persian—was built in 762 by al-Mansūr (the second Abbasid caliph) between the Tigris and the Euphrates Rivers, on a fertile plain often visited by merchant caravans. The city was devastated many times by floods, fires, and fearless conquerors but rose from its ashes every time. Today it is a megalopolis with more than five million residents and stretches over 190 square miles on either side of the Tigris. Thoroughfares indiscriminately cut through residential neighborhoods and the back section of the giant souk in the old city center. Concrete structures of various heights stand everywhere, sometimes intact, sometimes in a state of collapse, riddled with holes by the most recent bombs, bearing witness to the ambitious 1970s architecture that imitated Soviet monumentalism.

I was surprised that we were never stopped when we came to checkpoints. We drive alongside the Tigris, and I notice on its banks the "neo-Babylonian" architecture of the flamboyant villas belonging to Saddam's *nomenklatura*. During the weeks following the "liberation," all these villas changed hands. The former home of Tareq Aziz, former minister of foreign affairs and deputy prime minister of Iraq, dominates the famous Abi Nuwas Avenue, with heavy columns flanking its main entrance. It has become the residence of Abdel Aziz al-Hakim, the number-two man on the Supreme Council for Islamic Revolution in Iraq (SCIRI) and member of the Iraqi Governing Council, who returned from Iran after twenty years in exile. On the other side of the Tigris, set back somewhat from its pleasant shores, the former Qadisiya neighborhood, once reserved exclusively for the Baathist *nomenklatura,* now shelters Baghdadi pieds-à-terre for the heads of the two main Kurdish parties, the KDP and the PUK, both members of the IGC. It also houses the headquarters for their respective television channels. Jalal Talabani has taken up residence in a sumptuous villa that used to belong to one of Saddam's brothers. In the villa housing his satellite television station, KURDsat, a swarm of frogs croaks at the bottom of a half-drained swimming pool. As under the old regime, to gain access to that secured perimeter, you have to know the password. The Kurdish *peshmerga* have replaced the fedayeen.

Countless imposing piles of garbage with various miasmas carried by the wind, and concrete barriers trimmed with an entanglement of barbed wire outside every hotel and official building, add to the distressing overall impression. The structures sheltering the Americans, whether soldiers or civilians, are virtually inaccessible bunkers. Innumerable streets are blocked by metal gates "as security measures."

Ugliness is everywhere. I'm bewildered by the sight of it. It's the Friday ending the festivities for the Feast of Sacrifice after nearly a week of vacation, and almost all the street stalls are closed. Fortunately, business will resume tomorrow. As in Kabul, doctors and pharmacists display their degrees and specializations on signs and billboards that sometimes cover a building's entire facade. Many women of various ages sit begging outside mosques or in the doorways of central city restaurants. Mute, almost motionless, most are dressed in dusty rags.

The embassies, which lost their diplomatic staff in March 2003 on the eve of military action, came back to life in late April and have done their utmost to resume "normal" operations. Like all the villas in Baghdad, most of the diplomats' residences have been looted, except those that their governments took care to guard. Every organization that wants to go on functioning, whether official, private, humanitarian, commercial, or diplomatic, hires a large number of armed guards to oversee the security of buildings and staff. These guards are recruited locally or from abroad.[1] The many convoys of freight trucks on the long road from Amman, Jordan, or Kuwait to Baghdad also use them for protection. That new security "niche" is a profitable business for a number of specialized Western companies that jumped in as soon as possible.[2]

The rich El-Mansour neighborhood is home to most of the non-government organizations, businesses, embassies, as well as rich villas that resemble palaces from *The Arabian Nights,* lit up at night by humming, superpowerful generators. They are entrenched behind concrete walls and a maze of barriers, with lookouts watching from above, weapon in hand. After the attack that damaged its outer walls in January 2004, the Turkish Embassy, located on a busy thoroughfare, had a double concrete wall built that encroaches on the street and slows traffic. For the French Embassy, a beautiful red brick building from the 1930s located not far from the banks of the Tigris, having its street closed to traffic was not enough; it is now hidden behind a concrete wall covered by a large and colorful fresco, the work of students at the school of fine arts on orders from the ambassador. The French Cultural Center is closed to the public, since it is unable to guarantee security.

Barricaded behind its concrete walls, Baghdad lives in fear. Everyone is obsessed with security questions, especially expatriates, whether diplomats or not. The security measures taken hinder any other plan of action. Armed men whose status is sometimes risky to pinpoint comb the city, preventing ordinary citizens from gaining access to buildings containing Americans or other members of the coalition forces. The diplomats have strict orders not to venture out on foot in the city and are forbidden to move about the country as a whole. Episodes of general looting—heavily covered by the media—occurred in every large Iraqi city and shocked the Baghdadis, who entrenched themselves in their homes to defend their property. With their own eyes they saw the U.S. Special Forces position themselves around the Ministry of Oil to save it, whereas museums and archives were left exposed to looters. This behavior on the part of the "liberators" has not been appreciated. Another calamity is the electrical outages, a source of discomfort in daily life but also the cause of disruptions in public services. Some hospitals have had to shut down their operating rooms. Finally, uncollected garbage, telephone service limited to the immediate neighborhood, the unavailability of bottles of propane, and polluted, hence undrinkable, water make Baghdadis grumble even more.

———

The very urban Baghdad sometimes looks exceptionally rural. A few hundred yards from Paradise Square, where the statue of Saddam Hussein was toppled on April 11, 2003,[3] an old man passes every morning in his cart, drawn by a donkey whose desperate braying can sometimes be heard from one end of the residential neighborhood to the other. With his stick, the old man taps an empty propane bottle to alert the people who live there that he is going by.

The vegetables from owners of garden plots are sold at the souk or at the corner restaurant. Hence Al-Rif Café on Sixty-second Street buys most of its vegetables from neighborhood gardeners. This pizzeria is sought out by the elite of Baghdad society because one of the proprietor's sons, a computer scientist, has opened a cybercafé in high style there. With its light wood partitions between the tables of computers, its glassed-in upper level, its terrace encroaching on the sidewalk—fashioned by another son, a designer—the establishment attracts a diverse clientele, including many women. You can sip tea or coffee there or smoke a hookah while calmly surfing the Internet (at two dollars an hour). Every evening, I find businessmen urgently reading their e-mail, students subscribed to various chat rooms, and the Dominican friar Yusuf Thomas (see chapter 24), a true Internet "addict," who has exchanged his robes for a black leather jacket.

For the owner, a Christian engineer born in this neighborhood who still lives in his parents' home (built in the 1950s), business has been good since the "liberation." In fact, his workers are busy on a new construction site on the corner, where he plans to open an "Iraqi" fast food place as soon as possible. You'll be able to get a quick snack of rice and grilled chicken there. "The traditional restaurant, where they bring you chickpeas, vegetables cooked in sauce, ratatouille, hummus, and yogurt before you even choose the main course, has become obsolete," the man explains as he plays with an enormous bunch of keys. "That's one of the consequences of globalization. It's better to jump on the bandwagon, so I jumped! Even in Iraq, even in occupied or liberated Baghdad—in the end, it amounts to the same thing—no one really has hours to waste in a restaurant anymore."

Most often, however, when you ask the Baghdadis what has changed, they shrug their shoulders. Many curse the Americans, since it's easy to criticize them. Others have already adapted and don't even question the situation. But only a few express satisfaction, like the owner of Al-Rif. As in Afghanistan, the next country I will visit, even most of the wealthiest people would leave the country if given the opportunity.

Hamudi is thirty-four years old and has just gotten married. A secular Shiite from the chic El-Mansour neighborhood, he recently became a journalist on the television channel Al-Arabiya after years in the import-export business. He knows every nook and cranny of Baghdad, a city he loves and which he traverses in his boat of a car, an old red Chevy. But Hamudi no longer recognizes the capital. "The Americans have even taken over our parks; there's nowhere anymore you can rest and forget your stress . . . even though we really need that," he fumes. "Take Baghdad Island north of the city. People went there for its lake full of colorful fish, its soccer fields, its gardens, its wedding chapels, its observation towers. . . . Now it's in the hands of the Thirty-seventh Regiment of the First Battalion of the U.S. Army, which has rebaptized it the 'isle of bandits.'[4] We have only our zoo left, but hardly anyone goes there anymore because it's too close to the 'green zone,'* hence a potential target for the resistance. When they move around town, the U.S. military columns cause panic, especially if they're stuck in a traffic jam," continues Hamudi. He too tries not to stay long near U.S. weapons of war. He is exasperated by the Americans' presence: "What freedom are they talking about? The freedom of cell phones and TV channels? Of movement? I could travel to my heart's content under the old regime! No one in my family was killed or even imprisoned by Saddam because we knew the limits that were not to be crossed. Above all,

*The "green zone" is an enormous space of several dozen hectares located in the very center of Baghdad—it includes Saddam's former palaces on the west bank of the Tigris —which has become the headquarters of the U.S. administration. It is there that the Iraqi Governing Council held its sessions and where U.S. proconsul Paul Bremer had his residence, which is now the U.S. Embassy.

we knew we mustn't ever do business with them, much less openly criticize them. But I can now say that Saddam Hussein has quite simply
been replaced by the American oppressor."

In Baghdad, after you get used to the ugliness, you must adjust to the
traffic jams, which I will also have to endure in Kabul. They are a huge
inconvenience, and it's understandable why the Baghdadis sometimes
hesitate to leave their homes. No traffic lights are operating, and the
roundabouts are always jammed, hence difficult to get through. You
have to sit waiting amid the stench and the insistent and inopportune
honking of the heavy trucks. What are the reasons for the sudden urban congestion? The tenfold increase in the number of vehicles on the
streets,[5] the disappearance of traffic officers, and, above all, the new
regulations that give priority to the movement of soldiers and staff associated with the famous green zone at the expense of ordinary towns-
people. Anything likely to obstruct the movement of VIPs has been
barricaded or definitively shut down.

All along the central thoroughfares of Karrada Street, business is
in full swing. The market for household appliances, stereos, satellite
dishes, and used furniture has never been so good. At dawn, the merchandise overflows the shops onto the wide sidewalks, sometimes even
into the street. The demand is so great, especially for satellite dishes
(forbidden under Saddam), that whole truckloads arrive daily from Jordan, Syria, Turkey, and Kuwait. From private individuals to hotels,
everyone is getting set up. Cell phone stores proliferate as well: a private phone network covering Baghdad and the surrounding area has
just been authorized. Its merits are vaunted on enormous billboards,
and they are not alone. Advertising of every sort has invaded the city,
and the streets of the central urban area are covered with hundreds of
brightly lit billboards planted in front of Siemens and LG boutiques.[6]

Religious music wafts from loudspeakers attached to the minarets
of this neighborhood, with its Christian and Shiite population. A holiday is being celebrated. None of the young people squatting near the
entrance to the mosque on this calm sunny morning know what's going on; they listen to the sacred music without giving it much thought.

Under Saddam, it was strictly forbidden for mosques to use the loud-speakers on their minarets to broadcast music of any sort. "It's the very first time these young people are hearing this music," explains a young imam, delighted to be of use to me, "since it's the first year we can celebrate with such pomp and ceremony Caliph Ali's accession to power. It happened the day the prophet Muhammad died, fourteen hundred years ago." The imam, hardly astonished by the ignorance of the boys in the street, points out the need for young people to "relearn their religion." In honor of the holiday, pilgrims have left Baghdad on foot for An Najaf, where Ali's mausoleum is located. On all the doors of Shiite households, as well as on the heavy portal of the neighborhood mosque, people have attached a few palm leaves and red or green flags celebrating the return of the pilgrims from Mecca.

Now I'm on campus, in front of the language department at the University of Baghdad, where I've come to pick up forty-four-year-old Nahla, a professor of French. On the outside of the building, the words "Faculty of Languages" are written in English, French, German, Spanish, Russian, and even Hebrew. We go on foot to the Rashid Street souk in the historic city center, inaccessible by car since the "liberation." Nahla is single and lives with her younger brother in Adhamiya, a Sunni neighborhood in the northern part of the city, which is said to be the heart of Baathist resistance. It is there that Saddam was seen for the last time in public on April 9, 2003, haranguing the crowd on a public square across from the Abu Hanifa Mosque.

Nahla, a specialist in literature, devoted her thesis to André Malraux. She has come back from a month in Royan, France, at a training course organized by the French Embassy. Nahla is worn down, and for good reason: a year ago, one of her brothers, a shopkeeper, was murdered in the middle of the city as he was getting into his car. His assailants robbed him of a small suitcase full of money. He left behind a wife and three children, who have to be taken care of. Her elder brother had a law practice and recently left the country for Yemen, where he found a position as a law professor at the University of San'a. He could no longer tolerate the occupation. Nahla admits that if she could, she too would leave Iraq. I sense she is feeling lost, distraught, in the face of so many new things and the difficulty of reorganizing and inventing a future for herself.

We stroll through the area of booksellers, stationers, and printers. Through the open doors of workshops, I make out the silhouettes of monumental printing presses where people still work with lead type. Impressive color posters of the Shiite imams and their families are un-rolled on the shelves. Since the fall of the regime, their sales have mul-tiplied. I note as well the presence of calendars, also illustrated with the imams' pictures. But there are other images too. I see Ali al-Sistani, the Shiite spiritual leader of Iranian origin installed in An Najaf; Moham-mad Baqir al-Hakim, a Shiite cleric murdered on August 29, 2003, as he was leaving the mausoleum of Imam Ali in An Najaf;[7] Ayatollah Mohammad Sadiq al-Sadr, murdered by Saddam's thugs along with two of his sons in 1999;[8] and even Ayatollah Khomeini, father of the Iranian revolution, who died in 1989. Their dark-bearded faces and black or green turbans—a sign that they are *sayyids* (descendants of the Prophet)—are also reproduced on porcelain plates. Nahla, a good Sunni who advocates the strict separation of church and state, is shocked by that display of the Shiite faith, which, she assures me, would have been unthinkable a few months ago, at least in Baghdad. She's sorry that it's now possible to acquire these "souvenirs" somewhere besides the two holy Shiite cities of An Najaf and Karbala.

Right on time, the poster merchant turns up the sound of his radio to listen to the BBC news in Arabic. A portion of the sidewalk dis-plays the day's papers—there are a great many of them—spread out on the ground. One asks in a front-page headline: "Who Is the Strongman of Iraq?" above photos of George W. Bush, Paul Bremer, Jalal Talabani,* Massoud Barzani, and Ahmad Chalabi.[9]

In a café not far from Mutanabi Street, we have an appointment with Falah Kamel al-Azawy, a forty-year-old filmmaker who boasts of being "the last producer named by Saddam." He assumed his duties in the cinema branch of the Ministry of Culture in January 2003, that is, two

---

*Talabani is the Kurd who became the president of Iraq in April 2005, after the gen-eral election in January of the same year.

months before the fall of the regime. How does a state artist (he and the other fifty-six directors, actors, and technicians in that branch of the ministry) get along on a monthly salary of fifty dollars? Badly. That is why Falah has another occupation: selling old books. "Under the embargo, a great many families resigned themselves to selling their libraries. Sometimes there were thousands of volumes. I served as an intermediary between these families and the booksellers, but that saddened me a great deal. Selling books is a sign you don't want to read anymore. It's like a refusal to move forward, to evolve."

Even though the Iraqi Governing Council (IGC) has ordered two documentaries from him, the first on the marshlands (a zone in the southeastern part of the country drained by Saddam) and the second on the mosques, Falah is only partly satisfied. He would have preferred to make a fictional film on the relationship between Iraqis and Americans under the occupation, but the IGC refused: what if he got the notion to show the negative aspects of that occupation? Another dream—he lacks the financial means to realize it—is to show how, after thirty-five years of a totalitarian regime, Iraqi society again finds itself vulnerable because of the sudden upheaval imposed from the outside, even though Iraq saw itself as a "country of revolutions." "We have certainly been relieved of a burden, but the embarrassment of having tolerated Saddam for all those years persists, and we are, so to speak, hampered by that shame." Then he comments cynically: "After all, chaos is like surgery; blood has to flow. And now you can find a taxi at any hour of the day or night in the streets of Baghdad!"

It's Thursday evening, and there's a party at the Amurabi Restaurant in the Karrada neighborhood. They're celebrating a Christian wedding. Producing a deafening din that makes conversation impossible, a group of five musicians plays a mix of Assyrian and Kurdish music and Arab songs. For several hours the three hundred guests, as if hypnotized, stand in a circle, turning in one direction for a short while, then in the other.

Not far from the Turkish Embassy and its double protective wall stands a white cottage accessible by a simple porch. There is no outer wall, no barriers, no armed men suspiciously searching your bag. The only thing guarding the premises is a century-old tree. It's the Hiwar Gallery and Café, one of the bright spots of contemporary culture in Baghdad, a haven of peace and harmony. In the little garden filled with birds, we savor a *mozguf* (a fish from the Tigris cooked on the grill) skillfully prepared by our host, the seductive Qasim al-Sabti, gallery manager and artist. His full white shirt highlights his beautiful tanned skin. A wayward lock of gray hair grazes the top of his forehead.

Qasim has exhibited his paintings in France in 2004. He tells how, since the end of the first Gulf war in 1992, he and his wife, Iman al-Shouk, a painter and sculptor—along with a few other artists—have increased their efforts to ensure that contemporary Iraqi painting does not disappear. "We've held a hundred exhibits under the embargo, nine since the 'liberation,' because, in spite of the obstructed roads, pressures from the government, and propaganda, I want us to stay alive. Now, from morning till evening, students in the fine arts—painters, sculptors, journalists, and other writers—crowd inside to meet, drink a cup of coffee, and exchange news."

Because of the presence of the U.S. military on the long Abi Nuwas Avenue, the dozen galleries traditionally located in the neighborhood cannot operate normally. The Hiwar Gallery intends to be the exception. It reopened immediately after the war. Stubborn, and persuaded that "the terrorists are not taking Iraqi artists as their targets," Qasim refuses to yield to the paranoia that has rapidly developed in the capital and does his utmost to save what remains of Iraq's artistic heritage. "The Americans made a huge mistake when, smiling all the while, they incited looters to break into the Saddam Center for Culture and into the National Library. The week they arrived, I saw with my own eyes as they drove their tanks through the main entrance of the museum and invited the 'Ali Babas,' as they call them, to go about their sad business. Within two weeks, more than five thousand paintings by the 'pioneers' of modern Iraqi art had vanished, canvases dating back more than a century."

Qasim immediately set out in search of those trying to sell the stolen paintings but got only as far as the intermediaries: "I had ten thousand dollars available after selling some possessions, including my car. I used it to recover forty-seven canvases by masters, with no help from the Ministry of Culture, which I had contacted and which didn't even bother to reply. Along with members of the new Union of Iraqi Artists, for which I serve as vice president, I even met with the minister of culture. We tried to convince him that as many canvases as possible had to be recovered at a fair price. But he replied that the coffers were empty. The truth is it's the Americans, and not the Iraqis, who will decide the fate of those canvases." In the meantime, the paintings recovered by Qasim, a list of which he sent to the ministry, are being kept safe in his private collections until they can take their place again in some new museum.

How does the artist feel in this city under occupation? "The lack of security is frightening, and there are explosions and murders daily. The kings of Baghdad are the Americans and the looters." The situation is even blocking his artistic activity. It's not that the unrest doesn't inspire him, but, at a practical level, he can't work without electricity or a sense of security. "The situation is making me crazy. For fear of kidnappings, I take my children to school in the morning and ask one of the gallery employees to pick them up in the afternoon. During the last thirty years, art has been like a dream we were weaving: it has allowed us to escape daily life. We want to go on dreaming. Let's not forget we have ten thousand years of a rich and thriving civilization behind us. I have faith in the future. We're not just simple Bedouins busy with our flocks in the desert. We're intelligent people who settled along two life-giving rivers and built one of the first civilizations in the world. No one, not even the Americans with their unparalleled striking force, can take those origins away or destroy our culture!"

When I arrive in front of the imposing two-story red brick building that houses the Dijla (Tiger) Gallery, two sand-colored armored vehicles are posted outside the entrance, making it hard for cars to get by. Atop the vehicles, three young Americans, pimply faced under their helmets, attend to some mysterious business, looking worried and, as always, holding their fingers on the triggers of their automatic M16 pistols. Fortunately, I'm on foot.

Zaīnap Mahdi, who speaks perfect French, is a very beautiful woman
with chestnut brown eyes. She is dressed in a suede jacket, elegant gray
trousers, and fringed ankle boots. Zaīnap comes from a rich and powerful Shiite family with close ties to Faisal I (her father was his minister of education). She has been painting since early childhood. In 1977,
after serious administrative difficulties, she opened the Dilja Gallery on
the former family property on the banks of the Tigris.

"During the war, I was in Jordan with my three daughters, but I had
the gallery guarded by people I could trust, and nothing disappeared,"
Zaīnap says with satisfaction; then she complains about the moribund
state of the Baghdadi art market since the "liberation." "It's no longer
the Baghdad we knew, and after thirty-five years of dictatorship, the society has fallen victim to a great weariness." No sooner had she come
back than Zaīnap had to deal with a tragedy: her twenty-one-year-old
son was kidnapped for three days by a gang of eight, including two police officers. She was able to get him back safe and sound, but only by
paying a ransom of several thousand dollars. "These practices have become very common in the city, but no one can speak out against them,
since the police—we don't even know if they exist anymore or, especially, whom they're protecting—are in cahoots with the abductors.
When that happens, you have to manage on your own," the gallery
owner says with a sigh.

The vast Shiite neighborhood of the capital (with more than two million residents), formerly Saddam City, has been renamed Al-Sadr City
by Baghdadis, in honor of Mohammad Sadiq al-Sadr, killed in 1999.
His son, Moqtada, stood up to U.S. soldiers in April 2004 and throughout the summer. Cell phones don't work here. The residents are too poor
and have not been targeted as a financially solvent market by the rapidly expanding telephone companies in the capital. Al-Sadr City is an
enormous open-air dump where sacred images of Imams Ali and Hussein, photos of the martyrs al-Sadr, father and son, along with those
of Mohammad Baqir al-Hakim, share space with emaciated goats and
muddy sheep sprawled in the middle of the road or calmly grazing on
the piled-up garbage.

In honor of the tenth of *moharram* (the day commemorating the murder of Hussein, the third imam and grandson of the Prophet, killed in Karbala), processions were held along Bab-el-Mourad Street leading to the Al-Kazimiya sanctuary, one of the Shiite holy sites in Baghdad, which takes its name from the seventh and ninth imams, supposedly buried there.[10] On either side of the street leading to the cupolas, which are flanked by four minarets and covered with gold leaf, the closely packed crowd is noisy and attentive. They advance under the apparently indifferent eyes of U.S. soldiers seated on two armored vehicles. I really wonder what that procession means for these Americans. The crowd sprinkles itself with rosewater. It's an impressive sight: dozens of adult men, followed by children, rhythmically flagellate themselves from early afternoon till nightfall. Some events from Hussein's life are reconstructed. An old man depicting him appears on a richly decorated white horse. Two children walk beside him: they are his sons, who, according to legend, were imprisoned when he was murdered and sent to Damascus in the company of enemy soldiers. At dusk, rice and soup are handed out to all the passersby, including the Iranians, the oldest of whom are transported on the back of carts used for carrying merchandise. Mysteriously, they all wear white masks, as if they want to protect themselves from Iraqi bacteria.

At the al-Masbah police station, which looks like an entrenched camp behind three barbed wire fences and concrete blocks, the young Iraqi police officers in brand-new uniforms do not seem terribly busy. It's the quiet part of the afternoon, and five of them are playing cards in a hallway. "We're not the ones who put up all those blocks; it was the Americans. They imposed that so-called protection on us," explains a twenty-seven-year-old lieutenant named Habib, who was kind enough to talk to me without "official authorization." "We're not afraid and don't feel we have to barricade ourselves. That gives a poor image of the law. But the Americans are scared stiff!"

Habib receives me in a room sparsely furnished with a desk and two chairs. The odor of urine is overpowering. In the background, noise from the whirring generator obliges us to raise our voices. As for the looting, he notes, the situation has improved somewhat, because "in April 2003 we were catching about fifty thieves a day, compared with only two or three now." He criticizes the Americans for keeping all the information on terrorists for themselves and for not letting Iraqi police officers participate in the investigations. "They have no confidence in us; it's disappointing, because, as Iraqis, we know this country much better than they do."

Habib joined the police force four years ago at just nineteen, convinced that only that institution would guarantee him a future. But no sooner had he left the police academy when the regime fell. "The Mukhabarat and the Baath Party were spending their time watching us. Now we're more at ease. But we have to adapt to the Americans. They're extremely fussy and give orders we don't understand, either literally or figuratively."

Hence, after the "liberation," the Americans stayed on the premises day and night for two months before letting them operate on their own. "When we'd arrest a drunk or a prostitute, for example, they'd force us to release them at once. We definitely didn't have the same methods," he explains, still utterly astonished. Did he get something positive from that "cohabitation"? Habib smiles, a touch embarrassed: "New clothes, a new pistol"—he wears an Austrian-made automatic on his belt[11]—"generator units, air-conditioning for the offices, not to mention the pay, which went from twelve dollars a month under Saddam to three hundred dollars, a real gold mine." But the "runaway inflation reduces our purchasing power, and the uniforms, badges, cars, and weapons arrive at a snail's pace, as if the Americans hadn't yet decided how exactly to use us," he complains as his coworkers signal their agreement.

While we're chatting, someone brings in two rather excited individuals who have been shouting abuse at each other while waiting in line at a gas station. Apparently, it's nothing serious. Habib acknowledges that he is inundated by these minor infractions, attributable to the disorganized state of the society, when he should be focusing on arms trafficking and terrorism. The new Iraqi police officers are disoriented, caught between the resistance, which considers them "collaborators," and the oversight of a foreign power, which is sometimes difficult to accept. They no longer know whom they're working for, and that, he acknowledges, sometimes leads them astray. "Some of us are part of gangs of kidnappers who wreak havoc in the city. That will go on so long as we don't have someone at the head of the state who will establish order," he concludes.

In the Adhamiya neighborhood, to which I've returned this afternoon, the Sunni mosque Abu Hanifa, which contains the tomb of the "greatest of imams," summons the faithful to Friday prayer. An Iraqi flag unfurls its colors outside the white cupola, built by the Ottoman sultan Süleyman the Magnificent in 1535. In the courtyard near the main entrance, the sanctuary clock in a high brick tower is surrounded by scaffolding. It was seriously damaged by U.S. bombs on April 10, 2003, the day after Saddam appeared on the public square outside the mosque. Since that day, iron rails placed here and there prevent cars from parking on the sidewalk next to the religious building, and armed guards are posted on the porch.

Thirty-four-year-old Mohammad, assistant to the imam, has me visit the premises a few minutes before the beginning of prayer. In the gardens of the mosque, a cemetery of *shahid* (martyrs) was built in memory of the thirteen foreign Arabs and twenty-seven Iraqis killed while praying during the bombings. The sheikh still can't understand these "reprisals," since Saddam didn't even enter the mosque. Some of the faithful undoubtedly belonged to resistance movements, he acknowledges, but all the others were mere civilians. Although he is quick to accuse foreign journalists, especially Westerners, for the U.S. attacks—"because they gratuitously claimed that the resistance is everywhere, especially in the mosques"—Mohammad acknowledges that on that day he himself played the role of amateur journalist by filming Saddam—at the request of his superiors, he explains. His video is for sale everywhere and has made the rounds of the Arab world. In it the dictator appears in military dress haranguing a packed crowd, his right arm lifted in a salute, smiling and at ease. "Saddam was not observant and promoted atheism," explains Mohammad, who was arrested by

U.S. soldiers, then released after a hard-hitting interrogation about the resistance. "He had tactlessly invented a distant kinship to Imam Ali to establish closer ties with the Shiites, but no one was fooled by it. No one liked Saddam, but no one likes the Americans either!"

North of the city, in the Qahira neighborhood, a cottage that borders the expressway running along the east bank of the Tigris is crumbling under climbing vines. Before the road was built in the 1960s, the property and its many orchards were a haven of peace. A family of Kurds (a brother and his five sisters) from Dohuk, a town near the Turkish border, inherited their parents' house. They were all born in Baghdad, where they grew up and completed their studies. The brother and sisters communicate in Arabic even among themselves.

Ibrahim is thirty-eight years old and in charge of his thirty- and thirty-two-year-old sisters, as well as twenty-five-year-old twins. Their mother died fifteen years ago, and their father only three years ago: "He so would have liked to have witnessed the fall of Baghdad." The eldest sister, who is thirty-four, is married and lives in another neighborhood with her husband. When Saddam was deposed, the eldest son rushed to his father's grave to tell him about it. Ibrahim owns a perfume shop in the commercial district of Adhamiya. Aqil, his younger brother, supplies him with the merchandise from Kuala Lumpur, Malaysia, where he sought exile seven years ago with no intention of returning. "Aqil has adapted to a new way of life. Malaysia—where the Iraqi diaspora is very present—has become his second home. His import-export business in manufactured goods is growing, so why would he come back?" At his father's funeral, Ibrahim saw Aqil again and understood he could never readjust to the living conditions in their country. "I, on the other hand, embrace my Iraqi identity," says Ibrahim. "It's not easy, though, because Saddam turned us against one another until hatred erupted. No one dares to take on the responsibility of the surrounding chaos, and everyone hypocritically accuses the Americans. I'm a citizen of this territory, which is temporarily leaderless but is searching for its unity. Its anguish is my own," the young man with delicate features stubbornly declares, expressing himself calmly as one of his two green parakeets perches on his shoulder.

In the wide hallway leading to the kitchen, I discover eleven cages hanging from the wall, some holding several birds of the most varied species. "Their chirping is often unbearable," one of the twins whispers to me while the other busies herself setting the table, a bird on each shoulder. "At first, I kept them at the shop, then I brought them here. We can't leave the house for more than a day because of them," Ibrahim says with a smile.

In the living room, one of the twins turns on the television. After searching for a long time—the satellite dish offers an enormous choice —she chooses an Arab music channel. I take it she is irritated with her older brother, who sometimes keeps her from playing her favorite videos as loudly as she would like so as not to insult his precious birds. On the customary wood tray in front of the guest's chair, she gives us a glass of fresh water, a *piala* of sweet black tea, and a basket of fruit, still moist, with a small dish and knife. The young women, each more beautiful than the next, have long chestnut brown hair that highlights their regular features and a peaches-and-cream complexion. They wear very stylish pants (tight low-rider jeans) inside the house but abandon them in favor of long skirts to go out if their brother decides the jeans attract too much attention. Since the fall of the regime, the girls have made a point of wearing a head scarf (no one wears it within the home), and they no longer do their errands by themselves.

When I came in, I noticed large *x*'s of blue adhesive tape on all the windows in the house. "We were holed up here throughout the war, except when we decided to join my sister in El-Mansour, where we thought we'd be safer. We were wrong, because that's where most of the bombs fell!" one of the twins remembers with a laugh.

Fatima, the thirty-year-old sister, arrives. She has been a translator for the Governing Council since its creation, but "it's a secret." None of the neighbors or even family members have been told because "we're afraid they'll spread the news, which would put us in danger," she explains. Almost on a daily basis—no one has an accurate count—anonymous Iraqis are found killed by a bullet to the head. Later, people learn that they were working for the U.S. occupying force. Fatima is therefore taking an enormous risk by going into the green zone every day, but she believes it's worth it, financially and socially: "This work earns me four hundred dollars a month and teaches me methods whose very existence I had not even suspected. In addition, I'm making daily progress in English."

She translates archival documents from different Iraqi ministries—especially the Commerce Ministry—into English. "This work, in collaboration with civilians, gives me the impression that I'm doing my small part to rebuild our country. I'm aware of the many mistakes the Americans make because of their ignorance about the problems facing the Iraqis on the street: the lack of security, the regulations, the distribution of potable water, gas, electricity, etc. Along with my colleagues I do my utmost to identify these mistakes so that our superiors will take notice of them." She recounts with astonishment that Paul Bremer always greets them pleasantly when he runs into them at the canteen and stands in line like everyone else, plastic tray in hand. That aspect of democracy is rather agreeable to her.

Fatima's work ended on June 30, 2004, when sovereignty was transferred to the Iraqis and the Governing Council was dissolved: "Every day I receive offers of work from U.S. businesses present in Iraq, but for the moment I haven't made up my mind. Maybe if I find myself unemployed again." Fatima is happy: under Saddam, she had no work and had to stay home, since it was very difficult for a young Kurdish woman from Baghdad to be hired, even if she was highly qualified.

In the hot night, our car slips onto the highway between two access roads. Past the Jadriya Bridge, a strange crowd attracts my attention. About twenty cars are parked in a lot with all their headlights on. The wind tamps down the fragments of song and music coming to me in blasts. Indifferent to the security measures poisoning Baghdadis' lives, thumbing their noses at terrorists and occupiers, joyous people dance on the asphalt in the dark. In the center of the group is a delicate white shape in a long dress, gyrating lasciviously and sometimes catching the light. It's the bride.

9

A Dominican Friar

I visit the assistant priest at the Dominican convent in Baghdad, which houses ten monks. Brother Yusuf Thomas belongs to the Assyrian Christian community.[1] Born in Mosul in 1951, he completed his studies in Strasbourg and took holy orders at the age of twenty-five. He returned to Iraq in 1979 and opened a publishing house attached to the convent. He expanded the library, cleverly sidestepping regulations and bringing in books from Lebanon and Egypt. With his five-person team, he manages to publish four books a year, but the war against Iran and the devaluation of the dinar has forced him to file for bankruptcy. The friar is also editor in chief of the journal *Christian Thought (Al-Fikr al-Masihi)*. For the last forty years, ten thousand monthly copies have been published in Arabic and distributed to bookstores and churches.

Trained in computer-assisted publishing techniques, which he began using as soon as the convent acquired the necessary equipment, the friar oversees a library of seven thousand volumes in four languages (Arabic, English, French, and Assyrian),[2] entirely cataloged on the computer.[3] In early 2004 Brother Yusuf published a very beautiful illustrated children's Bible in Assyrian, a language he remembers speaking at home as a child. His dream is to create a people's university that would grant diplomas to all comers, including auditors. He has already sent a plan to Paul Bremer, with a budget totaling two million dollars. He awaits a response but harbors few illusions.

The service is over, and Brother Yusuf receives me in a white robe, cell phone in hand. Later, I'll often find him in jeans and leather jacket in one of the cubicles of the Al-Rif cybercafé, where he goes every day

—it's a short walk from his convent—to read his e-mail and surf the Internet.

According to Brother Yusuf, the usual opposition between Christians and Muslims is inadequate for characterizing Iraqi society as it now stands. "All of us here, Christians and Muslims, have that thirty-five-year dictatorship in common," the cleric says. "Let's talk instead about the two opposing worlds of East and West. The problems of national groups have always turned on identity and time: how to situate oneself in relation to these two notions, which neither religion nor sociology can help us apprehend. For us, as for our neighbors, with whom we share a language—even the Iranian language is permeated with Arabic—along with the same Shiite culture, the same Muslim culture, and the remnants of Ottoman culture, the problems of identity are worsening. The first seven centuries of Islam's development were centuries of extraordinary enlightenment, and they undeniably influenced Thomas Aquinas, the Reformation, and the Western world in general. For half of its history, Islam did fine work. The dividing line dates from the thirteenth century. It ought to be studied in the first place by contemporary Muslims mature enough and numerous enough to do the work. If they don't, they'll go on paying the price. The West has already paid the price for its identity—which no one here denies—by recognizing the rights of the individual. A month ago, I distributed fourteen thousand copies of the Declaration of the Rights of Man in our country, so that the Iraqis would realize for themselves what a tremendous Western accomplishment it is. If those in the Eastern world had drafted that charter, they would have called it Declaration of the Rights of *Men,* since we are communitarians, whereas the West is individualist. Here—and it's a catastrophe!—we don't nurture the individual. Muslims are suffering today because they did not bring up individuals to say loud and clear, 'I think, therefore I am.' Muslims see everything through communitarian glasses. We suffer from communitarianism and from our identity. Our true identity is not Christian or Muslim, Jewish or Arab, Sunni or Shiite: it is Man. For thirty-five years, Saddam Hussein killed the individual and the associated civic and moral values. As a result, some of us are capable of blowing ourselves up in suicide bombings, showing contempt for the value of man. For them, man as such has no value. He acquires value only by being part of a community. That is the sickness of the Eastern world.

"Oriana Fallaci would respond that the problem goes back to Muhammad, but she'd be wrong.[4] Because, in a certain way, all religions have the same value. The issue is what to make of it. If Christianity had not had theologians or synods or thinkers or reformers, that religion would have become rigid, hidebound. And today Islam is hidebound, since it has kept people from calling things into question, even though some wanted to do so. The other day, I was invited to be part of a committee made up of intellectuals and men of faith, Christians and Muslims. The Muslims asked me to show them how we interpret our books. In fifteen centuries, the Muslims have never practiced exegesis."

According to Brother Yusuf, time is another dividing line between East and West. "Look how it's managed in the West, and compare that with here, where it doesn't have the same value. When I go to France once every two years, I take a malicious pleasure in observing these differences. In France people get impatient when a driver takes more than five seconds to move after a light turns green. Yet during their famous 'business lunches,' no one consults their watches and they can talk on and on for hours. As for French ex–prime minister Lionel Jospin's notorious 'thirty-five-hour workweek,' for us that regulation seems to come from another planet. No one in the Eastern world can understand that by working only thirty-five hours a week you give work to others because 'time is money.' Here time has never been money. If that expression had been at the root of our religions, the prophets never would have accomplished anything," he says with amusement. We begin to talk politics: "Colonialism's time is past; now it's globalization's turn, and Iraq is first in line in terms of being 'problematic.' At present in Arab and Muslim countries, it's not just the threat of gerontocracy. Above all, every regime, whether republican or monarchical, bases succession on bloodlines. That's the case in Libya, Syria, and Egypt, where the president's sons are at the controls, and even in Israel, where Sharon gives his sons a wide margin for maneuvering. 'Daddy's boys' are on the job, and Saddam Hussein had plenty of his own. I forgot the example of Bush Senior and Junior, who both have a Gulf War to their credit."

Although Saddam was arrested and his regime overthrown, "his soul

remains," according to Brother Yusuf. "The people are demanding another dictator. Why? Because the people are obsessed with their personal well-being rather than with the big ideas that govern the world.
All it takes is terrorists raising the anxiety level about an attack and
people start calling for a 'firm hand.' Fear dominates the world. That's
nothing new in itself, but the methods are new. Fear has always been
used by religions, by politicians, by terrorists. The phenomenon of terrorism has changed. 'State terrorists' have more or less disappeared, and
Colonel Qaddafi looks like a choir boy compared with those wreaking
havoc today. The 'new terrorists' pay no mind to the notion of borders.
The United States is making many mistakes. It claimed to be attacking 'rogue states' even though it had nurtured those same terrorists in
the past. For the most part, the Arabs and Muslims who have emigrated
to the West, especially the United States, are exemplary citizens who
don't drink, don't party, and properly perform jobs no one else wants in
those countries. But there are all those who haven't become model im-
migrants and who fall prey to terrible identity crises. They belong neither to the West nor to the East. They've been dragged down by daily
contact with American society, which has gone to their heads. And the
chief thinker who's made them dizzy is Samuel Huntington with his
Clash of Civilizations.[5] Strictly speaking, it's is not a 'clash of civilizations' but a clash between one civilization and other cultures. Because
there's only a single civilization, the Western one, based essentially—
which is what gives it its power—on the mastery of technology and
of matter, whereas other cultures have no familiarity with industry or
with matter or with technology."

Brother Yusuf insists there is total incomprehension between the
two worlds of East and West. "You come here with your minds already
made up. We remain entrenched in our own positions and with our own
people. You throw bombs at us, we reply by brandishing slogans or Korans. Some dialogue! If the Americans remain stationed on their bases
here, which is most likely, we'll go on blowing them up and they'll go
on arresting us. Things can only end badly."

The general obsession with insecurity exasperates Yusuf Thomas.
When I mention the subject, he abruptly cuts me off: "You in the West,

you're scared too. They're afraid in America, everyone's afraid! Let's distinguish between fear and anxiety, and let's not forget their corollary: prudence. The West has gotten rid of its anxiety thanks to psychoanalysis, and I think of Freud as a prophet of modern times, but he created societies that suffer from egoism and loneliness. When I'm on a train, subway, or bus in Paris, I can't greet people, because it just isn't done, unless there's a dog: in that case, I can say a couple of words to it, and its master looks at me and smiles. But if it's a child, I must restrain myself, since the parents will suspect I'm a potential pedophile. In the Eastern world, human relations are both simpler and more sincere. Two men embracing for a long time in the street and expressing their good wishes are not suspected of being homosexuals; they're two friends."

The friar is outraged that the price of a barrel of oil, the barometer for purchasing power in all the oil-producing countries, is now determined in the West because of the globalization of economic networks. "And you expect terrorists won't be created by such a situation?" But the fiery cleric concludes his discussion of the two opposing worlds with a nice formulation borrowed from Daryush Shayegan, an Iranian philosopher and professor of comparative civilization in Paris.[6] Shayegan writes that the Arab world in the East must "steal and domesticate the sacred fire of the West." That "sacred fire," according to Yusuf Thomas, is nothing other than a profound knowledge of man and his limits.

10

A Resistance Fighter
and a Former Fedayee

The resistance fighter is a middle-aged university professor. The former fedayee (a member of Saddam's Guard) is a young father. Both live in the same neighborhood in the northern part of the capital, and both are profoundly hostile in the face of the events that have occurred in their country since the U.S. attack in 2003. One says he is secretly working in the resistance to get the coalition troops to leave—he hatches the violent plans, he's the brains. The other, skeptical after spending several years serving the dictatorship—for a long time, he committed acts of violence, he's the brawn—is attempting to refashion his life.

In an elegant olive corduroy suit and white shirt, despite his age and a slight limp, the man with the salt-and-pepper beard and careful way of speaking radiates a certain power. He is Sunni but is not inclined to say so, wishing to avoid playing the Americans' game: "Since their credo is divide and conquer, we're all supposed to identify ourselves in one way or another, so they can label us," he begins.

Abu Alhasan Albyati has written his name in my notebook in his beautiful round handwriting, explaining he has just chosen it. He has been a professor "of a scientific subject" at the University of Baghdad for five years and is the author of two books (in the most recent one, he addressed the relationship between Islam and Arab nationalism). His life is sharply divided between two causes: helping his wife get through her cancer and "avoiding civil war" by taking part in the resistance. "I dedicate myself to those two causes day and night; they've become my reason for being," he insists.

Since April 2003, Abu has led a group of about two thousand men, composed, he assures me, of Christian Iraqis, Shiite and Sunni Muslims, Kurds, and Turkomans. The group is divided into battalions, which are themselves made up of platoons. Within each platoon the smallest operational cell consists of five or six men, "the ideal number for urban guerrilla warfare," the professor and chief strategist of the group points out. "What hotel have you been staying at?" he asks me abruptly. I'm not at a hotel, I'm staying with friends. He seems reassured: "Some groups in the resistance have planned to attack all the hotels without exception. They're convinced that agents of the Mossad [the Israeli secret service] are hiding among the foreigners staying there."

According to the professor, the "resistance" is not guided by any organizing principle. Between twenty and thirty groups with various ideologies and methods exist in the capital, joined together merely by the same hatred of the occupation forces, which they seek to drive from the country. "Some want to get rid of the Americans because they're Christians and Westerners; others, because they're Jews; still others, quite simply, because they're occupying our country."

Abu is discreet about his own recruitment methods, but he does not hide the fact that his students put their trust in him. "They all have brothers, uncles, and cousins whom we put to use. The university is a very handy platform." The weapons? They come from the Iraqi army's stockpiles, looted long ago during the army's pitiful rout. More impressively, he claims that some men in his group, engineers from old Iraqi military factories, are manufacturing their own missile, dubbed Al-Khattab (after a caliph who succeeded Muhammad and is very popular among Sunnis), which could be used "in special cases." He will not elaborate.

The professor loathes "those who rode along with the Americans not because they hate Saddam but for the money." He names Ahmad Chalabi and Abdel Aziz al-Hakim,[1] members of the Governing Council. And he continues to air his complaints: "Under Saddam, it was forbidden to openly criticize the regime, but you could do it in secret. Today the slightest political criticism of a leader working for the Americans can get us wiped out by its militia."[2] The United States—and the CIA —are of course the focal point of all resentment: "Not only have the

Americans attacked our country militarily, they have attacked its culture and its religion, not to mention the civilians killed before the war by sanctions that smothered us. They haven't found the notorious weapons of mass destruction because they don't exist. What they want is to destabilize and weaken us. They constantly attack Islam. There's no other reason behind the reaction to the terrorist attack of September 11. They have a ready-made scenario: the CIA is going to cause panic by arranging the murder of al-Sistani, the religious leader of the Shiite community, to make the whole world believe that the former Baathists, the Sunnis, and the Shiites are killing one another, and that will allow them to legitimate their presence."

Suddenly giving a smile, he quotes "The Winner Takes It All," the title of a song by Abba, the Swedish pop group known worldwide in the 1970s. "Of course, the Americans possess the power of weapons, money, the media, and the United Nations, but if we go on doing nothing, that will never change. In Algeria, the Arabs have been fighting for 150 years. It's our turn." The professor lays claim to an "Islamic" democracy, whose seeds were already present in the Koran. "Before making an important decision, the prophet Muhammad always asked the advice of his close circle. That's the democracy we want, not the one the Americans want to impose on us, with their free economy, their free religion, and all sorts of other freedoms that lead to chaos. Those freedoms don't suit us; they're not acceptable to us here. And why do those invaders bring that democracy with their tanks rolling? Did anyone ask them to come and liberate us from Saddam Hussein? Weren't they more interested in our chemical weapons and our capacity to fight Israel than in our dictator? We didn't invade the West, proclaiming that Islam would be the best religion there. So why impose their 'democracy' on us?

"I lost my only brother in the Iran-Iraq War; that's the reason I'll hate Saddam for the rest of my life. And then, he's just a coward; we saw him when he was arrested. So don't tell me the resistance is pro-Saddam!" The professor divides the resistance into three groups: the Baathists; the Al-Qaeda subgroups, who arrived from neighboring countries through borders that have become porous; and groups "like mine," he insists, whose members were eager to join "not out of hatred for the Christians—that would be wrong and simplistic—but because an identified enemy attacked our culture." The professor saw the world turned upside down when the Soviet Union collapsed. "During the cold war, the USSR was like a huge cannon trained on the United States. It was an entity supported by Third World countries, including Iraq, in its battle against American ideology. The USSR imploded, and the threat emanating from the Soviets, which our enemy feared, has vanished."

Punctuating his speech with quotations from Samuel Huntington's *Clash of Civilizations,* he confirms that the double attack in Erbil on the day of the Feast of Sacrifice bears the mark of the Ansar al-Islam group. That allows him to compare Iraq's situation with Afghanistan's: "Here as there, the Americans have the same strategy. They impose their way of life, their way of seeing things. But at least in Iraq they haven't yet found the equivalent of a Karzai; that's a very lucky thing!"

The machinations of the secret service frighten him. CIA agents infiltrate the Kurdish community. In addition, the Iraqis in exile or the many Iranians found in the country—"since all the borders are open"—can easily be used by both sides. Six university professors, one of them known for his anti-Israel position, have been murdered. He fears it's the work of Mossad (aided by the CIA), which has increased its activities since the fall of the regime.

In passing, the professor laments the lack of knowledge among his base of support—"they're uneducated, hence sometimes difficult to control"—as well as the looting at the university, where computers, door and window frames, electrical switches, even green plants disappeared within six days of the "liberation." Like many, he blames the Kuwaitis, southern neighbors who were hated since the first U.S. intrusion in 1991.

What are his group's feelings toward the Baathist resistance? He does not think that getting rid of former members of the Baath Party by way of reprisal is an adequate solution. "Those people all have family who will take their revenge sooner or later...and that would lead to civil war, to the greater delight of the Americans," he concludes. "We don't want the Baath Party to return to power, but why ban it? That's what democracy's all about, isn't it? The acceptance of differences?"

———

Ali looks unpretentious. He welcomes us in the courtyard outside his cottage in an Adidas jogging suit, decides to change, and comes back in jeans and a T-shirt that clings to his muscular torso. I notice he has even taken the time to put on cologne. He prefers that we talk "on neutral ground," in some café in an adjacent neighborhood, since his family still doesn't know the details of his activities, much less of his exactions.

Ali is twenty-six. His lip highlighted by a fine mustache, eyes hidden behind fake Ray-Ban sunglasses, black hair cut short, he could pass for a student "in marketing," as he says. Until April 2003, this young man was first lieutenant in an elite unit, the Saffa Brigade, under the direct orders of Uday Hussein, the dictator's eldest son, who was known for his excesses, his killing sprees, and his debauchery.[3] It was for that sadistic master that in four years of "good and loyal service," Ali cut off thirteen tongues and about forty hands, by his own estimate.

Since adolescence, Ali, tired of studying the Koran at the madrasa, had dreamed of a military career that would allow him to be trained physically, to take courses at the academy, and, in short, to become a disciplined officer. At eighteen, he enlisted with the fedayeen, the regime's all-purpose men, known for their brutality. Three years later, he was selected to join the Saffa Brigade, specially charged with spying on Saddam's enemies. That elite role earned him a special identity card (which he has since burned) with Saddam Hussein's picture on it, personally signed in gold letters by Uday. Above all, it earned him a generous salary of seventy dollars a month. His mission was to murder, punish, or kidnap for "reasons of state."

When Ali recounts his previous work in detail, he chooses his words carefully, and, as if to minimize the horrors he is going to relate, his voice softens. About the tongues, Ali has precise memories. He and his confederates usually cut them out in the middle of the street. They worked in threes in front of horrified passersby and the families of the victims, who were paralyzed with fear. Dressed all in black, hooded, and equipped with shears, Ali tied up and blindfolded his victim. A second fedayee grabbed the poor fellow's head, and the third forced him to open his mouth: "We were always followed by an ambulance charged with dispensing first aid to the victim before taking him to prison," he remembers.

There was a punishment corresponding to each type of offense. Liars had their backs broken with a block of concrete; spies had their hands cut off; traitors were decapitated after being tortured at length on a secret base in the northern part of the city. Out of sheer sadism, Uday had most of these executions filmed; he possessed a video collection of his atrocities.

One of the last executions that Ali remembers took place in 2000, when the group decapitated thirty-nine people whom Uday had accused of setting up a prostitution network of Iraqi women, who were sold to rich Kuwaitis. "There were about fifteen women and twenty-four men," Ali recalls. "We divided up the work between those who cut off heads and those who collected them. Then the remains were thrown into the yards of their families' homes, to serve as an example. I was part of the second group." He bows his head.

Did he know at the time that Uday, to satisfy his deviant sexual appetites, participated in orgies in the company of Iraqi women, who were taken by force and handed over to him? "We all knew it; we were his bodyguards. How could we not have known his lifestyle?" he acknowledges at once. "But no one could go against his orders; the whole country belonged to him. He would have killed us. At the time, no one asked questions. It's only since the end of the war that I've realized what I did. It's inhuman." These words are his only expression of remorse.

Ali still hasn't fully come to terms with the fall of the regime. His unit was in charge of security in three Shiite districts, some of the poorest in the capital. The morning the U.S. Marines arrived, he was still patrolling in a Toyota pickup filled with men equipped with heavy machine guns. The fedayeen had received the order to gather information on the enemy's progress and to arrest anyone they felt was "not on the right side." Convinced that their commandos would easily defeat the Americans in bloody hand-to-hand street fighting, Ali is still waiting for that battle. "I didn't understand we were defeated until I saw some of my wounded colleagues falling around me. However unlikely it may seem, we were surrounded in the center of Baghdad by American tanks. My superior then declared we had done our duty and gave us the order to go home as quickly as possible."

Two days later, Ali went to Ramadi, a city in the "Sunni triangle," where he met up with friends. "We were all in a state of shock. We couldn't get used to the idea that we'd lost. Just the day before, we'd been dreaming of medals, villas, and cars that Uday would hand out to us to congratulate us for conquering the Americans."

Yet the former fedayee minimizes the U.S. military victory. According to him, it is not far-reaching, having been facilitated by the "purchase" of corrupt Iraqi officers in key posts, who ordered air civil defense not to fire on enemy planes. "On the eve of April 10, 2003, on the road between Samawa [a city in the southern part of the country] and Baghdad, I saw tanks and trenches totally deserted by our soldiers, who had received the order to clear out without a fight. What a waste, and just when we were so pleased with ourselves for having such a large number of armored vehicles," Ali bitterly laments. He shakes his head in confusion. "The hardest thing is that we uncovered saboteurs and spies right here. . . . And all for nothing! . . . But I didn't question things. I was defending my country and my leader, whose life had to be saved. Now," he snickers, "we live in 'wonderland,' with no leader and no homeland. We've lost all our dreams, all our hopes."

How does Ali see his future with his wife and two-year-old daughter? "When I was a fedayee, I wanted to make a lot of money and build me a house. But now . . ." He's trying to find work in a field close to his "specialization": as a bodyguard. "In protection, or whatever," the young man mumbles, embarrassed. "An Iraqi company will be quick to hire me, in the first place because I'm a professional, but especially because I'm a former fedayee." All the same, Ali is afraid of getting arrested by the occupation forces and lives very discreetly, always resisting the temptation to contact his former companions. Everyone is trying to save his own skin and integrate into civil society as quickly as possible. "Those who collaborate in one way or another with the occupier, which is to say, 80 percent of the population, are quite satisfied. They're paid well."

Resistance groups have already approached Ali twice, but so far he has refused to join them. "The sadness I felt when Uday died,[4] then when his father was arrested,[5] has completely dissipated. Now I think of myself and my family. I've banned TV from the house so we won't be depressed." A husband and father, Ali is resolutely trying to turn his back on violence.

I I

IN THE "SUNNI TRIANGLE"

In Baghdad I'm given to understand that going to Al-Falluja and Ramadi, two cities west of Baghdad that are considered fiefs of the resistance to U.S. occupation, would be reckless. The population, it is said,
has become extremely suspicious of foreigners, whoever they might be.
I keep to my plan, once more banking on the kindness and hospitality
of the people I'll meet—and on my lucky star.

The morning I leave for Al-Falluja, a bad wind draws up garbage
into a multitude of vertical whirlwinds and makes the leaves on the
date palms flap about noisily. As we are getting into the car, we learn
that a bomb has exploded in the center of the city, in a building where
soldiers from the New Iraqi Army, trained by the U.S. military, had
come to pick up their pay. Eleven hundred pounds of TNT killed
about fifty people and wounded another forty, all of them Iraqis. Like
the pro-Russian Chechens, considered "traitors" by the independence
fighters, the Iraqis who collaborate with the Americans are on their way
to becoming the chief victims of the conflict. Wisam, a thirty-year-old
Arab-Kurd who is coming along with me, has a slightly different interpretation: "The Americans are too well protected in their bunkers in
Saddam's former palace. As a result, the resistance has a hard time getting to them, so it's obliged to 'fall back' on easier prey—Iraqis."

We take the short trip on one of the ugliest highways in the country, which passes by Abu Ghraib. The prison was emptied of all its
prisoners on the eve of hostilities, and the United States is now holding coalition prisoners there in solitary confinement.[1] We come to the
city of Al-Falluja, which is so ordinary it attracts little notice. At ev-

ery jammed intersection, we are approached by kids selling bananas, one of the least expensive fruits. On the walls are the same signs as in Baghdad, vaunting private gyms with bare-chested men sporting ultrachiseled muscles. Along with the cyberclubs, these are the most popular sites in post-Saddam Iraq. There's a main street, single-story businesses, cafeterias where you can get a cup of tea on the run—and no American presence. The residents of Al-Falluja drove out the Americans a few months ago. Their only base is found on the periphery of the city, in one of Saddam's former residences. According to the people here, the Americans don't go out until nightfall, and then only within the framework of their "special operations." During the day, they're confined indoors because of the many attacks by the resistance.[2]

The family that welcomes me is celebrating the return of one of its eminent members from a pilgrimage to Mecca. The men are lined up on couches running the length of the walls in the guest room, to the right of the courtyard of this vast house in the central city. Twenty-seven mustachioed men are all similarly dressed in blue or gray dishdasha (long djellabas); those who are especially chilly wear a jacket over them. The men look somber under their white-and-red-checked kaffiyehs, which sometimes fall low on their shoulders. They chat quietly in front of glasses of orange juice served on trays by the youngest members of the family.

Gradually, the volume increases. One of the men, a former teacher recently dismissed because he belongs to the Baath Party, suddenly explodes: "The Americans are behaving like the Germans and their führer in Europe during World War II! In the former Ministries of Defense, the Press, and Information, as well as in Education, the de-Baathification of our country is beginning to look like de-Nazification. Why did they ban the only political party of ours that was known and renowned? Why drive out at least eight thousand of its members and authorize the creation and development of dozens of little parties that have no meaning and no legitimacy, merely on the pretext of democracy?" He adds in a calmer tone: "The cement works that were not looted because we defended our city are now occupied by U.S. soldiers, and the first thing they did was to stop operations. Do you realize what that means? They pillage, break, vandalize, and destroy everything in their path! Are they trying to guarantee that their companies—responsible in principle for rebuilding our country—won't be without work? They steal our wealth and prevent us from developing. What we need most in the world is work. We want nothing to do with the democracy they wish to impose on us, so long as it, like everything else they produce except bombs, is only virtual."

The somber faces stare intently at their glasses of orange juice. No one comments, but everyone acquiesces in silence. The group seeks to minimize the existing rift between Shiites and Sunnis, which is considered "one more tool of the U.S. administration to divide us and spread anarchy."[3] The free-speaking teacher resumes: "The Americans promised us a better life, but since they've been here, prices have gone up and we don't have any purchasing power anymore. Worse: they claim to be the champions of human rights, but they violate those rights—our rights—with impunity whenever it suits them. A gulf separates us, and it's getting wider from one day to the next."

The teacher pauses while other guests try to persuade me that yesterday's attack in Baghdad was done by the Americans themselves (a widely held view in Iraq). The media were banned from the site, and there's the proof, they assure me. Resentment is growing as well because of the house searches, which go on constantly and occur with no respect for Iraqi women—not to mention the thefts and destruction. "Can anyone explain why the U.S. soldiers always proceed by blowing out the gate with a grenade, then kick in our doors? Can't they just use their hands?" asks an old man with a dramatic goatee. He ran the neighborhood madrasa for twenty-seven years and was also dismissed within the context of de-Baathification. "One of my neighbors was a witness to their barbarism. One day, after blowing out three gates, the soldiers entered the yard and found a pregnant woman lying dead, her belly open. And we're supposed to support their inhuman behavior? How can we remain indifferent to these raids by vandals from another planet?"

"You have to understand. We were proud to belong to the Baath Party," the teacher continues, "because they were working for the people. Here, in Al-Falluja, we're not afraid to declare ourselves members of that party. We're like a big family, a big tribe, whereas in Baghdad they're holed up like rats." A wave of laughter surges through the group. "The Americans are killing us, humiliating us. But don't they understand that hatred toward them is growing?"

Away from the presence of their elders, the young people, freer to express themselves, do not deny the existence of a resistance within the "Sunni triangle," but they dispute that its "heart" is located in Al-Falluja. Twenty-seven-year-old Ibrahim has trouble accepting the reputation of a violent city, which is presented as the so-called refuge of the resistance in the western part of the country. Yes, it exists. "It's inborn and invisible, hence invincible!" he says proudly. "Of course, we all have contacts with groups actively working against the occupier, but we're at war, aren't we?" All the same, he seems to doubt that a serious plan to thwart the Americans can see the light of day in the current chaos.

A computer scientist, he ran a Web site on the city of Al-Falluja before the "liberation," but now he hesitates to download "data on the Americans' real activities in the region" for fear they'll arrest him and throw him in prison. He knows his site is under surveillance. Recently, during a chat group on the occupation for which he was serving as webmaster, the site was attacked by a computer virus that forced him to stop the session. He can't quite imagine the future anymore. The only thing he's sure about is that the Americans "don't keep their promises." It's not people "of their word" who invaded this country, where keeping one's word is critical. He's also not prone to accept their open pursuit of their own self-interest.

Eleven miles farther north, in the cob village of Al Karma, Sheikh Meshan Abbas Jumaili, head of the Sunni tribe of the same name, is also receiving a large number of guests to celebrate his return from the pilgrimage. It's time for lunch, which is shared by about fifty men in turbans seated in front of mounds of rice with chicken and almonds. When they're done eating, they'll begin once more to tell their beads, making a regular rattling sound that is both surprising and familiar.

Our conversation is constantly interrupted by long embraces, since every new arrival is obliged to greet the hajji ceremoniously. Dressed in an immaculate djellaba over which he has pulled a black coat with gold embroidery, the sheikh is striking looking. He too admits the profound unpleasantness of the situation. When he returned from Saudi Arabia, he was searched for a long time and felt very ashamed. From time to time, he readjusts his yellow scarf with a brusque gesture. Like every pilgrim returning from Mecca, he wears that cloth, placed simply on his head, in place of the usual black-ringed kaffiyeh, and he walks barefoot.

"One of the Americans' biggest mistakes," says the sheikh, "is that they didn't make friends with the local population. For example, they attacked my house with a rocket launcher, thinking Saddam Hussein had sought refuge there. I explained to them that I never would have taken him in, since his thugs financed the murder of my cousin Abd al-Salam Aref in the 1960s.[4] But it was no use; they didn't listen to me. According to their information, Saddam was supposed to be there in my house. They were disappointed they'd made a mistake, but they didn't acknowledge it."

I learn that the sheikh has yet another reason for not liking the Americans. In September 2003, they "inadvertently" killed two of his sons while they were repairing a tire on the side of the Baghdad–Al-Falluja highway, no doubt mistaking them for terrorists. Yet the sheikh, whom the interim administration asked to head a regional administrative structure, briefly occupied that post, then gave it up just before leaving on his pilgrimage. Since his return from Mecca, he no longer wishes to focus on anything but his religious obligations, though he leaves the door open.

"If things move in the right direction, I'll return to more political concerns. They chose me because mine is one of the most influential families in Al-Falluja. I agreed because I was afraid that a refusal would dishonor our clan, but I was wrong. For me, there's nothing more important in this earthly realm than justice, peace, and truth, values that have been shamelessly flouted by the occupier. With the Americans, there is no justice!" he laments. "Under Saddam Hussein, who in spite of everything was able to distinguish between an influential sheikh and something else—which the Americans are incapable of doing—we lived in a safer world. Now there are too many political parties and pseudotruths contradicting one another."

"The best regime for Iraq," he asserts a little later, "would be an Islamic state that did not distinguish between Sunnis and Shiites, and which would govern the people by the Koran and the Sharia."

The banks of the Euphrates are particularly fertile, and I see that men and women here divide the farming between them. As groups of men turn over the ocher soil and prepare it for seeds, women in groups of three or four—who, it seems to me, sometimes sit in the fields—harvest by hand the animal forage. On that rich western plain, raising livestock has long since taken precedence over truck farming. Every farmer owns a stock of steers, calves, and sheep, which graze peacefully on the thick green grass under majestic palm trees that have grown on these banks for fifty years.

Just before reaching Ramadi, we cross the Euphrates, crisscrossed by small boats—unlike the Tigris—and arrive in the village of Abu Haswa. Our taxi driver has been paralyzed by fear ever since he realized I'm a foreigner. For him, every Westerner is necessarily connected to the U.S. Army and therefore personifies the enemy. He's afraid someone has spotted us and is following, and that his car will become a target. Yesterday, the sheikh of his village was killed by strangers, and he's still in shock. As I talk to him about my likely visits to tribal chiefs with ties to the Americans, he strongly advises me not to undertake them.

For the time being, Wisam takes me to his mother's family. Abdullah, the head of the household, raises sheep with his son Saïd. Their house is located below street level in their little village. It is composed of a rectangular main building (a long hallway opens onto three unfurnished rooms that toddlers scamper through barefoot) and an adjacent cottage that serves as a kitchen and bathroom. There is no running water and no electricity. And as usual in rural Arab settlements, no demarcation indicates where the neighbors' property begins (neighbors

are usually members of the extended family). You can go from one property to the next without even realizing it. Outside, I noticed a few cows
and chickens. I heard a donkey bray, and for a few seconds its powerful
cry managed to drown out the chorus of locusts. Once again, I take a
seat in a long guest room, waiting for dinner. But here, instead of richly
colored carpets, there are raffia mats that are just barely comfortable.

Like most of my Sunni hosts, the peasant family who welcomes me
is eager to minimize its differences with the Shiites and to underplay
the inherent danger should Shiite leaders come to power after the elections. That prospect seems much more acceptable to them than the U.S.
occupation.

Because I'm French, someone mentions the "head-scarf affair" that
is causing a stir in France and that is relayed in great detail by the
Arabic-language media.[5] My interlocutors don't understand the French
president's decision to ban the wearing of the veil to school and consider it a further humiliation, a failure to take their ways and customs
into account. I quickly realize that my taxi driver's fears were not far-
fetched. My hosts too are afraid that the CIA is hot on my heels and ask
me several times if I've received authorization from that U.S. agency to
write my book.

We return to the subject of the U.S. occupation, and for good reason. Wisam's family recently lived through a nightmare. Three days before the end of Ramadan, two sand-colored armored vehicles belonging
to the United States crashed through a guardrail and careened down
a hill, making an infernal racket. They positioned themselves outside
one of the clay houses not far from here. It was *iftar* (the breaking of
the fast during Ramadan). The soldiers entered the house, separated
men, women, and children, killed two men at point-blank range in the
yard, and shot out the women's legs. One of the women was pregnant
(they made the Iraqi interpreter ask her "what she had inside, a baby or
grenades"). The operation was covered by two helicopters whirling constantly above the farm, and they killed five people aboard a Toyota
pickup. The reason for all that? No one knows.

The suffering is still acute more than three weeks after the incident,
and the details of the soldiers' behavior are permanently etched in their
memories. Yes, the U.S. Army seems to be acting contrary to any no-

tion of humanity, contrary to common sense, opening an unbridgeable gulf between it and the Iraqis. "In the end, we tell ourselves that to be able to commit such acts, the Americans must be worse than the Tikritis [residents of Tikrit, Saddam Hussein's native city and fief], the caste of Iraqi society that felt the most powerful and the best protected under Saddam, and which allowed itself to decide everything in the people's place," Abdullah concludes.

He too advises me against talking with certain local sheikhs accused of being remunerated by the Americans, hence untrustworthy. He does want to show me, however, the new houses with garish colonnades a few miles from the road between Ramadi and Al-Falluja. One of the "collaborator sheikhs" has just finished building them, thanks to the Americans' money. "Traditionally," Abdullah explains, "the primary function of the sheikhs was to represent the villagers vis-à-vis the state, but the coalition is now hesitant to make them its intermediaries, especially in a zone as 'dangerous' as Al-Falluja. Nevertheless," he continues, "whatever the behavior of the U.S. military in the streets of Al-Falluja, the sheikhs will always remain in favor of negotiations. And yet—though this process was already perceptible even before the war—the presence of a foreign occupation force has reduced their authority and left the field relatively open for aggressive young Islamists who organize to defy the occupier and call for jihad and rebellion."

We begin to talk about Saddam. My two interlocutors, a father and son, don't like him. They think the ruler may have made an agreement with the United States to time the invasion of the country by enemy troops in such a way as to be the most advantageous to him. "In any case, everything's moving in reverse," says the son. If people were afraid to speak under Saddam, now it's even worse, since the Americans are even less tolerant and more powerful. In the bitter aftermath of the fall of a man they abhorred, they admit that life "was sort of normal under his iron fist." For all of them, "the predictable aftermath" has now given way to a lack of security and an absence of faith in the future.

Since that iron fist was obviously unbearable to them, why didn't they overthrow Saddam themselves? The Americans would have stayed home. They don't seem happy with my remark.

Saïd, who raises sheep like his father, particularly deplores one unexpected consequence of the war: the opening of the borders. "There are no more rules," he observes bitterly. "People continue to buy sheep from us at the same price, but the merchants then sell them for twice that in Syria and Jordan, because the standard of living is higher there." He compares that to the situation with oil, a commodity that has always had an advantage in the parallel markets of the region. What shocks this simple man born in 1979, whose dangling kaffiyeh does not conceal his already deep wrinkles, is the ease with which some have gotten rich. Saïd is aware that the previous system has already been replaced, but he has not yet made any effort to adapt to the new rules of business. "Under Saddam," he notes, half reclining on a few small cushions brought in by the children, "it was much harder to get rich quick. Except, of course, for the border guards and other government workers who had access to the import-export networks. Now everyone's in business."

Saïd also wants "an Islamic state" for Iraq. But does he completely understand the implications of such a choice (for example, the importance that would give the Shiite population of the country, which by most estimates comprises more than 60 percent of Iraqis)? He knows very well, however, what he must condemn in Shiism, namely, the blind acceptance of the ayatollahs's fatwas, "as if they were military orders." That constraint shocks Saïd, who even refers to the Koran to explain that "it is contrary to the teachings of the Prophet, who always favored debate within his close circle before making a decision."

His mother, Fatima, has joined us for dinner. She says little but replies if asked for her opinion. Under her black head scarf with a heavy beaded fringe that conceals her forehead, her face, etched by the years, is impassive. Within the chaos that surrounds her, her greatest disappointment is that "the Iraqi police work not for the good of the community but solely to receive a salary from the Americans."

In the evening I retire to my room, where I will sleep with six other women and a swarm of children. My bed is already made (a starched blanket on a mattress), just next to that of the lady of the house. They have waited for me all evening, and they stare at me, their faces heavy with fatigue (without my interpreter, I can't communicate with them).

I sense a certain suspicion, and despite the silence I believe I can hear these women's comments and questions: So that's what a real Western woman looks like! Why isn't she dressed like in the movies, but instead simply, like us? Doesn't her similar clothing conceal something? Why does she scribble in her notebook from left to right and not in the other direction, like us? Why does she get undressed to go to sleep? Why does she brush her teeth?

Someone brings me a pitcher and a cuspidor so I can spit out the water after brushing. At the necessary moment, I turn my back on the captivated group. Appreciating my modesty, some laugh quietly.

In the end, what did I hear in that "Sunni triangle" that everyone is so afraid of? The same thing as everywhere else in Iraq: criticisms, suffering, an enormous disappointment in the Americans. Up north, in Kurdistan, the question of the Kurds' future was always an underlying theme, but the content of the complaints was exactly the same.

12

EN ROUTE TO AN NAJAF

Today my destination is An Najaf, one of the major Shiite cities in the south, where the headquarters of the *hawsa* (the supreme religious authority of Shiites) is located. I have taken my place beside thirty-eight-year-old Yusuf, a former Al-Falluja retailer who gave up his tannery business when production dropped precipitously as a result of the constant electrical outages, lack of water, and supply problems. He now works as a taxi driver at the wheel of his impeccable old white Mercedes.

During the whole first part of our trip, Yusuf's hatchet face remains somber. He and his family have been enduring a tragedy for the past week. Eight days ago, his sixteen-year-old niece was kidnapped by strangers. In a call to the family's satellite phone, the bandits let them know they were demanding a ransom of one hundred thousand dollars. Twice, his sister was able to speak to her daughter, who sobbed at the other end, begging her parents to pay. Yusuf's brother-in-law is doing his utmost to raise the money, but it's no use. He thinks he can manage about six thousand dollars, no more. Will it be adequate for the kidnapper? What can be done?

Talking to the police would be pointless, he thinks. They have too much to do elsewhere. In addition, some officers are involved in this filthy business, and a code of silence reigns.[1] Friends have advised him to talk to the U.S. military to test its will to help the populace. Yusuf refuses, beside himself at the idea that his niece might pay the price for such an "experiment."

Since that sad event, he no longer sends his four children (two girls and two boys) to the neighborhood school for fear that they too will vanish. The only thing matching his anxiety is his desire to leave the hellish central city and find a less visible, hence less dangerous, home in the suburbs.

We're passing through Baghdad when I notice watchtowers. Atop them, Iraqi soldiers equipped with Kalashnikovs are standing guard. The towers were erected in November 2003, Yusuf tells me. The mission of the lookouts is to identify potential terrorists who might get a notion to attack U.S. military columns, which are common on this road. At the south gate of the megalopolis, we pass in front of a giant dump of tanks, trucks, cars, and other vehicles damaged during the most recent conflict. All of these carcasses are piled upside down on the ocher soil, waiting to be crushed and sold for scrap iron.

As we head south, images of Imam Hussein in a green turban, his smooth face framed by a brown beard, proliferate along the road. At my side, the very devout Yusuf fumes that these portraits "were painted by man and not by God." The former retailer has written a book on "everything that the present-day religions of Iraq have in common." The completed manuscript is said to be in An Najaf, in the hands of proofreaders who will render it in proper literary Arabic before it is published. "In these troubled times," Yusuf confides in me, "I want to send a message of peace to the world." As a good Muslim, he believes in the Last Judgment and lives his time on earth in preparation for the moment when he'll find himself face to face with God for "the final reckoning." That's why he constantly works to do good, making himself useful to others. "Without the certainty that I'll speak with the Almighty, I'd be nothing, I wouldn't exist," he affirms with a slight smile.

In every township we pass through, the central police station is bunkered or entirely hidden behind concrete blocks, barriers, and high walls. Between urban areas, the palm groves become denser, interrupted by forests of reeds. Here and there the high smoking towers of brick ovens stand out against an obstinately flat landscape. When we

come to Hilla, we find that a huge traditional painting depicting Saddam Hussein has been replaced by a no less impressive one of Imam
Ali.[2] Jostled by a violent wind, young people stretching a calligraphed
banner (advertising their business) across the road almost fall from their
ladders. Many carts drawn by donkeys, laden with corn, lettuce, bricks,
or floor tiles, sway back and forth among Mitsubishis, Toyotas, and old
Mercedeses. At about half past noon, the streets are invaded by schoolchildren, girls and boys, dawdling on their way home. The girls wear
uniforms and tight scarves on their heads.

As I will notice in Afghanistan, the girls' elegance and modernity
(more noticeable than under Afghan burkas but still veiled by the black
abbaya) can be detected by their shoes. Here the most stylish are shiny
with polish or have buckles, and stacked heels are still a good value.

Between the piles of garbage common to all the cities we've passed
through, the entrance to a house is sometimes decorated with a tidy and
well-tended garden with a lawn and potted flowers.

13

A SHIITE FAMILY

As we approach the sanctuary of Imam Ali, its cupola, covered with 7,777 pure gold bricks, and its minarets, also covered with gold, sparkle in the distance. The black-framed posters of Ayatollah Mohammad Baqir Al-Hakim—killed on August 29, 2003, as he was leaving the mausoleum, where he had just been meditating—are becoming more numerous, Scotch-taped to every free space on street stalls or in restaurants. Everywhere, you run across cars and minibuses decorated with enormous green flags, a sign they are carrying passengers returning from the hajj.

At the central souk of An Najaf (population five hundred thousand) —a maze of arcades converging toward the main entrance of the mausoleum—the shopkeepers don't conceal their satisfaction. Since the opening of the borders, waves of Iranians and other pilgrims have invaded the city. Hotels and private homes are always full of visitors.[1] For the most part, they are lodged in the villas of former Baathists who have lost their jobs and need the income. Guests sleep on the floor with many others for $1.50 a night. One sign attests to the strength of the demand: on the market's main thoroughfare, traditionally occupied by jewelers and goldsmiths, many booths have changed their signs and are now selling fabric, ready-to-wear clothing, and lingerie, merchandise popular among pilgrims. Restrictions in Iran are particularly severe for that sector, to protect local production. A vendor of women's and men's underwear says he has tripled his turnover in the last twelve months. He used to go to Dubai twice a year to get his merchandise, but now he goes three times as often. The same observation is made by a man selling fresh-squeezed fruit juice as I enjoy a glass of pomegranate juice.

He has also noticed the surge in Iranians; they constitute four-fifths of his clientele. Shiites from Saudi Arabia, South Lebanon, and Bahrain, undoubtedly more concerned about the security problems, are becoming less common. In Baghdad I had also seen groups of Iranians, with white surgical masks over their mouths. Now here they are again, accompanied by women in dark-colored cotton chadors, sometimes with floral patterns. Some of the women are dressed in white. It is easy to spot the groups of Indians and Pakistanis, impeccable in their white or beige *shalwar kameez* (a traditional tunic).

All around Ali's mausoleum, a mixed crowd of people jostle with one another in the yellow dust announcing a sandstorm. Illegal peddlers spread out their merchandise on blankets on the pavement between their makeshift booths. They offer all sorts of items: battery-powered robots, green scarves embroidered with suras from the Koran, disposable cameras, and so on. You can hardly find enough space to move around freely. "Under Saddam, it was completely different," my companion Hamudi laments. "This type of business was strictly regulated." Closer to the sanctuary, I observe that the women's manner of dress has become stricter. Some, in addition to an *abaya,* wear black veils that completely cover their faces but whose fine mesh allows them to see properly. Others wear delicate black gloves pulled over their numerous gold rings.

Saddam's regime discouraged "religious tourism," and Shiite neighbors in Iran were particular targets of restrictive quotas. Every foreign visitor was charged three hundred dollars to enter the country and was placed under close surveillance throughout his stay. Today most Iranians visiting Karbala and An Najaf don't even have passports, since entry into Iraq is almost completely uncontrolled, and the influx of pilgrims is constantly growing.[2]

Unprepared for what some have already called an "invasion" (in Karbala, the language most frequently heard in the street is Farsi, the Persian language spoken in Iran), the Iraqi tourism industry, specializing in the holy Shiite cities, had to rapidly adapt to the situation as best it could. Of course, the security problems are increasing, but opportunities for revenue have increased tenfold. Karbala, Al-Kufa, and An Najaf[3] have very quickly become centers for tour operators serving a clientele from Iran, India, Lebanon, Pakistan, Saudi Arabia, Bahrain, and even the former Soviet Caucasia and central Asia. The trip begins in Karbala with the visit to the mausoleum of Imam Hussein, a central figure in Shiite Islam whose martyrdom has been commemorated since the seventh century.

The groups of Iranians, led by a guide brandishing a large green umbrella, circle slowly and at great length around the religious building before stopping in front of one of its entrances. I see them begin to pray, first standing, then sitting on the ground. Many cry, entering the tomb in tears. Not far from the men's entrance, a tight group of pilgrims intone a religious chant, tirelessly repeating Ali's name and striking their chests with their right hands. Oddly, that dull thud reverberates loudly. Then they sit down on marble slabs, and, slowly, the oldest one in the group begins to weep. Soon the fifteen or so men around him are also sobbing.

Accompanied by Hamudi's wife, Miada, I enter the sanctuary (forbidden to non-Muslims) through the main door framed by two gold-covered minarets. After my hips and belly have been patted down by a security officer (a measure implemented after the August 29 attack in response to the "terrorist threat"), I step into a vast courtyard protected by a high outer wall. A band of blue mosaics with elegantly calligraphed suras from the Holy Book runs its entire length. Cells reserved for doctors of the faith are situated all around the wall.

There are many groups, and the throng is rapidly growing. We leave our shoes in the courtyard at the sanctuary's door and go in. I'm constantly stumbling over small round stones made from the clay of Karbala (soil the faithful consider sacred, since it is sanctified by the blood of martyrs), where the Shiites place their foreheads during prayers. Kids armed with small knives toil away at the screens on the windows, removing all the green cloths tied onto them by pilgrims. They have obviously been told to tidy up.

Inside the sanctuary, we approach the catafalque, which stands in the center of a square room with crystal walls covered with Koranic suras. The women are becoming hysterical. They shove one another, holding their children—sometimes newborns—at arm's length above the human tide. They feverishly kiss everything that ought to be kissed as they go by, especially the gold or silver doors. It's a massive scuffle. Just as I did in Mashhad,[4] I feel I'm being swept away with the crowd, wedged tight in a dense mob, incapable of moving on my own power, anxious I'll fall and be trampled. The women emit loud gasps and cry out as they advance as best they can toward the catafalque (made of precious wood and encrusted with ivory) where Ali lies. The saint is protected from the pilgrims' fervor by impressive gold and silver gates. The women who've reached it tie on cloth ribbons after expressing a wish. We are separated from the part reserved for men (always calmer and more spacious) by a wooden balustrade. Green-capped guards on the men's side gesticulate and try to impose calm on the most excited women by tapping them lightly with multicolored feather dusters.

Outside, on one of the monument's facades, the damage from the bomb of August 29, 2003, is still visible. The building opposite has literally gone up in smoke. The lanes adjacent to the mausoleum are narrow and sinuous. There you find the humble offices—there is no external sign of modernity—of the Grand Ayatollahs and the different Islamist parties. Outside the one belonging to Moqtada al-Sadr, who, despite his youth, is both worshiped by his faithful and feared by his adversaries, are men young and old wearing dishdasha and black or green turbans. Some are here just to pay him a brief tribute, to have the singular honor, for instance, of kissing his hand or turban when he comes out of his reception room. Others, brandishing sheets of paper with various requests or petitions written on them, are trying to get inside. In the white-walled, unfurnished antechamber, they're prepared to wait for hours on end for the venerated man.

Across from a portrait of the cleric, a bookstore displays full shelves where calendars with pictures of the martyr Sadr, portraits of al-Hakim to affix to the rear window of a car, or posters of the Black Stone of Mecca surrounded by pilgrims are lined up. The bespectacled bookseller, a handsome beardless man with a high broad forehead, has run this bookstore for thirty-five years. From what he has observed, the works that are most in demand are the following: those that deal with current Islamic legislation (the various applications of the Sharia); the latest book by Moqtada; the CDs of his weekly harangues at the Al-Kufa Mosque; and a book forbidden under Saddam, written by a local cleric and dealing with the disappearance of the twelfth imam, a subject close to the heart of Shiites the world over.

Hamudi tells me under his breath that he believes many of the books stolen from university libraries following the Kuwaiti war in 1991 are now found on the shelves of the bookstores in the city center. Farther along, a peasant is handing out photocopies of his poems. The bookseller has taken a number of them and promises to pass them on to his customers. The "poet" is a devotee of young Moqtada al-Sadr's sermons and collects his CDs. "We're happy the Americans liberated us from Saddam Hussein, who did a great deal of harm to the Shiites, but now it's urgent that they leave the country," he says with a smile, repeating the credo proclaimed by Sadr in each of his sermons. Hamudi is troubled by the peasant's words but translates them for me all the same, explaining that the entire business center of An Najaf, inhabited by moderates, is closer to the "quietist" position of Ayatollah Sistani. It's more often the farmers living on the periphery, like this peasant-poet, who hold extreme positions. Hamudi believes Moqtada is too young to aspire to a leadership role.

The poem of our local Homer is merely a plea for rebellion by the Iraqi people. Here are some excerpts: "O Iraqi people / Let us speak of the occupier / He's the devil / Ever since the British generals in 1920 / people have claimed they want to liberate us / We know this democracy's a joke / That they want to profit from our riches / And eat the bread of our poor / But we have Islam / And that suffices for us."

As we are leaving the mausoleum, a patrol of Spanish soldiers, armed but without helmets, flings a tract at us, which we take through the open window of our car. It's publicity for the new Iraqi police, accompanied by a call for cooperation. "Don't let others fail to respect the law," says a stylized, resolute-looking "new Iraqi police officer" on the tract.

I arrived yesterday at the family home of forty-four-year-old Dr. Hamudi Rallah, assistant professor at the bookkeeping institute of the University of An Najaf. Hamudi teaches at the institute three hours a week; the rest of the time he is financial director for International Rescue Committee, a U.S. nongovernment organization. "The organization employs six expatriates from Australia and Niger and sixty Iraqis," he points out, anxious to banish all suspicion that he is "collaborating" with the occupier. Hamudi appreciates the "technical" work he accomplishes within the U.S. organization, which makes him feel that he is working for the good of the Iraqis.

In addition to the buildings devoted to teaching, the institute has fifty-eight identical single-family houses for the teaching staff. They are made of brick, attached to one another, and perfectly symmetrical. "The complex was built in the mid-1980s by Japanese workers," Hamudi remembers, adding ironically that Iraqis "would not have known how to do such a thing." For fifteen years, Hamudi has occupied one of these houses with his wife, Miada, who also has a degree in bookkeeping, and their four children (three daughters, fifteen, thirteen, and eleven, and little Mohammad, aged seven).

There is nothing stylish about the house. Inside, its plywood walls are yellowing. It is composed of an entryway, a vast living room—containing a telephone, a corner couch, and an imposing computer placed on a high table—a hallway, two bedrooms, a bathroom, a Turkish toilet, a kitchen, and a staircase leading to the terraced roof. Seated on the living room couch, I am amused to observe little Mohammad, who hoists himself up to the computer, slips off the green plastic cover, then gets absorbed in a game. As soon as the father returns, the child rushes to his lap. Later, during our endless discussions, all of us sitting on the floor in the parents' bedroom—which also serves as the dining room—he will stay pressed against his father's shoulder.

With the girls I climb the stairs to the roof. There is a cage on the ground with a bird hopping about in it. The bird is nearly mute, the children tell me. They want their father to buy it a companion "to make it happier," but Hamudi has other worries. A garden measuring a few square yards separates the house from the street. Hamudi's old car is parked on the sidewalk, rusted out and without tires. After the "liberation," he replaced it with a used Nissan station wagon that cost him twenty-five hundred dollars. On its trunk, the Nissan still has a sticker with "CH" on it, standing for "Confédération Helvétique," the Swiss Federal Republic. It's amusing to think that this vehicle, accustomed to Hamudi's aggressive driving in the deafening din of the fourth largest holy Shiite city in the world, once traveled the bucolic roads of Switzerland.

There is nothing superfluous inside the house. In the parents' room there are two mattresses placed on a board—which Hamudi and his wife share with their two youngest children—and a closet. I also notice a dressing table with swiveling mirrors, and next to it a small TV set with a satellite decoder, acquired as soon as it was allowed. Thumbtacked to the wall, a small poster depicts Ayatollah Mohammad Sadeq al-Sadr and his two sons, all three killed in a 1999 attack. The plastic clock is not working. An auxiliary electric heater makes a futile effort to heat the room. The only "extra" in the house, a second TV set, is located in the adjacent room, furnished with a single wardrobe and a wobbly table, belonging to the elder daughters. There aren't piles of stuffed animals or other toys cascading off the girls' wooden beds: they are bare. No shelves in the bathroom. The few so-called beauty products are placed on the floor, under the sink. I find the hand towel on the fuse box.

"We decided to stay in this ramshackle house for all these years only because the campus offers certain advantages," Hamudi admits.* Usually, the electricity and the water are never cut off, and the local telephone line has also never been out of service. I like the fact that the primary school for the two younger children is on-site and the two elder girls take the school bus to the high school in town.

In Baghdad my sleep was disturbed almost every night by Kalashnikov salvos (though they never came close to matching the noise lev-

---

*The Kurdish professors in "professor village," on the periphery of Erbil, also recognized this.

els of my nights in Grozny, Chechnya). In An Najaf, conversely, the
nights are absolutely calm and restful. This is also the only region since
the start of my trip where I run into a populace that on the whole expresses its satisfaction with its "liberation" and is fairly pro-American.
My host, Hamudi, is almost beardless (he has just the trace of a mustache above his fleshy lips), with a swarthy complexion, black eyes, and
a receding hairline. He is by nature demanding, and despite the generally favorable situation, he complains of the lack of education and the
naïveté of his fellow citizens. According to Hamudi, they are incapable
of apprehending the "notion of human rights," or of any "rights" at all
in fact, which entail a certain sense of responsibility. After the "liberation," when the rector of his institute was dismissed, only two people
were considered to succeed him: Hamudi and a colleague. Not wanting to fill that politico-administrative role, Hamudi ceded the position
to the other man, but now he deeply regrets it. The new rector turned
out to be incapable of making quick decisions to prevent the looting of
the institute that followed the regime's fall. Day after day, the professors' computers and company cars disappeared, without anyone looking askance. Hamudi was shocked by the behavior of a man he thought
he knew well.

Every significant war or political event has obliged Hamudi's family to vacate the premises on short notice, taking with them small objects of value and important documents, gathered together in a "special
attaché case." This undoubtedly explains why nothing personal adorns
the house anymore. In the spring of 2003, they fled again. A month before the invasion, Saddam ("who had no respect for civilians," Hamudi
points out) turned part of the institute's property into an arms depot.
"When we found that out, we got scared and packed our bags," he remembers. They took refuge with Hamudi's in-laws in the historic city
center near the mausoleum, a site that was considered safer. But the clay
brick house of Miada's family was struck by three missiles, and its roof
took an awful hit and collapsed. Fortunately, no one was killed.

After the fall of the regime, it was the Americans' turn to set themselves up on the grounds of the institute. They even barred access to it
for three months. During that time, a large share of the weapons was

stolen. When Hamudi finally reclaimed his house, it was in a woeful state: ceilings, cupboards, closets, beds, everything had been damaged. Miada pulls back the sheet to show me the large bed in the parents' bedroom. A few piled-up bricks are the only thing keeping it from falling over.

In the end, the U.S. soldiers left the premises, but CIA agents still occupy about thirty houses, which they have separated from the others by a checkpoint. "A few residents did go and complain that the presence of the Americans was an added danger to the people of the area, but they were rebuffed," my hostess explains.

The first time the couple had to clear out of the prefabricated house was at the end of the first Gulf war in March 1991, when the intifada began. Battles were raging between the regular Iraqi army, which had been defeated by the United States, and the Shiite resistance. For once, most of the fighting took place on the periphery of the city, on an enormous flat piece of land just behind the institute. Day by day the Iraqi army's shells became a more imminent threat. Not having a car, Hamudi fled with his pregnant wife and their eldest daughter, then aged two, on a donkey cart abandoned by a fruit and vegetable vendor. Before leaving, he was careful to place the Koran in the center of the house, hoping the Holy Book would protect it from intruders. He planned to stay in a village in the desert where one of his friends was living. When he arrived at his destination, he found the door closed to him. The friend in question had abandoned his house to the resistance. They ended up finding a place on one of the twisting lanes of old An Najaf, not far from the mausoleum.

When they got home three weeks later, they found that the Koran had been torn to shreds, its pages scattered in every room, and forty-three personal objects had disappeared (good bookkeeper that he is, Hamudi took an inventory before leaving). "We were looted by our Iraqi brothers," Hamudi continues in his gentle voice, "by Saddam's army and by some of our neighbors."

What does Hamudi think of the Americans now? Above all, he tells me, he considers them a people that reigns supreme over the world economy. As an expert bookkeeper, he admires their professional methods. "I just love their bookkeeping texts, which are clear and a pleasure to read. I have to say I'm as 'addicted' to that literature as a drug addict is to heroin. Their bookkeeping services are without peer." Nevertheless, Hamudi was shocked by the Enron scandal; he discovered that corruption is not the monopoly of Saddam's Iraq. "If that also happens in the United States, and on such a vast scale, we can't expect things to be better here at home," he comments.

Hamudi has a rather pessimistic view of the adaptive capacities of Iraqi society, its ability to change. He even doubts that the situation will improve in ten years, when his son is seventeen. Despite the values he inculcates in his children, he cannot fail to notice the bad influence of the schools and of public opinion or society in general, which is difficult to counteract. "When I try to persuade my daughters not to be satisfied with understanding the 'why' of things but to also understand the 'how,' the concatenation of circumstances, the complexity of causes, I can see that doesn't interest them," he declares with a sigh, obviously troubled.

An Najaf is a sanctuary for the martyrs of Shiite history, even in its most recent manifestations. As you drive around town, in addition to the venerated sanctuary of Imam Ali, you can't miss the freshly erected tomb of Mohammad Baqir al-Hakim, located a short walk from a busy intersection. A giant photo of the Shiite cleric stands in the center of the site, which is barred to the public. You can also cross the street where Mohammad Sadeq al-Sadr—Moqtada's father—and his two eldest sons were killed in a shooting on February 19, 1999.

Although very devout, Hamudi denounces the omnipotence of the Islamic parties, especially that of Abdel Aziz al-Hakim, who grabbed up most of the buildings abandoned by the old regime. A large piece of land in the central city thus came to house the mausoleum of his murdered brother. The Sunni mosque, built under Saddam, has just been completed by the Shiites. There are arguably other consequences of the fall of the regime. Under Saddam, the person in charge of the treasure in Ali's mausoleum was the chief of a powerful tribe in whom the Iraqi Shiite community as a whole put its trust. He was killed on April 10,

2003, under circumstances that still have not come to light. Today, according to Hamudi, the incredible financial windfall that treasure represents is in the hands of the hawsa. Hamudi explains that the hawsa of An Najaf has regained all its influence since the fall of the regime, even though under Saddam the city of Qom, Iran, was preeminent. In any case, "no one knows anymore where the money is going. Nothing is being done any longer to help the pilgrims or provide services." Others suspect Moqtada al-Sadr's group of wanting to lay claim to the mausoleum's revenues.[5]

Any trip through the city necessitates passing the old headquarters of the Mukhabarat, Saddam's secret police. But there is nothing left of it. Not even ruins of the building can be made out; it was vaporized by the explosion. The governor's office, the Baath Party's headquarters, the fedayeen's building, and the men's clothing factory (suspected of harboring stockpiles of armored vehicles) have also disappeared.

Hamudi tells me about his family and a little about his elder brother, who was killed by Saddam Hussein's secret service. This brother taught in Kut, where the family originated, and openly criticized the lack of freedom under the dictatorship. He avoided personal and direct attacks on Saddam, however. Hamudi frequently advised him to moderate his language, even to keep quiet, but it was no use. In the spring of 2003, when the archives were opened,[6] Hamudi received a letter confirming his brother had been executed in 1983 and revealing a few details to which the family had never been privy. Even now, no one knows where he is buried.

On leaving the city, you find one of the largest cemeteries in the world (about ninety-four square miles) stretching as far as the eye can see. This is Wadi'l-Salam, the Valley of Peace (as the locals have dubbed it). Since the earliest times, Shiites have been laid to rest there beside the "Prince of Believers," the prophet Ali. It's a real city you can travel to on foot, by car, or by bus. In 1991 the cemetery became a nexus of resistance to Saddam. After the bloody repression of the intifada by the dictator's troops,[7] he tarred over hundreds of sepulchres, creating a wide paved road to discourage any efforts to regroup.

During the long years of Saddam's dictatorship, the Shiites who had

left Iraq were not permitted to come back and bury their dead. Many
of the dead were "temporarily" interred in neighboring countries such
as Syria or Iran before being transferred to An Najaf. Every tribe has a
man in charge of sepulchres, whose office is in one of the lanes of the
cemetery. The position is profitable, since families are generous with
their gifts to ensure that their beloved dead will be buried as close to
the mausoleum as possible.

We head toward the sepulchre of Mohammad Sadeq al-Sadr. Under
Saddam, the building was constantly under surveillance, since the regime wanted to keep an eye on its visitors. Today the thugs of the Army
of Mehdi have limited control of the area around the grave.[8] Three buses
parked in front of the sanctuary discharge tourists arriving from the
southern provinces to pay tribute to their martyr. The tomb is a simple
concrete building on which green flags are flying. Billboards depict the
sage flanked by his two sons.

Despite severe Koranic restrictions on the matter, the tombs sometimes vie with one another in their fanciful architecture. Humble brick-
and-cement structures stand side by side with real mini-mausoleums
with domes; color photos of the dead, often retouched, stare intently at
the living. Some structures take the form of stairs rising several yards.

Hamudi shows me a very tall one that resembles a miniature mausoleum: "This is undoubtedly the tomb of a highly placed member of
a tribe. The Koran forbids making distinctions between tombs, since
we are all equal in death, but people don't respect what's written in
the Holy Book. I discussed this with clerics, who deplore the practice
but think nothing can be done to counter that state of mind. A Shiite scholar even recommended that tombs not exceed ten to twenty
centimeters [four to eight inches] in height, but no one listens to him.
People think the higher their tomb, the better they'll be treated in the
next life."

Hamudi takes me to the home of forty-year-old Hayder, a rich businessman from An Najaf and a moderate Shiite. He has an imposing villa
in a residential neighborhood, with two stories and a well-tended garden. The huge living room is furnished European style. Set here and
there on wooden trays are the ubiquitous boxes with ornate covers filled
with perfumed handkerchiefs.

"Under Saddam Hussein, the growth of my business was limited because Shiite businessmen were subject to special restrictions. When I inherited my father's companies (selling oxygen supplies for hospitals, automobile tires, and spare parts), I settled for a modest profit with the sole aim of not displeasing Saddam's family and accomplices. All real competition had been abolished," says Hayder, convinced that he would be wealthier today if Saddam and his anti-Shiite Baathist regime had not prevented him from prospering. Like many Shiites in southern Iraq, his father, accused of being of "Persian" origin, was arrested and expelled to Iran. Hayder's two older brothers left Iraq, one for Canada, the other for the United Arab Emirates. Hayder stayed behind to take care of his parents. "You could be suspected of anything; you could be thrown in jail just for installing a satellite dish—which we've had since 1995, stashed away in the chicken coop. The laws were sometimes interpreted capriciously by those in power. Even now the body of laws we need hasn't been established, but at least we're free," he says with a sigh. "In fact, thanks to the absence of laws, the lack of import quotas and taxes (which rose by 200 percent under Saddam),[9] I've gotten into the automobile import-export business, which is currently the most lucrative kind. If I buy an Opel Omega for two thousand dollars in Amman, I can sell it for a thousand dollars more here."

Hayder is planning to build a commercial center specializing in spare auto parts, but for the moment he prefers to wait for the political situation and the level of security to stabilize. He's afraid he'll be the victim of extortion, especially by the thousands of thieves Saddam freed in November 2003 under a general amnesty. When he leaves on a business trip, even for Baghdad, his wife and three children become very anxious. The children are now driven to school.

Hayder is convinced that if the Americans were to leave Iraq, there would be civil war, since "the Iraqis don't know what they want." Like all Shiites, he wants elections, but "not too soon," since "the recently formed and inexperienced political parties would put forward candidates who are without experience. Those who have real political experience do not work within the parties," he laments. Hayder considers the Islamist extremists dangerous, but he is confident. The United States won't allow Iraq to set up a regime like the one in Iran.

A little later, Hamudi drives me to the home of one of his former pupils, now a student of religion in one of the many schools and institutions of the *hawsa'lmiyya*.* I go through the gate and into a small courtyard as chickens and roosters run between my legs; then I enter the living room decorated with devout Shiite imagery. A canary is hopping about in its cage. Thirty-two-year-old Mohammad Saffar Malif sports a thick beard and an imposing white turban, a sign of his religious devotion. Like all who are respected for their religious authority, he is called sheikh. He explains how the curriculum of the hawsa is organized. It comprises three phases that entail no time limits, unlike traditional studies: the introductory phase, the intermediate phase, and the research phase. The *marja'iyyat* (a group of the most influential *marja,* or Shiite clerics, and those best known to the community of believers) decides when each student will move from one phase to the next. In addition, every marja is a "source of imitation." It is recommended that students seek constant inspiration from his marja's intelligence and knowledge.

Six years ago, after six months in the introductory phase and three years of intermediate studies, Sheikh Mohammad became a doctor of religion. He is now entirely free to participate in the long and bitter discussions that precede the promulgation of fatwas by the marja he chose for his own (Grand Ayatollah Sistani),[10] some of which are made public only after months of elaboration. He cites a recent topic for reflection: Is it possible for a Muslim to say his prayers in the home of a Christian? Will the prayer be valid? The response is not simple, since one hadith authorizes it and another does not. "In any case, ev-

*Literally, "apprenticeship territory." This Shiite religious seminary is the oldest in the world (established in the ninth century). It produced the ayatollahs who played key roles in the history of the Middle East, for example, those who encouraged the 1920 revolt against the British colonial power and those who fomented the 1979 Islamic revolution in Iran. For a precise documented study of the Iraqi Shiites, see the excellent report by the International Crisis Group on the subject: "Iraq's Shiites under Occupation," September 9, 2003, www.icg.org.

ery argument has to be analyzed, broken down, and discussed," the
sheikh insists, and no one is "objectively" right or wrong, since each
marja's opinion can be different. The marja who has been most influential will be heeded. Nevertheless, Mohammad assures me, "given two
fatwas on the same subject, it is always the more conservative one that
prevails."

Mohammad is satisfied with the quality of his studies but adds that
in Iran seminarians are also taught the rudiments of computer science,
the operation of computers, and other subjects related to the human sciences. For the moment, An Najaf has fallen behind. Mohammad hopes
to achieve the rank of marja soon—*"insh Allah"* (God willing). He is
pursuing intense research so as to be worthy of his masters' confidence
and to earn the right to interpret legal texts in such a way as to draw a
lesson for the present.

"Grand Ayatollah Sistani was already renowned under Saddam. The
number of faithful inside and outside Iraq is huge, but one mustn't
overestimate his influence within our country. He could turn out to be
less powerful than we think. The Americans chose him as their man in
Iraq only to divide and weaken the *marja'iyyat,"* Mohammad explains.

It is true, he adds, that the Iraqis are weary of all the fighting. Perhaps the tragedy of civil war will not come to pass. In any case, he rejects
the "Iranian" variant: "The regime of mullahs made many mistakes,
and we Iraqis are not Persians. We are very different. The Persian leaders pursue only their own state interests, that's all." Mohammad truly
hopes to see the society of his country federated some day: "In Islam
there's a golden rule: an addition is always better than a subtraction.
That's why our religion can and must play a role in politics and why
our president, whether secular or religious, will be a Muslim. I'm convinced that that man exists. It's just that with the Americans occupying not only the territory but also the political and social space, he has
not yet had the opportunity to show himself."

What does he think of the future elections? "Sistani should modify
his views and call for elections as soon as possible." Mohammad is impatiently awaiting a fatwa to this effect. Otherwise, he predicts, "other,
more radical Islamic leaders, such as young Moqtada al-Sadr, who are

dissatisfied with Sistani's 'peaceful' resistance to the occupation government, will take advantage of the great master's 'weakness' and use
violence to force the Americans to revise their positions." (That is exactly what has happened.)

The young cleric's concern for moderation extends to other religions: "We respect Christianity and don't want any problems with the
Christians of Iraq," he affirms. "We should follow the example of European countries with Christian majorities, which treat their Muslim minorities well. That won't be easy. We'll have to keep repeating
that Imam Ali and his faithful were always courteous toward Christians
and Jews, and that anyone who does not adopt that behavior is not a
self-respecting Shiite." As for liquor stores, traditionally run by Christians, "they should not be banned," says Mohammad, "but they also
shouldn't be promoted."*

When I get back out on the street, I notice five enormous cast-iron kettles set on tripods. Three men armed with giant kitchen utensils are
tending them. Mohammad's next-door neighbors are celebrating the
head of the household's return from Mecca. The pilgrim's family and
tribe welcome him home around dishes of rice, white beans, and meat,
all cooked in a tomato sauce, and the entire neighborhood (about a
thousand people) has come together in jubilation to pay tribute to the
new hajji.

This year, more than forty thousand Iraqis were allowed to go to
Mecca,[11] says a young man in a white turban. He is the hajji's son and
also made the trip. For the most part they are Sunnis, and their Shiite
fellows have seen them praying for the dictator to be liberated and returned to power. Worse, fumes this religion student, "they accused us
of abandoning the resistance. They don't understand that our way of resisting is different from theirs, because Shiite territory has suffered too
much." As often happens, a circle of gawkers has formed around us. The

---

*Sheikh Mohammad is referring to liquor businesses run by Christians, most of
them in the southern city of Basra. After the fall of the regime, they were looted by
fanatical Shiites, who killed some of the shopkeepers.

sheikh's tone is firm. He declares that he "suffers personally" from the "poor image the West has of Islam as a result of the ravages of terrorism," even though in his teachings in An Najaf, Grand Ayatollah Sistani recommends that his students "respect the Christian ethic." That bitter observation is met with total silence.

A neighbor speaks up. He is pro-American, provocatively so. "I'm ready to have them plant the American flag on all our buildings.... Without those foreign soldiers, there'd be civil war here. I'm even for offering them part of our oil wealth. Before they got here, Saddam's police force conscripted our young people to fight them. I'm sad when I hear an American soldier has died, and I don't understand why France has not joined the coalition forces. Bush, okay; Jacques Chirac, no!" he exclaims, roaring with laughter and staring intently at me.

Under her black hijab, her eyes hidden behind thick glasses in plastic frames to correct for nearsightedness, Kawkab Mawmood Ali is a determined woman. She obviously runs her organization—created "by women for women," as she points out—with a firm hand. (Under Saddam Hussein, that type of organization was forbidden.) A scientist by profession, for a long time she taught at a secondary school. Then her husband, a biology professor and a very observant Muslim, was imprisoned and later killed because his faith had become "too conspicuous" at a time when the regime was doing its utmost to make Iraq an atheistic society. In 1980, widowed and pregnant with her second child, she left Baghdad with her daughter, then two, for the holy Shiite city, where she hoped to live in relative peace. To support herself, she ran a pharmacy, which is still in business.

The aim of Kawkab's organization, Islamic Faith and Koranic Science, launched in September 2003, is to "teach the Holy Book to women who cannot study it at home or in religious schools and who are eager to learn." Kawkab has noted that to live by the "correct interpretation of the Koran," it is certainly necessary to have studied it, but above all, to have studied it "in a favorable climate."

Her activities are independent of the hawsa, which dispenses more academic learning, "at a level much more complex than ours," she concedes, adding that they are not in competition. Four volunteer teachers are educating 150 women. "We pay them when possible, sometimes with the help of operation grants we've received from the hawsa and the services of Moqtada al-Sadr, among other donors. Or we share gifts in kind with them that the organization receives. Our teachers often refuse to take payment and prefer that the money be used to equip the offices," she explains. At that precise moment, I notice that I am sitting on a particularly uncomfortable couch. A table and the chair my interlocutor is sitting on make up the rest of the furniture.

Kawkab explains why she wanted to create this organization: "I felt that the values of the Koran were disappearing from our society, even though they are the foundation of everything. The Koran is like a constitution and we must respect it. It serves to guide our lives." While she is speaking, a veiled young woman frequently interrupts her, handing her documents to sign, then slips away like a shadow. "In their homes, the women read and learn certain suras by heart. We would like the Holy Book to become their practical reference guide in every circumstance of daily life." They must first learn to read the Book correctly, "which is not to be read any which way," Kawkab points out. They are also inculcated with the rudiments of computers and English, if they so wish. Classes meet every day, including Friday.

Her dream? To expand her organization and develop it into a network outside the capital—a vast area extending into the desert to the border with Saudi Arabia—and then even to Sunni territory perhaps. Asked whether she supports Ayatollah Sistani's "quietist" attitude or the openly provocative behavior of young Moqtada al-Sadr, Kawkab replies with these words of Imam Ali: "If you are not my brother in religion, you are my brother in humanity."

Kawkab doesn't feel any lack of security, thanks precisely to the Koran. "The Holy Book has made me stronger in every situation." Her only worry: the incessant quarrels among political parties, which she often asks her God to settle. As for the occupation, she is utterly against it. "The gulf between us and the Americans is enormous. They occupy our territory and therefore our lives, whether we want it or not. No Iraqi worthy of the name can be satisfied with that situation. We must there-

fore act to put an end to it," Kawkab affirms calmly, thus assenting to
the aggressive positions of the radical young cleric. She adds finally:
"We Iraqis possess the spiritual power of our faith, which can be much
more devastating, should we so decide, than military power. That is our
form of resistance, that is our refusal to accept the occupation. Our re-
jection of the American army is psychological, since we cannot consent
to being under the control of non-Muslims. We reject our past, that
is, our fate under Saddam Hussein, just as forcefully as we reject this
Americanized and 'democratic' future."

She harshly criticizes the way that the candidates in the municipal
elections were chosen by the Americans, who, according to her, want to
impose people "no one knows and who don't represent anything." All
the same, she will not be apathetic about the electoral campaign, since
she wants to prevent other people "loyal to the occupier" from taking
over the city. "It's a global tactic on the part of the Americans to try to
give a democratic facade to any effort of theirs to rebuild a society after
war. Look at Afghanistan. But we are not dupes!"

How does she respond to the proliferation of suicide attacks and
violence, which affects her compatriots more than the U.S. soldiers,
since they have entrenched themselves on their bases? "Thank God, we
haven't yet gotten to a situation as desperate as Palestine's, but if the
Americans continue to ridicule the aspirations and needs of the Iraqi
society they are claiming to help, anything is conceivable," she concludes harshly.

I have returned to Hamudi's home, and, sitting on the floor next to the
rickety bed, I am watching television with the family. After channel
surfing for a long time, Hamudi selects a channel from the sultanate
of Oman, in which an Iraqi commentator and an Egyptian political
scientist discuss why the U.S. administrators, after barring the Baathists from holding power,[12] have surrounded themselves with former
Baathists who immediately set about resuscitating their networks. The
last piece of information shocks Hamudi, who has never worked within
the Baath Party. The children, for their part, want to change the channel. They take advantage of a moment of inattention on their father's

part to get hold of the remote control and switch to an American program full of spectacular police chases, broadcast by a Bahrain channel and subtitled in Arabic. Exasperated by all the noise, their father switches the channel. The children settle for an Arabic cartoon from the local cable channel.

Hamudi talks to me about this satellite television. Like many others, he was tempted and bought one as soon as he could. But from his perspective as an observant Muslim, it shows Western culture at its most reprehensible: men in elaborate costumes, women in tantalizing dresses. (The weather forecasts, however, are presented simply.) High fashion is everywhere, coupled with the vanity of gala evenings such as the Oscars, which "the rich" invented to pass the time. These are so many insults to Iraqis' traditional way of life and their current existence, which has been turned upside down by the war, not to mention the countless shocking variety shows with half-naked women, who are necessarily perceived as a symbol of Western depravity. Hamudi has begun to channel surf again while his wife irons his jacket, placed on a piece of cloth on the floor. When she's finished, she puts the iron back on a patch of linoleum on a corner of the dressing table.

Hamudi is an enlightened television viewer. Insatiable for news, he's interested only in the foreign channels that offer continuous news programming, which allows him to compare their coverage. On a daily basis, the bookkeeper goes over the BBC and Euronews in English, in addition to Al-Jazeera (a channel from Qatar) and Al-Arabiya (from the United Arab Emirates based in Dubai). But he accuses them of being less than objective. "Just before the war broke out, when we were living in terror of what was going to happen, journalists on these channels praised to the skies 'the Iraqis, the heroes who dare defy the Americans.' You could feel the propaganda mounting bit by bit," he remembers.

Quick to make fun of the still unpolished ways of his compatriots, Hamudi tells a story that supposedly unfolded in a village south of An Najaf. A little girl, on seeing an enormous rat bolt out from under her neighbors' fence, panicked, fell, broke her leg, and had to be taken to the hospital. Through the intermediacy of tribal chiefs, her family demanded that the neighbors pay her medical bills, since it was their fault that the daughter found herself in the hospital. A few weeks later, the little girl's father waited for the rat to come out of its hole and killed it with his rifle. The neighbor was thrilled, demanding—and receiving—damages for the "murder" of an animal belonging to him. For Hamudi, this anecdote is proof that a different cultural level must be achieved. It is not enough simply to change the political system. In other words, the Americans may well install the regime they want and call it democratic, but it will be of no use. People's ways of thinking are not about to change.

Every day, Hamudi checks his e-mail in a cybercafe in the central city (single servers are still too expensive, and the institute's connection is reserved for American employees of the CIA). Before Saddam's fall, two official cybercafes were open in An Najaf, but most of the sites were artificially blocked. There are six today, all operating independently of the government.[13]

Hamudi believes the coming local elections are altogether premature, since the population already has a great deal of trouble participating in any real way in the democratic process the occupying power has endeavored to set up. "As far as candidates go, they're not notable for their intelligence or their professionalism, and they don't have the slightest idea what 'service' means," Hamudi declares. "Our society is not accustomed to election campaigns, even less to debates. No one has in mind a precise platform on precise issues. They go on and on, of course, but they're wasting their breath. I heard an Egyptian political scientist on TV say that the 'Arabs ought to learn to hear and to listen to others.' She's right, no one respects others here, and everyone meddles in everyone else's affairs." I find Hamudi's lucidity and civic-mindedness striking. I learn, however, that yesterday he rejected an offer from his institute: they wanted him to take over the financial management of the school. Hamudi prefers merely to dispense advice without assuming administrative responsibilities. Why? Because he clings to his independence and because, despite his desire to be useful to his country, he is afraid of getting "dragged into networks of corruption" that he'll be unable to manage.

Hamudi's income has greatly increased in recent months, which has allowed him to make plans for the future. During the last two years of the regime, he taught classes for fourteen hours a week at a salary of barely $80 a month (and $10 before that). Since the dictator's fall, Hamudi has been paid $150 a month and $400 since January 2004, a considerable raise that was given to the entire teaching staff in Iraq. In addition, as financial director of a foreign NGO (his second profession, which he has practiced since June 2003), he earns $700 a month. Thanks to this combined income, he manages to support his wife (who has no work outside the home) and four children.

In the future, Hamudi would like to leave the house at the institute and move somewhere else. Fourteen years ago he had a house built on land that the state distributed to teachers in the 1980s in lieu of salary. Several times he has been kind enough to lodge families in desperate straits, but he has been taken unfair advantage of. "First, there was an individual who presented himself as an engineer whose wife had recently died. He was just an impostor, out of work, and I had a lot of trouble getting rid of him," says Hamudi. Unable to be impolite, let alone threatening, he had to ask his brother-in-law to help him throw the interloper out. "More recently," he adds, "a neighbor asked me for shelter for three months. He's now been there for nine months, and not once has he paid me the thirty-dollar rent." Hamudi would like to sell the house, where in fact he's never lived, buy another property, and build two places, one for himself and the other for his son ("he's still little, but you have to plan ahead").

No sooner have I expressed the wish to meet a former official of the Baath Party than Hamudi, beaming, announces that nothing is easier: the head of the family in the house next door is a former party member, suspended on May 16, 2003. The man welcomes us in his living room, an exact replica of Hamudi's but slightly more middle class in its furnishings, with drapes on the windows and decorative plates displayed in glass cases.

Hussein Jamil Ghalif, a bookkeeping professor like his neighbor, is a tall, handsome man of forty-seven with an impressive salt-and-pepper mustache. I suspect he has put on his best suit to meet with us. He's the father of eight children, but I catch a glimpse of only the youngest, a four-year-old who occasionally escapes from one of the rooms where the women have ensconced themselves. Of the women themselves, I hear only their voices. Hussein begins, adopting an intentionally plaintive tone to justify joining the Baath Party, claiming he had no choice. He enumerates all the calamities his country has gone through since the early 1980s, bringing with them a whole series of repressive measures against the Shiite population. "It was then I became a Baathist, in 1994, not for love of Saddam, but to protect my family," he pleads. He does not conceal the fact that financial motives also played a role, since Baathists were paid better than other people.

I suppress a fierce desire to cite his neighbor Hamudi as an example. He was in similar circumstances, but he had the courage to make a different choice. But since I am a guest, it is not my place to interrupt him. I would offend both my host and Hamudi.

Hussein began as an ordinary member of the party,[14] then became a *farqā* (a higher-ranking official) in 2002. The promotion, he insists, was also "wholly pecuniary," though it required, in addition to his regular activities as a professor, that he stand guard at the party's headquarters once a week and organize and supervise demonstrations in favor of Saddam. When he received his dismissal letter from the institute in 2003, Hussein felt an enormous sense of injustice, especially since "in the Sunni regions and in Tikrit, the local administrations have disregarded that decree and former Baathists continue to receive their pay, whatever their rank in the party." Hussein Jamil draws a sharp distinction between Baathists in the south like him, who were forced to join, and genuine "Saddamists," Sunnis in the central and northern parts of Iraq. Only the latter, in his view, deserve to be excluded from public service.

When the Americans he was supposed to fight arrived, he fled with his family to Al Kufa. "What could I have done against their firepower, equipped as I was with only my service weapon? We were so sure we'd win by the sheer force of our propaganda," he groans. Today he acknowledges that "it's not easy, especially psychologically," to live with CIA agents at his back, literally and figuratively. Both irritated by their presence and afraid he'll be targeted by the resistance, Hussein has headed various movements denouncing the prolonged presence of the occupier within the institute's wall. He even met with a member of the military as a delegate for residents of the complex, but the man laughed in his face and threatened him. "Not only don't we intend to leave but, should the resistance attack, you will immediately be held responsible, since you seem well informed," he was warned.

Hussein Jamil lost his privileges, but he is happy about Saddam's fall for his country's sake: "Now people can speak freely and go to the mosque. . . . It's democracy," he declares, smiling again and a touch ironic.

Hussein has no regrets and has stored away his olive green Baathist uniform and his weapon in a closet. Unable to return to his old university post, he would like to teach abroad in a friendly country—Libya, Jordan, or Yemen. Moreover, the University of Al Kufa will undoubtedly take him. Was his past as a *farqā* ever mentioned? "They didn't ask me anything, I didn't say anything precise," he replies, a thin smile on his lips.

14

A FORMER ADMIRAL

"September 11 is my daughter's birthday. On that day in 2001, after watching the towers collapse on television, I gathered my men together and told them I had good news and bad news. The good news was my daughter's birthday; the bad news was the terrorist attacks in the United States, which in my view were going to provoke a rapid military response in our region. That evening, I even authorized them not to sleep on the base because I was so afraid something would happen."

Until April 6, 2003, Adnan Karim Bhaya was an admiral in the Iraqi fleet based in Basra—called Bassora in ancient times, the home port for Sinbad the Sailor's fabulous voyages. Because he is a former military man and a former Baathist, he has not had the right to work since the "liberation" and lives off his wife's salary. She is an English teacher at the local secondary school. The forty-nine-year-old former soldier has two children (a son, fifteen, and a daughter, twelve). He is short and stocky with rather close-set chestnut brown eyes, a broad and somewhat fleshy face, a flat nose, and a thin mustache, graying like his sideburns. During our first meeting, he is at the steering wheel of his black Toyota all-terrain vehicle with tinted windows. He is dressed in a three-piece navy blue suit and gray tie and is wearing cologne.

Adnan is obsessed with the war and immediately returns to the details of the last days of his life in the military. "How can you defend yourself with a Kalashnikov against tanks and planes? It wasn't a war, it was a farce. . . . 'We're not going to be such idiots as to mass on the approaches to the main thoroughfares,' Saddam said. 'They'll serve as an expressway for the invaders. So we must put pressure on the major

cities.' That amounted to giving the green light to street fighting, almost house to house. I was one of the people who retorted that we
didn't have enough troops to defend all our big cities. They could keep
the enemy out of our territory only for an area of two hundred square
kilometers [125 square miles] maximum. The Iraqi army was divided
into five corps, based in Diyala, Kirkuk, Mosul, Amarra, and Basra.
Each army corps was made up of three divisions, themselves divided
into three brigades and subdivided into three battalions. The navy was
composed of four battalions that, in anticipation of this war, were
trained for land operations," Adnan explains.

"Unable to guess where the Americans were going to begin their
attack, we were obliged to wait. We had received the order to defend
Basra, An Nasiriya, Fao, Umm Qasr, Al-Falluja, Ramadi, Tikrit, Nineveh, and Baghdad. The propaganda wanted to make us believe that
the millions of Baath Party members would join in the fighting, but
we knew it was a lie and that we would have to rely only on ourselves.
According to Saddam, the invader's three chief targets would be Baghdad, Basra, and Kirkuk, but he acknowledged that his first priority was
Baghdad. Obviously, he was thinking only of himself. Even the ultimatum from the United States [the ultimatum to Saddam to leave the
country] would not make him comply, we were sure of that. The day
the United States declared it would come by any means necessary to
verify the existence of weapons of mass destruction, we understood that
war was inevitable. We feared that the Americans would invade us by
way of Turkey and march on Baghdad, and that we'd be unable to prevent it, since we had received the order to remain entrenched and to
wait. In reality, once the borders were crossed, the Americans were in
no hurry, because they too were afraid. For five days, you could sense
them wavering. Our troops took advantage of that hesitation to fight
here and there, but they were too weak. Our reconnaissance service was
unable to pass on the necessary information, and we had only an imperfect idea of where the enemy was.

"I was the fourth in command of our troops in the region of Basra.
Twice I wanted to try a surprise operation in Umm Qasr, on the border
with Kuwait. Twice I was prevented. On March 21, perfectly well in-

formed of the enemy's coordinates, I asked my superior to prepare six ground-to-ground rockets to attack forty British tanks, two planes, and eight missiles. In Baghdad they claimed the target was not worth the trouble and that we'd be better off saving those weapons for a more important one. When the U.S. troops arrived in Umm Qasr, I had at my disposal a brigade of three battalions [about 350 men]. On March 23 a regiment commander informed me that he could attack the Americans at night and save Umm Qasr. I agreed and immediately called the Ministry of Defense in Baghdad. The minister, who knows me well, gave me the green light. I also needed that of the general in charge of the southern sector. I called his people and they put him on. He refused, even threatening to kill me if I attempted that attack. I was beside myself and asked if we were here to have fun or to make war. These two refusals in a row deeply upset me.

"Then the military situation turned against us, and it was too late. On March 24 the enemy troops were almost in Basra. Our soldiers immediately started deserting. Filled with shame, they went home, but in many cases their families forced them to return to the front. We hardly knew what to do with them. Finally, I had the idea of gathering some of them together as volunteers. In that way, I obtained about a hundred men—sergeants and officers—whom I divided into groups of two or three. I gave them Kalashnikovs and antitank grenades and assigned them to 'special missions.' Between March 24 and April 5, they were active from evening till morning, complementing the regular troops I commanded during the day. Every night we completed six or seven operations to prevent the Americans from penetrating Basra. We did manage to delay them. Only my local superior was aware these special groups existed. I was obsessed with the thought that they'd be executed as deserters, when in fact they'd been extremely useful to me. Thanks to them, we destroyed about fifteen tanks and five planes (three of them unpiloted) and dynamited a bridge. When British troops were alarmed that all of Basra was fighting against them, it was actually only that very motivated alternative group.

"My last phone contact with Baghdad took place on March 23. After that, nothing. We were awaiting precise orders, and there was nothing but silence. Among ourselves, we officers were so ashamed of the situation that we no longer knew what to say to one another. We'd been left to fend for ourselves, surrounded by the British in our southern fief. On March 29, as a last resort, we received reinforcements, the Eighteenth Amarra Brigade led by Ali Hussein Majid [known as "the Chemist" and since arrested], but they were incapable of fighting: they were a tank unit! Our artillery fired blindly, without the slightest information about the coordinates of the units to be bombed.

"I had of course warned the minister of defense that our plans were wrong, but, out of respect for my rank, I had no intention of surrendering. On April 4, when we saw on Iranian and Kuwaiti television stations that U.S. tanks were on the outskirts of Baghdad, we understood it was the end. On April 6, at seven in the morning, the British troops took Basra. I told my subordinates to stay home. As for myself, at ten in the morning, still at the Admiralty, I took off my uniform, put on civilian clothes, and quietly went home on foot, escorted by my driver and my aide-de-camp. They were able to go home to Karbala after three days. Two weeks later, I decided to return to Baghdad. During those days I was devastated because I realized that these events had ended my military career. But I'm not ashamed. I would have thought Saddam could have found a way to avoid that war, but I was wrong. So then I defended my country without bringing dishonor to my rank. Now when I talk to former soldiers like me who are hiding out because they're afraid or ashamed of their war deeds, I cite John Kerry, the Democratic candidate in the U.S. presidential election in November 2004. There's a man whose entire popularity rests on his conduct in Vietnam. So what would we have to be ashamed of?"

Adnan is a Shiite. His parents are from Hilla, south of Baghdad, and belong to a very influential family of *sayyid* (descendants of the Prophet). In 1974 his father, a mechanic specializing in diesel-fueled vehicles, closed his shop for good. Business had fallen off considerably because of the oil crisis. He then moved to Basra. That year, at the age of seventy, the patriarch was finally able to make his first pilgrimage to Mecca. He had raised and married off his six sons and three daughters

and had built a house for each of them. His job was done. Before his father left on pilgrimage, Adnan accompanied him to the imam in charge
of calculating the *zakat*:* $750, which the patriarch was allowed to pay
in four installments. In accordance with the law, only his "unused"
property was taken into account: for example, his second television, the
initial value of his house and not its current value, and so on.

In 1974, at the age of eighteen, Adnan left Iraq to study naval engineering at the Kirov Military Academy in Baku, USSR. He stayed
there for five years. In 1979, at twenty-three, he was an engineer first
lieutenant and began his career as a squadron leader in Umm Qasr. "We
were destroying Iranian tankers to prevent them from exporting their
oil," Adnan recalls, explaining that the Iraqi navy possessed French
Super-Frelon aircraft equipped with Exocet missiles, as well as Super-
Étendard planes. In 1984, at twenty-seven, he returned to the USSR,
studying at the Grechko Naval Academy in Leningrad for eight
months. Adnan received the Medal of Courage five times during the
war with Iran and was promoted to commander six months early. He
was barely thirty. Then he went to the military school in Baghdad for
a year and a half and became a captain four years later, in 1991, at the
age of thirty-four. He was the first of his class to attain that rank, which
was awarded a year early. Until 1995 he taught "strategic planning
of naval operations" at the military school. Achieving the next rank
was more difficult, since there were no positions available in Baghdad.
To pursue his career, he returned to Basra. Adnan was hoping to rise
quickly through the ranks to get the benefits of a full military pension
at the end of his service.

At that time, he became commander of Basra navy headquarters and
trained officers. He was finally awarded the rank of rear admiral in 1997
and should therefore have been named an admiral after four years, that
is, in 2001. But to achieve that rank, he had to agree to accept a higher
rank in the Baath Party, of which he had been an ordinary member since

---

*A legal tithe constituting a Muslim's third religious obligation. It is proportional
to one's assets, and its aim is to clear one's property from the taint of sin.

1974 (joining the Baath Party was a necessary condition for leaving for Baku). Adnan therefore returned to Baghdad and became a *farqā* and member of the military's executive committee. "I didn't want anything to do with being a farqā, since that meant being responsible for a group at the mercy of Saddam's thugs," he says. "In the 1970s, criticism within the party was possible and discussions free. But when I returned to the Soviet Union, Saddam had just been elected president and the organization was becoming more rigid. Things got worse with the war against Iran, a further pretext Saddam used to get the party and its many branches under his heel."

Finally, the rank of admiral was conferred on Adnan on January 6, 2002, a year before the most recent war. "In Iran, when the Shah eft and Khomeini came on the scene, there were rumblings of revolution, and that frightened us." Adnan draws a map showing the location of the Shiite population in Iraq and Arabistan, one of the southern provinces in Iran, where Arabic is spoken. This former territory of Iraq was handed over to Persia in 1905. "Saddam attacked first because he knew Iran was already invading us ideologically through a sustained religious propaganda campaign. Immediately, we penetrated 40 kilometers [25 miles] into their territory over 300 square kilometers [200 square miles], that is, an area larger than Lebanon. The Iranian army was formidable, but we knew it had been somewhat marginalized by Khomeini in favor of his personal militia, a mistake Saddam was smart enough to take advantage of. Saddam wanted the whole world to recognize him as the architect of peace in Iran. He was waiting for a political opportunity to propose that peace. But the Iranians launched a military response. They led a counterattack between 1982 and 1985, reaching our marshlands and killing thousands. They got within 5 kilometers [3.5 miles] of Basra, and for two years, between 1986 and 1988, they occupied Fao, our only deep-water port. During those years, we remained massed on the border there, awaiting hypothetical orders. Increasingly, the military advised Saddam to change his tactics. He needed to attack and take prisoners. Saddam didn't want to hear of it and even demoted and replaced the most highly ranked officers. Finally, in 1988, he decided to attack again. In the south, my men and I surrounded the enemy forces while covering their advance with our infantry. We retook Fao in March after two days of fighting. It was the first step toward ending the war.

"By way of response, the Iranians attacked Halabja, Kurdistan, because they wanted to destroy Darbandikhan Dam and flood Baghdad. We didn't allow it. We asked the people of the area to leave and allow us to attack. In one night, more than fifty thousand fled. Some five thousand remained, taken hostage by the Iranians. Our artillery owned weapons from Russia, Brazil, France, and Austria. We bombed with chemical weapons. Three days later, our army entered Halabja. The Iranians, who had taken photos after the bombings, immediately accused us of genocide.[1] But Khomeini, who had first declared he would rather drink a large glass of poison than end the war, signed the armistice sealing our victory on August 8, 1988. For me, the war against Iran was unjustified, but Saddam had just come to power—Khomeini as well, in fact, and he was preaching international revolution. As Iran's immediate neighbors, we were the most affected. Saddam didn't want a religious leader to take power in Iraq. The Shiite revolution frightened him. The West also feared the contagion effect and openly supported Saddam.

"In 1991, after the first U.S. attack against our country, we launched rockets against Israel. Israel did not counterattack. They had no doubt received orders from Washington, which feared a regional war with Israel. That was precisely what Saddam had in mind. He would have loved to liberate Palestine in the same way that the Americans had liberated Kuwait.

"We consider Ahmad Chalabi and the other exiles who returned to Iraq riding along with the Americans agents of the United States. They don't represent anyone here; they never worked for our country. In addition, Chalabi is an international crook. As for the U.S. occupation troops and the civil employees who have accompanied them, they are perfect ignoramuses about politics. We will never accept the 'American lifestyle.' According to my sources [which he won't name], twenty-five hundred U.S. soldiers wrote to the Senate in Washington expressing their desire to go home as quickly as possible. Maybe they haven't been heeded, but I've observed recently that vast numbers of troops are being relieved. In addition, several hundred Americans have deserted to Syria and Turkey with the help of Iraqis who smuggle them across the border."

Adnan distinguishes between two types of resistance. First, there is that of the "Islamists"—"terrorists," according to journalists and politicians—who kill blindly, using suicide attacks, among other methods. "They're not Iraqis; they receive their orders from fundamentalist organizations such as Al-Qaeda and Ansar al-Islam," he declares. "The only objective of Al-Qaeda, in fact, is to weaken U.S. power and prevent it from ruling the world. The Americans invaded Afghanistan so that they could designate an enemy and show they could defeat it. In that way, they can justify the existence of the prison camp in Guantánamo Bay. But what are those three hundred prisoners compared with the hundreds of victims killed daily by their imperialism in Iraq?" The former military man fumes. "By occupying our country, they want to take control of the whole world. That's true globalization. To effectively fight terrorism, they'd have to have a military presence in every country in the world, and that's impossible. So they concentrate on a few, such as ours and Afghanistan, or, for example, the Philippines, where they helped the state fight Abu Sayyaf, who never fomented anything against them.

"The second form of resistance is found among former Iraqi soldiers," Adnan explains to me. "They fight the 'invaders' but have no political plans. They are only reacting. Whom and what are these groups resisting? Those who want to impose a calendar, a political plan, a constitution, a government council, an interim government. There are also malcontents among them, unemployed Sunni civilians and Sunni clerics worried about a potential strengthening of the Shiites. They will remove their masks when the time comes, in five or ten years, when the Americans have lost their influence and retreated to their bases.

"I don't believe the Americans came to Iraq to help us. Rather, for me that invasion marks the beginning of World War III, since in coming to fight in Iraq, they have in some sense imposed their will on the rest of the world. Uzbek president Islam Karimov, who heads a state

rich in gas and oil and a dictatorial political regime similar to that of
Saddam Hussein, has been eager to bow to the wishes of the U.S. military, which is now also present in his country. That is proof of the new
power of the United States. From Iraq they pull the strings in Syria,
Iran, and Saudi Arabia. Collaboration with Turkey has become pointless, since the Americans already occupy Iraq. And they have gained access to lucrative oil markets. The Afghanistan war was strategically less
important, since it was simply retaliation."

We are driving on the old corniche road that borders Basra, the Venice
of the Eastern world. It overlooks the wide and majestic Shatt al Arab.
The road winds past the huge Sheraton Hotel. After the damage caused
by the war, only an imposing burned-out skeleton remains. Adnan
shows me what is left of the hundred bronze statues erected to the
glory of the heroes (officers and junior officers) in the war against Iran,
about twenty of whom he knew personally. The pedestals are bare.
Everything was taken away, stolen by vandals who sacked the city.
"They'll have sold the bronze for spare parts in Iran to make a little
money." As for the warships, still operational barely a year ago, they too
have been looted and savagely smashed all along the quays where they
were berthed.

From the city of Basra all the way to the sea, along both banks of the
Shatt al Arab (currently authorized for navigation only by coalition
craft and some trawlers), hundreds of lateral canals have been dug. They
empty and fill with the tides every six hours. Under the embargo, these
canals were the site of all the smuggling activity, especially of oil des-
tined for Iran. To get into the business, you had to pay off the Iranian
intelligence service. They then closed their eyes to the boats filled with
barrels of crude, flying the Iranian flag as they went up the river. With
the occupier, such schemes have now become much more difficult, the
people of the region complain.

The multicolored fishing boats riding at anchor are almost completely neglected. They don't seem to be waiting for anyone. Beside
them, *shakhtura,* flat-bottomed boats used to shuttle between the two
banks, bob up and down with the waves. How remote those days seem

when charming wooden pontoons housed seafood restaurants for tourists! In these makeshift bars along the banks of the Shatt, men spent whole afternoons playing dominoes. Today those same men are idle, smoking cigarettes and sitting back on their heels in front of the boats. Furious but resigned, they know that the diesel fuel needed to go to sea is still rationed and that the new governor hands out boating licenses at a snail's pace.

Across from the customs building is a children's playground that looks brand-new. It had just been built when the war broke out, but two of the five yellow-and-green slides are in pieces. The opposite bank is Iran, and the hundred statues of heroes toppled by the war once pointed threatening fingers at the enemy country.

At dawn, traffic is heavy on the bridge, built by the Iraqi army in 1986. It is the only border post controlled by British troops, who discreetly keep surveillance with almost indifferent eyes. The naval yards that were swarming day and night with various activities before the war seem to be frozen in time. As the month of *moharram* and the commemoration of *Ashura* approach, black streamers are proliferating on the doors of traditionalist Shiite families. They are sometimes combined with the green or white flags of hajjis. On every street corner, garbage is piling up. Sometimes scattered into the street by the wind, it prevents cars from passing. (During my entire journey, An Najaf and Karbala were the only places where I observed municipal street sweepers, who managed to keep the central city clean.)

Sadly, we visit a cemetery where all of Adnan's friends may be lying. The former admiral wants to drive over to look at the buildings in Basra destroyed by the enemy air force. It's always the same ones: the headquarters of the Baath Party; that of the Mukhabarat; the headquarters of the oil company in the southern region. "They even bombed the yacht club twelve times. It housed the president's personal fleet. Their tenacity was ridiculous, since they knew very well there was no one aboard," Adnan points out in a reproachful tone.

We hear the strident sound of an approaching police siren. We are passed at top speed and in a deafening racket by a Toyota pickup. In its bed stand five Iraqi police officers, automatic pistols pointed at the populace, fingers on the trigger. "Exactly the way they learned to do it during the single week of training with the Americans," Adnan comments, amused.

We are now driving in the vicinity of the Admiralty. The row of beautiful houses where ranking officers were housed is now occupied by poverty-stricken families who arrived from the marshlands during the wave of anarchy following the "liberation" of Basra. Here in front of us are the vast grounds of navy headquarters, one of the oldest Iraqi bases. It was built in 1937 and bombed twice by the enemy air force during the most recent war. At its entrance, the Iraqi insignia and the militarist slogans painted on the outer wall are still visible.

It's the first time the former admiral has returned here since April 2003 (our visit took place on February 20, 2004). The devastation of the place is stunning. "Hordes rushed in after we left. They broke everything and sold it as construction materials," Adnan sadly observes. Sheep and a few goats gambol around us. Adnan is still mortified by the memory of the vandals who virtually took over the city in the space of a few days, and he assures me that only a minority of soldiers participated. "Those who tried to prevent the looting were called Saddam's men," he remembers. "There was nothing to do but to let it go."

We park the car among concrete blocks and set off on foot in the ruins, stepping over the debris. Adnan insists on giving the grand tour: "Where we are now was the dry dock. Everything has disappeared," he says with a sigh. "They had to sell the twenty-five boats that were still here. Even the landing docks have vanished. . . . Of course, there was the bombing, but most of it is the result of human folly, which is much worse than a bomb. . . . That's the location of the old prison ship. . . . There's the skeleton of a ship destroyed during the Iran-Iraq War. It had remained berthed since that time. At least they haven't touched it."

I notice a group of six men leaning against their cars, looking as if they're waiting for something. They are former officers from the base who have decided to stand guard to prevent the pipelines and water pumps from being stolen. "Otherwise, the neighborhood will be a complete disaster," Adnan explains, signaling to them with large gestures as we approach. Along the way, I ask him how he feels to be here again. He sighs. "Bad, very bad. It makes me want to cry. What does all that mean? It's not really Iraq." And in fact Adnan looks distraught.

Setting aside their sullen expressions for a moment, the men seem happy to see Adnan again and exchange greetings for a long time. They confirm they have organized into six-man teams to stand guard day and night. Since the taking of Basra, all of them have been unemployed. They remain idle, consumed by bitterness over their ravaged past.

Some kids, attracted by our presence, emerge from the ruins and come up to us. They're constantly afraid that an authority of some sort will evict them, and they surface to get the news. Now more and more come running. One of them, in rags, finds the courage to speak: "We're very poor, homeless, and out of work. Some of us came here from the outskirts of town, others from the marshlands. First we came just to look, then we decided to stay. We're hoping for a better life. Our mothers would like to be able to feed their children and send them to school." They are now packed so tightly around us that we have trouble getting back to our car. Adnan is not at all convinced of the honesty of these "squatters." He assures me that most of them make their home elsewhere, in the rural areas, but they want to take advantage of the opportunity of being in town.

A few hundred yards away is the port administration, or rather, what's left of it. Adnan heads straight for the warehouse, where he managed to hide eight land-to-sea missiles a few days before the outbreak of hostilities. He boasts that none of the weapons inspectors discovered these Chinese-manufactured twenty-six-foot rockets used to attack the port of Kuwait City from Basra. "They were concealed in refrigerated fish containers. There were seventy-six of them, most unusable because they were too old. One of them even exploded on the launching pad, killing two of our engineers."

According to official information, the port has resumed a semblance of activity. We find everything quiet and exposed to the elements. On seeing two British army jeeps lying in ambush in an alleyway, we decide to turn around.

From a distance, Adnan points out the building of the navy's general staff, one of the first to be targeted by bombs (it was thus emptied early on). "We had five buildings in different neighborhoods throughout the city, including the basement of the navy club. We changed location every three days," he recalls. We reach the site of the old naval academy, not far from the airport and university (taken together, they constituted an ultrasecret military zone barred to unauthorized civilians). Now raw-boned cows are grazing between the concrete blocks, and the old campus is unrecognizable. Laundry is hanging out: here, too, someone has taken possession of the ruins. Adnan casts a distressed look at the ragged villagers with deep-lined faces, now oddly in charge of this place where for many years he studied and taught. He prefers to keep quiet.

We return to the center of the city. We've given a ride to a student who is preparing her doctorate in molecular biology and whom we found patiently waiting for the bus. "We're like a football that the players endlessly pass back and forth among themselves," she complains. "At the university, the political parties, especially the Islamic ones, have taken over, and I'm very afraid it will be for a long time. Nothing is sure anymore, and I don't know whether I'll be able to continue my research."

A month after the war ended, Adnan asked to see the civil governor of Basra to tell him that, as a former admiral, he was ready to "make a contribution toward reviving the Iraqi army." The governor had nothing to suggest except that he write up a plan for the British authorities. Adnan has received no response to the report. The copy sent to the head of the provisional coalition government in Baghdad was also never acknowledged. Last December, however, Adnan was summoned to the green zone in the company of about ten of his colleagues for a meeting with U.S. Army colonels, "in a consultative capacity." They asked the Iraqi military men their opinion, for example, about potential reforms to be made at the Ministry of Defense and its leadership. Should the minister be a civilian or a member of the military? Adnan, finally listened to, was generous with his advice. He recommended that the Americans "stop patrolling the streets like arrogant conquerors" and entrust the patrols to the Iraqi army, which had to learn to command respect again. He urged the occupier to call on the best officers in the old army. According to the former admiral, it is urgent to reconstitute the Iraqi armed forces. "When our army was created in 1921, it was under the supervision of the British," he reminds me.[2] "Why not repeat that process?" The Americans said that within two years they wanted to create an army corps made up of three divisions. Adnan said he wanted three corps formed. But they refused. "They don't trust us," he points out. "They know we are not supported by the political parties, which are terror-stricken by the idea that the new Iraqi army might deprive them of powers they have too easily acquired.

"No one knows who our future head of state will be. It would be desirable to hold elections. At least then all those many parties would come in contact with reality. In some sense, the elections would also serve to poll the population. That's what al-Sistani wants, and we support him." Adnan reminds me that the Shiites were in power for only a brief period in Iraqi history, under the socialist Abd El Karim Kassem, who was soon assassinated. "The United States fears the advent of an Islamic regime in Iraq, as happened in Iran," he continues. "But that fear is ridiculous, since many Shiite Iraqis refuse to link religion and politics. The Americans trust only the people they know and who they're sure will be loyal to them; that's their biggest mistake. They don't want any newcomers on our political scene. They want to make us 'manageable' like the Germans and Japanese, who have housed their bases for a long time. When the first British detachments invaded us from their landing site in Fao in 1914, they too claimed to be 'liberators' and wanted elections. In 1922–1923 Ayatollah Mahdi al-Khalasi issued a fatwa barring Muslims from voting under a military occupation regime. He was exiled, but the people respected his will and boycotted the elections. Today al-Sistani has the same authority as that ayatollah, but he won't call for the people to rise up against the occupier because the Americans are much more influential and much more powerful militarily than the British were in their time."

What has Adnan believed in all these years? "In Iraq, in my family, in my land, in my history, in my Islam," he says without hesitation. "Beginning in 1958, they made us become members of one party or another, the Baath Party, the Communist Party, or some other one. The Communist Party was atheistic and didn't suit me. I became a Baathist in 1947 when I joined the military, undoubtedly because of Nasser's role in the liberation of Palestine. An announcement in the newspaper vaunted the possibility of pursuing military engineering studies abroad (in France, Yugoslavia, or the USSR) for those who agreed to join. I applied. Three months later, I was on my way to Baku. I had always dreamed of becoming an engineer. And then, I wanted to leave Iraq, something that was almost impossible at the time, especially for a penniless boy like me. But I didn't know that Saddam Hussein was going to drag us into three wars. . . . I came back to the country in 1979, the year Saddam became president. He was known to be a friend of many Western countries, including France. He was thought to be intelligent. People said he would lead the charge in industrializing the country. In fact, the president thought only of himself, and his entourage was a regular royal court gravitating around his person as if he were the sun.

"For a while, I planned to become the administrator of the naval academy, but a Sunni from Tikrit was named in my place: another example of the religious discrimination practiced under Saddam. The wars engrossed me. I didn't want to participate in the one with Kuwait because I understood we were taking the wrong path, but the war with Iran was another matter."

We leave the huge urban area of Basra (population 1.5 million). On either side of the road, on plots of land devoid of vegetation, are numerous concrete building frames. Construction on them has been abandoned. Our destination today is Safwan, a village on the border of Kuwait. Sheep are sprawled on the asphalt, and their shepherds feed them a little straw from a pile in the center of a large black tire. Dump trucks are parked on the side of the road. I've seen many of them on the periphery of the large urban areas, offering, as they do here, sand, gravel, and other construction materials.

We pass a U.S. column of fifty heavy trucks with Kuwaiti and Saudi Arabian license plates. They are transporting rubber tracks for tanks and other military spare parts. "Seeing them is like being stabbed in the back," Adnan tells me. "I cried about it for the first time when I returned to Baghdad with my family after the fall of the regime. But I was happy that Saddam was gone." As much as possible, he tries to avoid this highway, which passes not far from Imam-Ali Base (a former Iraqi military base, now the largest U.S. base after the one in Kuwait).

It is precisely on this road, between the last houses in Basra and the Shatt al Basra, that very bloody battles took place over a period of ten days.[3] The gas and oil complexes on either side of the road are now operating perfectly, as the gray smoke escaping from them attests. For lack of funds, however, the swing bridges over the tributaries, destroyed during the 1991 war, have still not been rebuilt by the Iraqis. "Of course," Adnan exclaims, "that was what the Americans wanted, to safeguard the oil." The production of crude is now under the coalition's control.

We follow the same path taken by the Americans after they landed in Kuwait, but in the opposite direction. At the border, the 2.5 miles between Safwan and Abdaly, Kuwait, are nothing but a vast open-air bazaar where Kuwaiti shopkeepers vie to sell anything that may have fallen into their hands, from an ordinary blanket to kitchen utensils to cars from Dubai. There are an impressive number of sinks and bidets, which form a colorful fresco on the ground. The used bidets (if they were new, they'd be too expensive for Iraqi customers) are an amusing symbol of a lost modernity that needs to be quickly recovered—the tawdrier the better.

In the midst of the huge sidewalk sale, you barely notice the Iraqi customs buildings, destroyed in 1991 and since abandoned. At that time, Iraq and Kuwait were on very bad terms, and the border post was officially closed. Its control then passed to the United Nations. It was reopened in October 2003 after a decision of the Iraqi Governing Council. Although Kuwaiti shopkeepers don't need a visa to enter Iraq, the reverse is not true. For the most part, Iraqi citizens must carry a visa and prove that they are visiting members of their families living in Kuwait. Four pot-bellied Iraqi border guards invite us to have a cup of tea in their sentry box. They're still fuming about the "occupiers," whose long convoys returning from the Kuwaiti base on "their" road they can make out in the distance. What about the new government? It's a shadow government that doesn't pay them (they haven't received their salaries since October) and "doesn't give a damn about its borders, hence about its own existence." Nor is the minister of finances spared: he's "a banker rolling in money who doesn't even know his own country" and is incapable of equipping them with official vehicles. "We can't get around anymore. We don't even know who our superiors are, whom to report incidents to. Iraq no longer exists." They are bitter, and Adnan readily shares their bitterness.

We have returned to Basra. After asking for directions several times, we finally find the impressive stone church that serves as the house of worship for the Seventh-Day Adventists. According to Adnan, it was closed for thirty-six years. In 1968, he says, the monitoring devices of a Soviet ship cruising in the Gulf intercepted suspicious conversations. Their analysis, conducted with the help of Iraqi intelligence, allowed them to break up a network working for the Mossad and based precisely in the Seventh-Day Adventists' church tower. Seven people were hanged, their bodies exposed on the city's central square. The church was closed by the Mukhabarat.

I will later learn that Basim Fargo, the current secretary-treasurer of the Seventh-Day Adventists in Iraq, completely discounts this version. According to him, it was fabricated out of whole cloth by the Iraqi government, then disclosed by a Kuwaiti newspaper to delegitimate the church in the public's eyes.[4] In fact, the house of worship has always remained open (except between 1993 and 2000), and six ministers have served there in succession. It is not currently holding services, but that's because the last minister, Johnny Masasian, left in 2002 and has not yet been replaced.

In the 1980s, Basra had a large Christian population, but once the war with Iran broke out, they began fleeing to Mosul, Baghdad, or abroad. A second wave of emigration, this time for English-speaking countries (the United States, Canada, and Australia), occurred after the first Gulf war. Barely two thousand Christians are left in Basra. "The Muslims are protected by the tribes. That is not the case for the Christians," Adnan points out.

In the new part of Basra, Shar-al-Watan, we pass rows of padlocked street stalls, the shops of Christian liquor retailers who preferred to shut down and leave the region after some of their own were murdered by Islamists. The sale of alcohol in restaurants and nightclubs was banned in 1992 in a sudden crackdown by Saddam Hussein. These former shops stand next to bars and discos that closed in the 1990s "because they were getting fewer and fewer customers," Adnan confirms, proof of the slow rise in power of fundamentalist tendencies in the traditional southern Shiite society.

Father Souleqa Zacharia, a Syriac priest, welcomes me to his neighborhood church. He is clearly irritated by the fact that I am wearing a Muslim head scarf to hide my hair on the street. His irritation also manifests itself when women ask for his permission to recite a Muslim prayer inside the church while facing Mecca. He asks me on the spot to take off my scarf and responds to the women's wishes with a categorical refusal. Then, mollified, he explains to me that he also highly recommends that these Muslim women, who have come to meditate, "remove their veils in this holy place." To hear him talk, it appears that large numbers of Muslim women come here. They light a candle to the Virgin Mary— "Maryam" in Arabic, one of the "pure" women of Islam. As the mother of Jesus, she is the only woman to have lent her name to a Koranic sura.[5] Some confide their family problems to the priest, as if they trusted him more than they trusted the imams, he notes.

Father Zacharia even remembers a Muslim woman whose daughter had gone to Jordan without permission and had not been heard from since. As a last resort, the mother came to the Syriac church to ask Maryam to return her daughter to her. "She cried for three hours and promised to keep me informed. Two days later, the runaway was back." All the Muslims who come to meet with Father Zacharia question him about the Crucifixion of Christ, an episode related in the Koran, but differently from the New Testament. Supposedly, another man took his place on the cross, and Jesus (Issa) is still alive in a "primordial state," outside time and the world.[6] If his visitors have no objection, Father Zacharia hands them the Gospels in Arabic, but he never forces anyone to take them. Some Muslims saw their Christian neighbors abstain from stealing, looting, and destroying when the city was being sacked. "You're better than us," they have come to tell the priest. "Christ is the true spirit of God, whereas Muhammad is only a human being," Zacharia invariably reminds them.

Like most of the Christians in Iraq, Father Zacharia is a native of the northern part of the country, Mosul to be precise. He has lived in Basra since 1992. He confirms to me that there are five active Christian churches in the Shiite southern capital: a Catholic Syriac church, an Orthodox church, a Chaldean church, an Armenian-rite Orthodox church, and this Seventh-Day Adventist church. "The history of Iraq," he tells me, "has been characterized by religious tolerance. But today we sense that most Shiite Muslims want to take advantage of the power vacuum to turn the Iraqi state into an Islamic state." He is not terribly afraid, but he is wary. Above all, he fears that "the extremist current, no longer restrained by Saddam's iron fist," will feel they have a completely free hand. The ghettoization of his city worries him a great deal. It's a far cry from the 1960s, when brotherhood and cooperation between Christians and Muslims were the norm. Now a Christian will choose to live in a neighborhood of his fellow Christians "for the sake of security."

The priest stubbornly rejects the idea that the foreign soldiers have come to "occupy" his country. In his view, the Iraqis ought to be less cold, ought to cooperate more with the Americans and thank them for putting an end to a dangerous regime. But there are countless misunderstandings. "The Americans came here with their minds already made up about the Iraqis, and their ideas didn't correspond to the reality. They mistrust them and constantly fear they'll be deceived. The Iraqis don't understand the Americans any better. They don't accept their way of seeing things, their lifestyle. They blame them for not being able to stabilize the situation; they're terrified by the idea of collaborating. Yes, the situation is complex."

This evening, in the Sunni family of twenty-two-year-old Innas, one of the wives of Adnan's younger brother, the discussion turns to Saddam

Hussein's upcoming trial. There are two camps. Adnan clearly doesn't want the trial to proceed "because Iraq would again be obsessed with Saddam for two years at least, and that would prevent us from moving forward." Innas and her mother are altogether in favor of the former dictator's being tried and convicted. Innas's mother is unusual in that she is a descendant (through her two grandfathers) of "first-class Anglo-Indian" citizens, which gives her the right to British nationality. As soon as the dictatorship fell, she applied for citizenship.

Adnan has a disapproving look on his face. "Whether for Saddam or for anyone else, I don't believe that capital punishment should exist in our country. It's only by the will of Allah that someone should perish."

Then the following discussion ensues.

Innas (outraged): "But Saddam killed thousands of people; he must be done away with. [Her mother nods in agreement.] Psychologically, his death will free our whole society."

The mother: "Basically, I don't even think there will be a fair trial. The CIA has probably already plotted with him to set him free or to give him a lenient sentence in exchange for his silence on embarrassing subjects. There's no shortage of them! The U.S. policy in Iraq in the 1990s, for example."

Adnan: "And you think Saddam will agree?"

Mother and daughter (in unison): "To save his skin, of course he will!"

Adnan: "But then, what's the point of trying him?"

The mother: "The point is to free ourselves from a burden that is still dragging us down psychologically. That's all. . . . As for the rest, what control do we have? None. We're involved in a chess game that we haven't mastered."

Adnan: "And you'd like that game to go on?"

The mother: "It will go on whether we like it or not, because the Americans won't be so quick to leave Iraq. But with Saddam under lock and key, we'll be able to think more of *ourselves* and move forward, with or without a trial. Of course, the Americans didn't find weapons of mass destruction, but doesn't Saddam by himself represent *the* weapon of total destruction?"

Innas: "Precisely. As for me, I'm convinced that we need that trial to come to grips with the fact that the 'Saddam era' is truly behind us."

Adnan (pensive): "Yes, the Americans will stay. But they'll have withdrawn to their bases, and that will still be better than seeing them patrolling our streets."

The mother: "Saddam was a nightmare. He spent all our oil revenues to procure weapons."

Innas: "We learned all that much too late."

The father arrives home from work. He's a civil engineer and collaborates with the British troops. He apparently hopes to put an end to the discussion. "The Islamists who came back from Iran clearly want to impose a regime on us similar to the one in Tehran, and that's unacceptable. So whatever people say about the Americans, we need them."

It's the first day of *moharram,* and it looks like rain. We are headed toward Fao, south of Basra, the only deep-water port in Iraq, strategically located at the mouth of the Shatt al Arab. Fao suffered greatly during the wars. It was a bridgehead for British troops during World War I and the conquest of Mesopotamia and, later, the site of one of the most memorable battles in the Iran-Iraq War. Ninety years later, the city has played an equally prominent role during the second invasion of British troops in Iraq.

Again we follow the path of the invaders, British this time, and again in reverse. From time to time we stop so that Adnan can show me the observation posts his own troops used during the conflict with Iran. Sixteen years later, most of them are still here. "For that war, we had forty-five observation towers between Basra and Fao. They served no purpose, since the enemy came by air for the most part," Adnan recalls. Opposite the village of As Shiba, behind an undulating mass of reeds, we clearly make out the tubular structure of the Abadan refinery, the largest in Iran. On either side of the road is a yellowish gray desert. "On March 18, 2003," the former admiral continues, "our plan was to attack the enemy by sea on what were supposedly commercial boats. Once again, at the last moment, we received the order to do nothing," he laments. Saddam Hussein supposedly ratified the plan, but the minister of defense made him change his mind. Some officers, including Adnan, even believed at that moment that Saddam's about-face meant that an agreement had been signed and that war would be avoided. In the end, the four commercial vessels were stopped by the U.S. military forces, and their crew of soldiers were taken prisoner. A total fiasco.

On the road stretching out toward the sea, it's impossible not to stop in front of a giant concrete billboard on which the following is painted:

> Dear visitors on the road to Fao, watch over this land, pay heed to this soil and treat it like a friend. It has been nourished by the blood of the brave 52,948 Iraqi soldiers who defended and then liberated Fao in the battle of *Ramadan Mubarak* on April 17 and 18, 1988. Let us honor that blood, thanks to which the 120,000 invaders from Iran did not succeed in taking possession of our country. 6,890,690 Iranian bombs of various kinds fell on Iraq between 1980 and 1988, perhaps more, according to some figures. Despite that, this land is and must remain Arab and Iraqi. We are engaged in a new humanitarian mission: good health to the residents of Fao!

A prayer to the memory of those who died on the battlefield follows. In very large letters, the words "ALLAH AKHBAR" (God is great) end the text.

Behind the billboard, the drab grayness creates so much confusion that a steamship seems to be gliding over the sand.

We will pass three more replicas of the large concrete billboard in the twelve or so miles that separate us from Fao.

As we enter the city, police officers at the checkpoint are hanging an enormous black banderole on their building in honor of *moharram*. They have completely forgotten the road traffic. Beside me, Adnan is recalling many memories of the war he was robbed of: "For the invasion, British troops used the oil-drilling and storage platforms, which are less than a dozen kilometers [seven miles] off the coast. Their planes were able to land there, and they also installed their water-jet-propelled hydrofoils. On March 21 and 22, I wanted to bomb those platforms and blow them all up, but we weren't given the opportunity." Adnan is dejected. "I would rather have died than witness that battle," he says finally. "After he reclaimed Fao, Saddam lost no time in building two mosques, a stadium, and many official buildings there. But he forgot the people. He didn't give them anything that would have allowed them to rebuild their roofs or their lives, and this is the result."

Inside the city, the official buildings look empty, devastated. The marble plaques commemorating the liberation of Fao on April 17, 1988, were stolen after the other "liberation" of 2003. On the opposite shore stands the Iranian mausoleum in memory of those who fought the Battle of Fao. "Every year on April 17, while we on this bank were in jubilation, we had to bear the mourning across the river conducted by the mullahs, the weeping of Iranian women hired expressly for the occasion," Adnan remembers. "Depending on the wind, the lamentations, amplified by powerful loudspeakers, could sometimes drown out the official ceremony on the Iraqi side. Some of the women in black chadors who were grieving the deaths of their sons watched us with binoculars." During the two years of Iranian occupation in Fao, three bridges were built over the Shatt. All were destroyed by the Iraqi army in their final counterattack. Now the two banks watch each other in silence.

Dreamy-eyed fishermen, barefoot and with the sleeves of their woolen jackets rolled up, are covering the hulls of their boats with a coat of glossy black rustproof paint. Since the previous Gulf war, disputes over fishing zones have resumed (more with Kuwaiti neighbors now than with the Iranians). Adnan shows me a hospital built by the Iranians and used by the Iraqi army until that war. The area adjacent to the port is strewn with blockhouses whose darkened apertures are flush with the dried-out land. On one of them is this inscription, undoubtedly recent: "Down with Saddam Hussein!" At the entrance to another, a sumptuously calligraphed *Allah* stands out in white paint against the muddy black background.

We cross the many canals, along which a few houses with reed hedges have been constructed. We are approaching the sea. We pass an old mosque with a strange silhouette: its minaret was cut in half during the war with Iran. The paved road has turned into a dirt path, which narrows before us. The road was built by Adnan and his men and was supposed to take them to the Iranian post. After a bit, at the point where the Shatt al Arab, shimmering blue and pink, flows into the Persian Gulf and then into the Arabian Sea, the path quite simply stops, running into the sand. If you want to get a glimpse of the open sea, you have to finish the journey on foot.

Intrigued by our presence, two robust young fishermen wearing filthy, tattered sweatpants and ancient camouflage jackets appear out of nowhere. We had not noticed them hidden in their boats, slender as gondolas, deep in the reeds. They've spent ten days in these remote swamps, attempting to catch a fish apparently coming from Australia. The only provisions they've brought with them are about a hundred *khobuz* (a delicious, delicate flatbread called *nan* in Afghanistan and cooked in an outdoor oven). Otherwise, they make do with what they find here.

On this thin Iraqi inlet, no noise reaches us from the city. Boats simply glide by on the Shatt in one direction or the other, passing one another without difficulty in its wide riverbed. Some politely wait their turn to go through the Iranian customs procedures at the mouth of the river. For the time being, the Iraqi checkpoints have ceased operation. I count at least three vessels, including the enormous steamship *Marina Express*. Its hull is painted the three colors of the Italian flag, but it is flying the flag of the United Arab Emirates and is laden with cars and trucks. A boatload of passengers zigzags past it, shuttling between Dubai or Kuwait City and the major Iranian ports, without stopping on the Iraqi coast.

As we head back toward Basra, Adnan wants to stop at a military base built on the banks of the Shatt, where he apparently had some good times. Walking along the river, we disturb an eagle and then myriad other birds, which take flight in a noisy flapping of wings. The water is sparkling and almost babbling, and the panorama of the river is bucolic and charming. Military motorboats for "special operations" have been replaced by boats with oblong oars, and the fishermen aboard patiently cast their lines. A family from the marshlands has moved into one of the ruined buildings on the base. The family has eight children, four of them very young. I see them playing barefoot on the hardened mud. When we first appear—for only a few seconds—the new householder panics. He has broken into the building, but he also knows very well that in Iraq today, no one has the right to keep him from being where he is. Climbing a staircase in ruins, he follows us to the second floor, which has been exposed to the elements since the large picture window was smashed. Doors and furniture have vanished. Adnan, indifferent to the man's presence and to my own, is overcome by a tremendous nostalgia. He reminisces aloud about returning from patrols with his boys at dusk, when there was nothing more to do than to fling oneself on the soft couch in the living room, facing Iran. It was a time when one could open a good bottle, smoke a cigar, and, in short, savor one's happiness.

15

A MAN OF THE THEATER

Forty-five-year-old Tariq al-Etharei is director of the theater department at Basra University and also runs the university drama club. His clothes are resolutely Western. A cotton jacket opens to reveal a nice checked shirt, and his belted linen pants accentuate a slight rotundity. His round face with its sparse mustache, illuminated by magnificent blue eyes, is open and generous. Tariq does not complain about the past or about the uncertain future. For him, there is nothing more precious than to safeguard what he already possesses, namely, a certain knowledge of the world acquired through his readings and experience. In his astonishing library, he has Gaétan Picon's *Panorama de la nouvelle littérature française* (Panorama of the New French Literature), an Arabic edition published in Beirut. He can declaim whole poems by Paul Éluard in Arabic. He tells me that he knows almost by heart all the French, English-language, and Russian classics and dreams of creating a troupe that would perform his favorite authors in productions of his own imagining.

For the three days following the "liberation" of Basra, the buildings of the faculty of humanities were laid waste. Electrical wires, air conditioners, doors, windows and their frames—everything was torn out and no one made a move to stop the devastation. When the professors and students returned, they were alarmed to find that the destruction had been the work of local looters (a vicious rumor spread in this southern region, still marked by the first Gulf war, that they had come from Kuwait). In his memory, Tariq has retained the image of a delighted woman he ran into outside the department building. Clutched to her chest was what she thought was a television set, though in fact it was a computer. "I pointed this out to her. She seemed upset but didn't put it down. She even started running," he remembers. "Farther on, I also saw a young boy with a scanner in his arms. He was having a lot of trouble carrying it. Did he know what exactly he was carting off? No, of course not. For the next three months, this merchandise was available cheap at the market. At first the locals had some scruples, but they quickly dismissed them, and we were treated to a regular frenzy of appropriation." Eleven months later, the British army financed the refurbishment of the university. The hallways have just been repainted, and a few windows have been put in. Tables and chairs are expected to arrive soon.

A small poster Scotch-taped to the wall at the entrance to the department warns in English: "We are on the side of the religious leaders who demand free elections for the entire Iraqi people." Another, accompanied by a photo of Mohammad Sadeq al-Sadr (Moqtada's father), threatens in Arabic: "If a woman reveals a single strand of her hair, it's as if she were stabbing me with a knife. Anyone who allows his sister, wife, or female cousin to unveil her hair can expect to be disgraced as much as Umar Ibn-Saad, murderer of Imam Hussein!" These small signs have proliferated since the "liberation." The political parties are taking over the universities, and no one seems to be looking askance at them. Tariq, however, is dismayed.

We leave the university, and he takes me home with him. As we are winding along a narrow street in the central city, he points out his house, almost entirely concealed under a flowering pergola. A police station stands two blocks from his residence. As we go by, apparently good-natured British soldiers are having a great deal of trouble unloading a giant headless statue, no doubt of Saddam, from a truck. I hear them joking about what they are going to do with it.

Once home, Tariq shows me photos of Jean Cocteau's *Antigone,* a play he managed to stage in 1990 and which all the critics considered "a lesson in democracy." Here is a photo signed by the British theater director Peter Brook; here is Tariq standing next to the French playwright Armand Gatti, whom he met in Geneva. In a photo taken in 2002 in one of the presidential palaces in Baghdad, he is next to Saddam, who stands in the center of a group of a dozen artists. Tariq still can't grasp why he was summoned to that gathering of handpicked actors and directors. It's the only time he met Saddam.

His three youngest children (he has five) are in charge of the household in their mother's absence. She is in Baghdad finishing her doctoral thesis. The adolescents are playing "Hotel California" by the Eagles as background music. The living room where we are chatting has been entirely redone by the eldest son, aged twenty, who has discovered his talent as an interior decorator as well as a fashion designer. Couches and ottomans have been reupholstered with orange fabric. Curtains of the same color conceal the cold walls; the woodwork is white. The room is utterly lovely. The second son, aged eighteen, is a student and a fan of computers. The third is still in secondary school. The eldest daughter, twenty-two, is about to be engaged, and the second is still an adolescent.

"Every human being is fascinating because of what he is in his own truth. Saddam's generals' stars and military helmets don't interest me. It's the man who interests me," Tariq continues. After a laborious search in his library, so overrun with books that some are piled up on their sides over the rows standing upright, he pulls out John Reed's *Ten Days That Shook the World* in an Arabic edition published in Moscow. "God created us naked so that we could look at one another directly and without shame. That's why I pray at home; I don't go to the mosque. Between my children, my wife, and me, everything is transparent; we hide nothing from one another."

Tariq allows his eldest daughter, Shaheen, to meet her fiancé under his roof as often as she likes. It's a liberal attitude, Tariq being by nature benevolent and generous.

At the same time, however, he keeps his eyes open. He has given the young couple a year to get to know each other well, and he observes the young man, who visits his future in-laws almost every day. Tariq pays particular attention to Wisam's attitude toward money. "If a man is too captivated by money and lives only to earn it, he won't be a good husband because he won't properly love his wife," he explains with great seriousness. "I've allowed him to come to our home because our family is very different from his. Here we attach a primordial importance to culture, less to religion, which I consider a private matter. My goal is to see how my future son-in-law is adapting to this new environment."

Although Tariq is a happy father, the turbulence affecting his country worries him a great deal. He too acknowledges that during Saddam Hussein's time, the dictator had the merit of restraining the Islamist parties. He tells me that in Basra all of Saddam's portraits have been replaced by those of religious party leaders. "They were able to slip into the breach of power, and they aspire to fill it. We particularly fear their excesses, which can't be controlled. . . . In addition," he continues, "I've noticed that in this new context my students have become wary. In discussions, they avoid certain subjects. They're not the same ones as under the dictatorship, but there are still things that are left unsaid. No, I don't feel very comfortable in this society. In addition, I have the impression that educated and cultivated people no longer matter here." He shows me his two books on the history of theater in Iraq, which he was supposed to have published in Jordan. Suddenly, in a playful tone, he quotes Napoleon: "As the emperor said, everything under the sun is possible; one has only to persevere. So we're trying to get our brains working. Yesterday I finished an article called 'Theater and Democracy' for the daily paper *Azzaman*."[1]

Despite thirty years of good and loyal service in teaching, Tariq has not received his salary for the last three months. The political situation, which he calls "hazy," does not really inspire him. "Of course, now all the doors are open to students, but where can they go?" He doesn't understand why the U.S. troops are doing such a poor job of "conquering hearts" (how many times have I heard that same disappointment expressed?). "But they should know that the word 'democracy' has no meaning here," continues Tariq. "They should emphasize rebuilding a street, a school, or a building, but not democracy; that's much too abstract."

At the souk, I observe that many black banderoles have been deployed in honor of the *Ashura* holiday. On the street stalls of picture framers,

posters of Imams Ali and Hussein are liberally displayed. Tall and slender, with flamboyant hair, the most beautiful brown mustaches and
beards, and green turbans flowing in the wind, they prance about on
white horses or stand straight and majestic, flanked by a panther and a
lion. Looking at a poster on which two angelic tots are kneeling beside
Hussein, I find the resemblance to idealized depictions of Christ striking. Tariq also regrets the profusion of devout images in public spaces.
"Under Saddam, that was forbidden, which was much better."

He was able to keep his position as a university professor only because he was simply an ordinary member of the Baath Party. His wife,
a *farqā,* was dismissed. She is taking advantage of her free time to finish research on her doctoral thesis in theatrical studies. It has merit,
Tariq tells me. "I truly believe she'll never be able to teach again in Iraq.
But that may be a possibility in Syria, Jordan, or Yemen. When she became a ranking member, she was not asked for her opinion," he notes.
"She was selected and congratulated. The party supposedly needed
her." Of course, any refusal would immediately have ended her career.

In the car we listen to Radio Sawa ("together" in Arabic), a frequency
financed by the coalition. Arabic music and Western (that is, American) "hits" alternate judiciously. Beyond the canals spanned by rickety
bridges, Tariq takes me into the narrow streets of the old city. We visit
Ahmad, one of his colleagues, a singer of *maqām,* ancient melodies accompanied on the lute that are embellished and revised over time by
their interpreters. Tariq himself sings the maqām, which Iraqi young
people, he tells me, appreciate less and less.

At Ahmad's home we find an old friend of Tariq's, Dr. Abbas Jawad.
In 1977 Dr. Abbas left for Kuwait, then emigrated to Great Britain. In
the same year he wrote and defended a thesis in theatrical studies at the
University of Portsmouth. After twenty-five years away, he came back
to Iraq "to serve his country." Dr. Abbas is now trying to secure a position as assistant professor at Basra University, but the school requires a
great deal of coaxing and is slow to recognize his British degree. He is
impatient to share his knowledge with the students, who are hungry
for new things. Dr. Abbas got rich in Kuwait during the war with Iran.
Since his return, he has purchased six houses in the center of the city

and has rented them out. The rather courageous choice to return is his alone. His wife, accustomed to European comforts, doesn't want anything to do with Iraq anymore. His children are British subjects and will also not return.

"How long will I stay here? Ten years? More? No one knows. But even though the situation is unstable and I run the risk of getting killed tomorrow, I'm the happiest man in the world since I've found my old friends here. I'm free to argue with them, free to try to change the way people think. My priority is to talk and talk and talk, constantly explaining what I've acquired, and to argue," he forcefully declares. Dr. Abbas is also unusual in that he has long been a member of the Iraqi Communist Party—the oldest party in the country, created in 1934. "And we have a representative on the Iraqi Governing Council," he reminds me.

This colorful man has a great deal to say about the problems of artists in his country, now and in the past. "It's not easy being an artist," he concedes. "But nothing was ever written against the arts, either in the Koran or in the hadith, the commentaries of the Prophet. As far as paintings go, still lifes have always been allowed—faces no, but the ban is not written in the Koran; it's a purely human tradition. Yet many of us Muslim artists have a deep-rooted conviction that our religion has clearly pronounced itself against certain forms of artistic expression and that they are reprehensible—purely Western—phenomena. The secular dictatorship absolutely did not manage to destroy religious rituals. And the Iraqis in the south, who suffered more than the others, found their only refuge in religion. It's as if they no longer needed anything else." His tone is accusatory.

"As for Saddam," he goes on, "he banned the commemoration of *Ashura* during *moharram* for the following reason: Yazid the First, the second caliph of the Umayyad dynasty, killed Hussein, of course, but he also killed thousands of other innocents. The comparison between Yazid, murderer of the seventh-century imam, and Saddam Hussein, dictator of contemporary Iraq, was self-evident. When Shiites wanted to criticize Saddam, they called him Yazid, and everyone knew what that meant.

"Even though my friends and I—like Tariq here—are Shiite Muslims, we drink alcohol, dance, and flirt openly. Most of our compatriots hide away to engage in the same behavior. In this country, homosexual men and women live in secrecy and fear being discovered. It's a strictly taboo subject. Let's hope that thanks to freedom of information, everything will change over time. I believe that the satellite and the Internet are the best weapons against the religious fundamentalists, particularly the Shiites," he says frankly.

"Our traditional theater has always been a powerful force," he continues, "but the real problems began with the intrusion of politics into our lives, when all strata of the population, including artists, had to be in the service of Saddam Hussein and his regime. And even though everything might seem to be settled now, we still can't do theater because we're afraid of being killed . . . and to top it all off, nobody would care," he laments.

Why has Iraqi society turned its back on men of the theater to such an extent? "Because thirty-five years of dictatorship and twelve of international sanctions inevitably leave a mark on the way people think. Saddam spent our entire budget on his wars and distributed his money only to his own clan. Teachers and other government workers, none of them were decently paid. They could hardly make ends meet; they became taxi drivers or shopkeepers. No one could allow himself the luxury of caring about culture and the arts anymore. Those things were relegated to the background."

This evening, Tariq has invited his friends home to sing maqām. When they arrive, the six men joke about the risk of getting arrested by the new Shiite religious militias. In this month of mourning, singing and dancing are officially forbidden.

In the first place, there's Dr. Al-Hakim (of the same tribe as the religious leader by that name), graduate of a prestigious London university. He had to give up his position as professor of pharmacology at Basra University because he was a *farqā*. He wears his fifty years and his big belly well, dressed in an elegant suit and tie, smiling behind a salt-and-pepper mustache and smart eyeglasses. In addition to music, he now devotes himself to his pharmacy business.

Ahmad Ibrahim, the *ustad*,* has lackluster skin and raven-black hair and mustache. He provides me with a few explanations. He has first chosen a Baghdadi singing style, the chorus of the maqām. He explains the use of quarter-tones, a particularity of Arab music. Of the five strings on his lute, three allow for double stopping. His impressive voice is full and sweet.

Mustapha is another ustad from Basra, a professor of song and the rudiments of music in the music department of the faculty of fine arts. The voice of this unassuming professor also becomes magnificently expressive as soon as he starts to sing.

Dr. Abbas Jawad, cell phone in one hand and briefcase in the other, has just arrived. At the first notes, he closes his eyes and blends his voice with the others.

Finally, we are joined by two of Tariq's students. The first is studying music with Ahmad Ibrahim and seems a little constricted in his new pearl gray suit. The second is in jeans and a T-shirt. He is an interpreter for the commander of the British troops in the sector, and Tariq informs me with a laugh that working for the coalition pays. His student is earning four hundred dollars a month, a tidy sum for southern Iraq. In twelve months, the boy has bought a car and two houses not far from the city center and is now looking for a wife, since he's become a "catch."

Between songs, the young man relates that the British soldiers know they are more appreciated than their American counterparts and take advantage of certain situations without qualms. Photos of Americans being insulted by the Iraqi population or mistreating civilians[2] are thumbtacked to the walls of the base. Apart from that, in the department where he works, soldiers are often curious to know how popular they really are but never ask questions about local ways and customs, much less about religion, a subject that seems of no interest at all to them.

---

*"Singing teacher." Iraqi youth now prefer contemporary music, and fewer and fewer singing teachers are acknowledged by their peers. According to my hosts, there are only about ten in Basra (including Ibrahim) and about fifty in Baghdad.

Ahmad has taken up his lute again. The group falls silent and listens reverently to the first verses sung by the ustad. With eyes half
closed, his hands barely brushing across the strings, first in a leisurely
fashion, then faster and faster, he gradually takes flight for horizons
known only to him. Then another man's voice rises and swells, then another. Everyone knows the words. Anything can be used to accompany
the singers: some snap their fingers in rhythm; the interpreter grabs the
empty canister of crackers and beats on the bottom like a drum; others
whistle or tap on the table. The music dates back to time immemorial
and, more than anything, is a collective act marked by joy but also by
power and serenity. Now the six men are communing intensely through
the maqām. Looking at them, listening to them, I see they've forgotten all the rest.

PART II

In Afghanistan,
after the U.S. Military Victory of December 2001

16

EN ROUTE TO KUNDŪZ

On the road south to Dushanbe (Tajikistan), there are many police checkpoints, and we have to submit to them, even though it makes us lose time. On both sides of the black tar macadam, stretching out as far as the eye can see, are cotton fields with flowered female silhouettes stooped over their labor. Old and young, all delicately drop the balls of white gold into large burlap sacks carried by broken-looking men with deeply lined faces. We pass many bicycles with two people on them: the Tajik women ride sidesaddle on the luggage racks of their men. I have also been told that accidents with cars abound.

When we arrive in the small town of Chilikul, on the Afghanistan border, a huge iron statue of the Tajik president, Imomali Rakhmonov, steals the spotlight from a small, classic sculpture of Lenin with his arm extended, pointing an accusing index finger. A rusty, warped sign announces menacingly, in Russian and Tajik, the beginning of the "border zone." It makes no difference. There are just as many bicycles, and they are just as nonchalant. They swerve gracefully in front of our vehicle, and someone sticks out a flowered leg for balance.

The road toward the Russian border post of Nijni Panj is lined with reeds. We are now driving on piles of freshly harvested rice, deliberately placed on the roadway by peasants in the region so that the wheels of the vehicles will separate the grains from their husks. Since the disintegration of the Soviet Union in 1991, modern tools have become rare, and people have had to adapt. (I observed that method throughout the former Soviet regions of south central Asia, especially Tajikistan.) "Tajikistan is my country!" proclaims another sign in Uzbek as we are passing through a village composed of that ethnic group. The cotton plants have been burned by the summer sun: red ocher, sometimes black and stunted, they do not stand proud. In addition to the bicycles, we pass many light carts drawn by donkeys and driven by children.

Once we have passed Nijni Panj,[1] I find myself once again in a rusty bus in the company of fourteen men, ethnic Uzbeks, Turkomans, and Tajiks, all carrying Afghani passports. Davlat, a Tajik journalist who is accompanying me to northern Afghanistan, explains that they are seasonal workers who have come to harvest medicinal plants, which they will sell on the Afghan market. The Afghans joke among themselves about the unvarying visa procedures they must go through, even though they cross the border almost every day under the Russians' impassive gaze, who are used to their complaints.

My French passport and my presence in that zone stun the Russians, however. They bombard me with questions, more out of curiosity than with any express intentions. The bus is supposed to deliver us to a ferry (dating from the Soviet period), which will take us across the sandy waters of the Panj River, which forms the border between the two countries. As if on purpose, the mustachioed and copper-skinned Afghans are all wearing the same red-and-white-striped imitation Adidas shoes with the English inscription "good luck" on the heels.

Parked on the north shore, we wait to be allowed aboard the ferry. Across from us lies a yellow and dusty landscape: Afghanistan. Before our eyes, a small boat flying the Tajik flag is towing an enormous barge in the direction of Afghanistan-Tajikistan; it reaches shore, and, from the vessel, five tanker trucks from the natural gas deposits of northern Afghanistan are pulled out, making a huge racket. Laborious maneuvers are needed to get the dangerous trucks, heavy with propane, back onto the bank. Resigned and united in our wait under the early afternoon sun, which is still very hot, we sit in the dust. A fully veiled old woman suddenly appears from the boat and struggles to get on the bus we have just left and which will take her back to the border post, accompanied by the tanker drivers. A Tajik border guard is wearing an American cowboy hat that clashes with his military uniform. I pay ten dollars (in U.S. currency) for my passage, a "special foreigner's" rate that fortunately my Afghan traveling companions do not have to pay.

It's finally our turn. The ferry rocks slightly. We slip almost noise-lessly from one country to the other, a few yards south. On the deck, where we have all taken our places behind other trucks, empty this time, a curly-haired, potbellied man of about thirty wearing a jacket and tie busily pulls from his overnight bag karaoke cassettes he hopes we will listen to. But there is no tape deck aboard, and in any case the crossing does not last long enough. Then he goes on to something else, insistently asking an old man squatting beside him if he can cut open the watermelon that sits in front of the man and which is obviously tempting him. The old man in the beret stubbornly refuses. Finally, the man in the jacket and tie, clearly in search of new friends, offers his neighbors *nan** cakes, which he has kept folded in four at the bottom of his bag. The atmosphere is relaxed. The sputtering deck being raised by hand—the crew seems somewhat out of breath—and the rising noise of the motor help me realize that I am slowly leaving the famil-iar territory of the former Soviet empire and approaching the unknown.

---

*The *nan* is a delicate Afghan pancake essential at household meals. The balls of dough are flattened and applied to the walls of a cylindrical wood oven called a tandoor, which is usually dug in the kitchen floor—or in the yard in urban areas. When the bread is cooked, it detaches itself from the tandoor wall. The cake, succulent when warm, has the peculiar quality of remaining fresh for many weeks.

17

A TEACHER

We reach the southern bank of the Panj River; we are in Afghanistan. The procedures on this side are much less burdensome. We have to go on foot to the top of a wind-beaten knoll, where my passport and visa are inspected by a bearded and silent Afghan official. He is seated behind a simple wooden desk and equipped with a rubber stamp.

I am admiring the all-terrain vehicles with tinted windows that have come to the riverside to pick up their cargo or their guests, and especially the proud Afghans in turbans and light sandals who are getting out of them, when we are addressed in Tajik by a man convinced he is speaking to compatriots. It's true I'm in Tajik dress, that is, in multicolored baggy trousers and a large flowered tunic, both fairly loud and hardly corresponding to the notorious discretion of Afghan women. Hence Hajji* Kabir, a former teacher of French from the township of Kurgan-Tyube in southern Tajikistan, nearly faints on learning that I'm French. Once he has gotten over his surprise, he laughs at his mistake.

To earn a better living, he has begun a new career as a technical manager for Acted, a French nongovernment organization (NGO) in Taliqan (a city in the province of Afghan Badakhshān). Kabir is wearing Afghan clothing "so as not to be harassed," as he quickly confesses, but he is counting the days until he can return to his country, that is, to the other side of the river. Like my Tajik guide, he is excessively crit-

*An honorific term designating individuals who have returned from the hajj, the pilgrimage to Mecca, one of the five pillars of Islam.

ical of his neighbors to the south, who, in case he's forgotten, nonetheless offer him an opportunity to earn a better living. To hear the two of them talk, the Afghans are "very dirty" and "much less hospitable" than the Tajiks. I am shocked by these words: the Pashtun Afghan family with whom I spent my first night was clean and welcoming, as was everyone who offered me hospitality in the former Soviet regions of central Asia.

On the path leading us toward Kundūz, the largest city in northern Afghanistan after Mazār-e-Sharīf, disorder is the norm. Kabir, whose job is to keep the NGO's fleet of automobiles in good working order, complains that the professional Afghan drivers do not know how to drive, that they have "bought" their licenses, and that the vehicles have to be constantly repaired. As if things were not exactly the same in Tajikistan! Once again, I observe the lack of real objectivity people have about their immediate neighbors. Of course, to travel from one country to another and to take stock of the situation oneself, one must have money, a passport—a very rare and expensive commodity—as well as the means to pay for a visa,[1] but especially an open mind.

Traffic is heavy in town: the 4×4 Jeeps of the international organizations and those of the mujahideen (Afghans who fought the jihad against the Soviets between 1980 and 1989), for whom they are the outward sign of wealth par excellence, mingle with the yellow-and-white taxis, which drive with no concern for the rules of the road, and with motorcycle taxis, which backfire as they drag their little trailers—not to mention the horse-drawn carts adorned with red and white pompoms, which are surely the most common, and which always signal their passage with a long stream of ringing bells. It seems to me that everything here is much shabbier and smashed up than in the former Soviet regions of central Asia, where, however, the standard of living is not much higher. Could seventy-five years of Soviet dictatorship have left a few positive aftereffects north of the Panj which are missing from Afghanistan?

Gulbuddin, aged fifty, is Pashtun and the father of seven children. He says he migrated from his native region in the south (not far from the border and the tribal zones of Pakistan) to the Tajik region twenty-three years ago, at a time when the government was encouraging the Pashtuns to populate the ethnically diverse north. He is a teacher and is proud that under the Taliban regime, he continued, illegally, to give private lessons to some two hundred students, both boys and girls, in their homes. He was paid three hundred afghanis a month (close to six dollars) by their parents. "I'm quite satisfied with what I've accomplished in my lifetime. Teaching mathematics and geometry for thirty-two years is no shame, and if I compare myself with today's businessmen, at least I'm not dependent on anyone, I've lived very freely, and the most difficult years of my life are behind me."

Eight months ago, Gulbuddin decided to begin a new job at Health International, an international NGO financed by the European Union, among other groups, and specializing in increased public awareness about malaria and other illnesses. He knew its director, whose children had been his students. "So the director had a high opinion of me as a person and hired me," explains Gulbuddin. "I don't earn any more money than before, but at least I have job security, which is not the case when you're a teacher, because the Afghan government doesn't really exist. My salary is paid regularly, and that makes a great difference psychologically. Teaching is good but not one's whole life, especially not under the harsh conditions we have here."

Is he satisfied with the measures the new government took in education? "No, it could do much more, but its members have decided to give priority to other problems, for example, the disarmament of the militia and of those who have blood on their hands. Our people are in favor of freedom, of course, and of modern technology, the arts, and education, but those who have kept their weapons—and there are still many of them—are opposed to all that. President Hamid Karzai is caught between the Americans and the mujahideen, the former warlords.[2] He's in a difficult position. The Afghani government isn't powerful enough yet to ensure the population's safety. Of course, the government came into existence without us; it's all the result of schemes by the forces occupying us."

Our conversation is taking place in the presence of a large number

of other people, all men. Sitting cross-legged on carpets in the room reserved for guests near the entrance to his mud house, his sons, nephews,
sons-in-law, and cousins, all younger than Gulbuddin, listen to us re-
ligiously. Someone hands me a blanket, and I readily wrap myself in it:
sitting on the floor in that unheated room, I'm a little cold, and it seems
to me—to them as well, since they suggested it—more appropriate to
conceal certain parts of my body under the blanket, even though they
are nearly invisible under the Tajik clothing.

We speak of the postwar situation. Gulbuddin, bitterly observing
that the mujahideen, who still possess many weapons, are disinclined
to turn them in, acknowledges that the disarmament plan under way
in Kundūz satisfies no one: "If you turn in your weapon in exchange for
two hundred dollars and they give you no guarantee of work, it's really
not worth the trouble. The effectiveness of that plan will have to be analyzed over time. Fidel Castro said that a man's most loyal friend is his
weapon; he was right, but when the individual in question has no experience except that weapon, unfortunately he may turn it against himself and, more broadly, against his country. That's what's happened to
us: weapons replaced the Koran, and as long as that's the case, nothing
will change."[3]

In the late afternoon, his sons bring us a TV and a VCR from the
women's quarters so that I can have some fun, and perhaps so that I'll
stop talking politics with their father—after all, in their eyes, I'm still
a woman and my curiosity sometimes seems strange to them. They persuade me to watch an Indian film with them. As for Gulbuddin, he
wants to show me a poem (since the end of the Taliban regime, he's begun to write poetry), in which he urges young Afghans to exchange the
culture of guns for the culture of writing.

In the end, we go on talking and no one is really looking at the television, which has the sound turned down. The youngest men, designated to serve us, bring tea in a plastic thermos, then dinner, which we
savor on a piece of oilcloth that has been folded in eight and that is unfolded on the floor before our eyes. In its center, the women have placed
warm nan cakes. We feast on peas with rice, marinated beef, fried zucchini, and fresh mint.

All of a sudden, an electrical outage plunges the whole neighborhood into darkness. The power station in Norak, Tajikistan, which provides electricity to northern Afghanistan, is immediately blamed. Someone lights candles and oil lamps. Gulbuddin is still soliloquizing: "Every Friday at the *jumah namaz* [the midday Friday prayer, which includes the sermon], the mullah tries to top himself, telling us over and over again that we must not let our women leave the house without their burkas. There's no consensus about their education, and I sense reservations about the duty to send girls to school, as they do in the West. Let's take my wife as an example: we got married because her father was my mother's brother, hence my uncle. It's the custom here to marry within the family. I would have liked her to go to school, but that didn't happen." He declares with a laugh: "It's a pity, because if wives were educated, I'd have two or three!" He then recounts that until recently (even under the mujahideen, before the Taliban government), girls received instruction only from women in their own families, and the mullah taught them at most to read a few passages from the Koran and to understand the rudiments of their religion.

"Women represent half of humanity and, like men, they have the right to an education and to work. I have always been opposed to the Taliban's idea that the wife should stay home to educate the children. She can't do that unless she herself is educated; that seems obvious to me!"

The next day, emboldened by my presence, Abi Nullah, one of Gulbuddin's former mujahideen sons-in-law who fought the jihad against the Soviets, summons me for a "discussion." It's a rare opportunity for him to approach a Western woman with whom he shares a language—Russian. At forty, bearded and wrinkled, he looks ten years older than he is. His Russian is good. He studied it for six years at a military academy in Ryazan', south of Moscow, during the Soviet occupation. He is still full of hatred for the Red Army. "The American soldiers today behave better than the Soviets at that time, since they're adapting better," explains the former soldier in a faltering voice. "But here, people in the rural areas don't see any difference; they don't understand that these foreigners wish us well! Because they came to help us, one mustn't forget that. As far as I'm concerned, it's a good thing the soldiers from the international security assistance forces (ISAF) are stationed in Kundūz.[4] Without them, the anarchy would spread. In fact, so long as Iran and Tajikistan continue to get involved in our affairs, so long as our borders with those countries remain open, everything will keep going downhill, since those two neighbors don't wish us well."

For the moment, Abi Nullah has decided not to accept a job with the state, since "it's still too dangerous and there's too much potential for instability." But later on, why not? "I'd like to go on serving my people, the way I thought I was doing by being a mujahideen. The residents of Afghanistan can't back a man like Hamid Karzai or Burhanuddin Rabbani,[5] the former president; they're politicians from the past. We'd like a new and younger man." As in the case of his father-in-law, Gulbuddin, he thinks that disarmament and security constitute the real problems of the day.

Before going to Afghanistan, I had read and heard a great deal about the women hidden under burkas, those notorious "fleeting shadows" deprived of all rights, even the right to walk in the street with their faces uncovered. In a country liberated by the military coalition forces, I was not expecting to see so many of them. Yet they are certainly there. In the streets of the multiethnic Kundūz, the first Afghan city I passed through, all the women I met (Tajiks and Pashtuns, but also Uzbeks and Turkomans) were veiled from head to toe. The only exceptions were the very young, the prepubescent girls—and even they wear a veil, though not necessarily a black one, over their dark hair—and the very old, women nonchalantly wrapped in a large piece of fabric, often white, which is pulled over their heads. All other female forms disappear under a piece of fabric with a thousand pale blue or white pleats (only once did I see a dark green burka) radiating from an embroidered skullcap. It might almost be a pleasing garment if the anonymity it imposes were not inhuman. Under all those vertical pleats, the shape of the body is no longer apparent, of course; but they also serve to elongate the already unreal silhouettes, which become almost phantasmagorical. Sometimes, squatting as they wait for a bus, some of the women will discreetly pull up the front part, which may come down to their feet but may also stop below the waist. In doing so, they uncover their faces. For the others, you're reduced to directing your eyes at their calves, which are sometimes dangerously bare, and their shoes. They often wear rudimentary worn-out plastic things but sometimes unexpected polished pumps, and you catch yourself imagining a different woman, more refined, more beautiful even.

Since the Tajik outfit is decidedly too gaudy, I decide to dress like the Afghan women. I go to the souk, accompanied by Abi Nullah, whose job is to advise me in my choice of a local outfit—which, in fact, turns out to be made in Pakistan. Three women in blue burkas who are also doing their errands seem to be amused under their veils by the exotic presence of an unveiled foreign woman at the local market. They follow in detail the bargaining conducted by my chaperone and seem to approve of our choice of a long tunic with sleeves, made of khaki-colored cotton and embroidered on the front, with matching pants and a wide, colorful, pleated veil. Beside that merchant, where the three blue ghosts have come to make their purchases, I suddenly see one of the conical shapes making extensive concealed motions near the top of her chest and neck, before holding out three crumpled bills in her hand—bare but for her rings—in the direction of the imperturbable vendor. She's gotten her money out of her bra, that's what it is, thus sparing herself the trouble of carrying a handbag or wallet, very impractical accessories under the burka. To my enormous surprise, in exchange for these few afghanis the three customers leave with a fitted black leather jacket, which, as Abi Nullah explains to me, one of them will wear exclusively under her veil or at home, in view only of her parents, brothers, uncles, and cousins.

As I am leaving the souk, another woman is posted there. Mischievously and to better satisfy her curiosity, in a sudden and somewhat provocative gesture, she lifts the front part of her veil over the top of her head. For an instant, I discover a beauty with pale eyes and brown skin, giving a little smile.

18

EN ROUTE TO BADAKHSHĀN

We start out at dawn on a stony road heading east. Moving in the opposite direction from our minibus, dozens of men converge toward the central area, that is, the bazaar, accompanied by their donkeys, often with heavy packsaddles. Here and there, a white or blue form is quietly seated sidesaddle on the mount. Outside almost every cob house in the villages we go through is a pile of more or less round stones of similar size, collected from the riverbed not far away. They will be used to build the foundation for a new dwelling. From time to time, window frames painted blue or green indicate slightly wealthier families. But most are ocher, earth colored.

We leave behind the pleasant plains and enter a rugged and unforgiving landscape, the valley narrowing as the hills become steeper. In every direction there are sheer mountaintops, jagged walls that let the traveler pass only grudgingly, or so it seems. On either side of the road, which is reaching increasingly dizzying heights, stand carcasses of disemboweled and rusted armored vehicles: no doubt the remains of Taliban tanks that faced the forces commanded by Ahmed Shah Massoud's successor during the attack of the Northern Alliance in October 2001,[1] or older debris from Soviet armored vehicles dating to the major offensives of the 1980s.

The minibus driver is very proud of his new acquisition, which cost him seven thousand dollars at the largest automobile market in Afghanistan, in Herāt, a major city in the west of the country.[2] We are swaying back and forth without a second's respite, the asphalt having long since disappeared. The jolts are sometimes so powerful that they knock me right out of my seat. As we come around a mountain curve, I see a labyrinthine open-air coal mine from which ragged workers are emerging, not even wearing helmets.

A little farther on, I see a colored spot on the ocher mountain: it's a group of women traveling on foot to the sound of tambourines, heading for a neighboring village to celebrate a wedding. At the approach of our vehicle, which can be heard from a long way off on the path, some of them quickly move aside. Any vehicle is a danger and causes panic, since it contains strangers to whom one must not show oneself. These mountain women, who do not wear burkas, feel even more vulnerable than their sisters in town and are even more withdrawn. They simply hide their faces by turning their backs to the road or squat hastily and bury their faces in their skirts, patiently waiting until we have passed. I turn around in an effort to meet their gaze, discern their features, or observe if they are coming back onto the road as soon as the bus has passed, but the cloud of dust that surrounds our vehicle removes all visibility.

In each village, the only permanent structures are the schools, often built on the periphery, plus the buildings for humanitarian aid organizations and the medical centers. Bits of colored fabric hanging from sticks, all surrounded by a clay wall, are enough to indicate a cemetery. Under the noonday sun, a peasant hitched to his makeshift plow makes his furrow.

"Why should I put a Karzai poster on my bus? He hasn't done anything for our country. At least Massoud has accomplished something," the driver declares defiantly, throwing two bills—which blow away —to an old man squatting along the roadside who has said a few words of prayer as we pass. Sometimes the conical structure of a brick oven breaks the monotony of the landscape. There are signs that someone is building houses; smiling young people mold the cob, a mixture of clay and water, to which must be added straw carried by donkeys. Indeed, every minibus we go by has a photo of Commander Massoud taped to its windshield. He is venerated in the region.

We stop in the township of Kishim to get something to eat. On our arrival, all eyes are fixed on me. Very much against my will, I am the center of attention. I am sitting cross-legged on a platform not far from the restaurant entrance, following the example of all the other customers, for the most part travelers like us. I wait for someone to bring me bowls of rice with *bamyan,* the delicious little fried zucchini. Fortunately, a Bollywood action film in Urdu (the language of the Pashtuns in Pakistan) steals the spotlight away from me. Inside the restaurant, everyone is glued to the television screen; another, smaller screen is even set up outdoors so that no one feels deprived. Above the wooden door, a color photo of President Karzai, an official portrait of sorts, is flanked by two photos of Massoud.

Still farther to the east, the landscape has become lunar: from one end of the horizon to the other, I see only countless pebbles, stones, and rocks with sharp ridges. Often the road does not even exist anymore, and we must slowly make our way along a dry riverbed. From time to time, on signs written in English, Pashto, and Dari, the Halo Trust organization indicates the presence of land mines on either side of the road. The line not to be crossed is drawn with small white and red pebbles. Everyone has long since forgotten who put the mines there: the Soviets, the mujahideen, the Taliban? In these hostile places where history repeats itself, everything is all jumbled together.

As if rising up from nowhere, three or four children in rags throw a few shovelfuls of sand onto the path as we approach, wanting to prove that they are making themselves useful in their way. They look crestfallen when our driver does not throw them a few coins as we pass; he argues he cannot make everyone happy.

Collapsed bridges have recently been restored by humanitarian organizations, as explanatory signs indicate in English. Other buildings, which have not been so lucky, are miraculously still standing, patched up by the local population with, for example, rubber tracks recovered from tanks. A pulley bridge serving the opposite bank (we are passing alongside the Kushka River) is sensibly tucked away on one side of the road.

The driver and his friend insist that we stop several times so that they can say their prescribed prayers. I observe them as they first wash their feet deliberately near the river, then kneel in the direction of the setting sun. Each of them removes his *patu** from his shoulder and throws it on the ground in front of him, then prostrates himself on it. When the prayer is over, he pulls his socks up and gets back on the minibus.

For fun, a muddy brood of kids attach themselves to the back of trucks that slow down to go through their village. I have never seen so many children working in the fields and on the construction of various buildings, right alongside the adults. On the walls are inscriptions in the local language declaring that "the cultivation and sale of opium are forbidden by Islam," signs of the growing drug problem.

*A large woolen rectangle, often beige or brown, which men wear on their shoulders and in which they wrap themselves when it gets cold, covering their heads.

19

AN ENGINEER

Faizābād, the capital of Afghan Badakhshān,[1] has never been occupied
by the Taliban, or by anyone else for that matter: the northern province
is too far away from everything. It is linked to the world by only a single unpaved and particularly dangerous road—through Taliqan and
Kundūz to Kabul. The road from Salang to Kabul was built only in
1964. It has taken us ten hours straight to travel the 106 miles that separate Taliqan from Faizābād.

At dusk, as the Toyota pickups honking and even knocking down
passersby in the steep lanes of the old city transport me in my mind
back to the Casbah in Algiers, we find Hamid at home, at the end of
a maze of narrow lanes (his street stall was already closed). A forty-
three-year-old Tajik, Hamid lives with his family—parents, brothers
and unmarried sisters, children, and in-laws—in Faizābād's old city,
constructed entirely of cob and separated from the "new city" by three
miles and two bridges, the first built forty years ago. His house has two
stories, which is fairly rare, and is built like all the others, of baked clay
bricks. Nevertheless, since its walls are covered with paint inside and
out—a sign that the family is well off—it looks like a permanent structure. After going past a porch so low we have to duck our heads, we are
received in the room designated for guests, immediately to our right.
Adorned with carpets and *kurpachi* (a colored mattress filled with cotton, also found in Tajikistan), it is rectangular and its windows sport
closed curtains. Hence the guests do not see what is going on in the
yard, and vice versa. On the central carpet, someone opens the *dastarkhan,* on which are set out the tea thermos, glasses of warm milk,

crusty nan, and almonds. Hamid, our host, has Uzbek blood, which is obvious by his almost slanted eyes and his good round face. Across from the room we are in is the medical office of Dr. Hajira, his elder sister, a gynecologist who is supposed to return from the United States any day now.

Hamid is an angry man: angry at his government, which he considers weak and cowardly; angry at the international community, which is not making the right strategic choices in Afghanistan; and angry at his fellow citizens, who are not managing to reason any differently from what the recent historical situation has inculcated in them. "It's pointless for the United Nations, through the World Food Program and the local NGOs, to still be distributing flour to us, since we're all planting wheat. That will make the prices drop for lack of competition. Those soft prices incite our peasants to grow poppies instead, which immediately brings in much more money. They sell their crops to middlemen at the bazaar, who then resell it to guys in cahoots with the 'commanders.'* Along the way, everyone deducts his share. In certain remote villages, the trade is well established: the 'commanders' hire people who ensure the safety of the heroin-processing labs. So long as they're heavily armed, no one can prevent them from engaging in that lucrative trade. And those people are interested only in money; they don't bother with ethical questions. The central government has no grasp of what's happening here, and less so in the neighboring villages. In fact, even in Kabul, Karzai has no control over anything. It would seem that even the ISAF has fallen into the deep pockets of the 'commanders,' who are the only ones able to guarantee the security of foreign soldiers. That's the last straw! As for the Taliban, they're still around, but they're discreet. Those Taliban are a real poison, which seeped into the ranks of the mujahideen thanks to the Americans, after they financed both groups throughout the 1980s and 1990s. Perfectly trained during the jihad against the Soviets, all the mujahideen had to do was continue:

---

*"Commanders" are what the Afghan population calls the former mujahideen who took up arms in the 1980s against the Soviet army and who were then at the center of the civil war that erupted in 1992. Some of them became Taliban beginning in 1996.

the Americans didn't teach them to build a state, so they've gone on doing what they know best, making war."

According to Hamid, there's a fine line between the mujahideen and the Taliban. In terms of Islam, they are hardly different at all: the Taliban are in favor of a radical Islam, precisely the watchword of the mujahideen at the beginning of their struggle. In Hamid's view, the difference is rather ethnic in nature and corresponds to the line of demarcation between the Pashtuns and the other ethnic groups. Indeed, in their hunger for power, the Pashtuns have always been pro-Taliban, he assures me. "I remember in Kabul in 1992 when the mujahideen took over, a former Communist soldier said he knew nothing about Islam but that he wanted to stay in power, a privilege of the Pashtun ethnic group for 250 years." The question of ethnic diversity leads him to declare himself in favor of a federal system. He recognizes it is difficult to live together but declares the Tajiks are "ready to share." Despite his open-mindedness, Hamid has trouble accepting the decisions made by the U.S.-led international coalition, which put Hamid Karzai, a Pashtun, in charge of the country and which backs him as the future president (see note 2 of chapter 17). He denounces it as too rapid a process, unrealistic, and, above all, an American maneuver designed to ensure the future leader's loyalty to the United States.

"The coming elections have no chance of being genuine, and people are already laughing about them. We all know in advance that Karzai will be elected. He lived in the United States for eight years, and many members of his family are still there. It's obvious to any Afghan that Karzai is the Americans' man. As for the Pashtuns, they don't care: he's a Pashtun, that's the only thing that counts. They've also got hold of the Ministry of Finance, hence of banking and trade. As a result, for us the Tajiks, the term 'Afghan' sounds like an insult: an Afghan is above all a Pashtun. Should we change the name of our country? I don't know.

"The Loya Jirga has turned out to be a sham.[2] The delegates don't really serve much purpose, since no one listens to their advice. It's clear now that the council was organized just to legitimate the democratic facade desired by the West. The Americans closed our military academies, our own army is still not trained, and our former soldiers have become construction workers or businessmen!"[3] America is completely foreign to him, and he doesn't understand the mentality or the way of life. "We have the impression that we're being manipulated," the engineer says, "as if the issue had never been humanitarian aid but rather political stakes greater than us. For example, we believe that Saddam had the right to remain president of Iraq and to defend his country against the military invasion, since that's a question of honor. In fact, because of that policy, his detractors have now become his allies and he looks like a hero!" All the same, Hamid acknowledges that the Americans claim to be helping them to "live differently, without weapons." According to him, however, it's a hollow wish: people here still buy weapons to protect themselves, at the bazaar or from the "commanders," because they still have no confidence in the state.

He concedes two other positive aspects of the occupation: "The responsibility to rid our country of what they themselves produced, that is, fundamentalism, and the obligation to help us, since we're a poor country. Of course, the standard of living has improved: under Rabbani, a worker was paid fifty cents a day; now it's six dollars. The average salary is thirty dollars a month for government workers and about twenty dollars a day for a highly qualified specialist such as a painter or a mechanic, but no one gets paid regularly. There's generally a delay of three to four months." He keenly regrets the fact that the Americans "are imposing their way of thinking as well as their lifestyle."

Hamid offers the example (which caused quite a stir in Afghanistan in the autumn of 2003) of a young Afghan woman, winner of a beauty contest in the United States, who has incited the wrath of the various political and social institutions of his country, even the intellectual strata. She paraded in front of an audience (hence in front of men she didn't know) in a swimsuit, an unforgivable sin according to the Afghan code of conduct. He insists: "In emphasizing activities uncharacteristic of our society, that is, the marketing of a woman's beauty, she provided a bad example for our young women. Afghanistan ought to find a 'middle course,' which would be neither that of the Taliban nor that of the Northern Alliance."[4]

The following evening, Hamid, who has decided never to take off his baseball cap (it adds an amusing modern touch to his Pakistani dress), goes on at length about Massoud, "the Lion of the Panshir": "The Americans, of course, could not have gained a foothold so easily in our country if Massoud were still alive," he declares. "Nevertheless," he adds sarcastically, "I find that his death is convenient for everyone, and in the first place for Defense Minister Mohammad Qasim Fahim,[5] who would never have become what he is today if his leader had not died. Massoud was an unparalleled strategist but a wretched politician; that's our bad luck. But for me, our problems are essentially due to our inability to close the border with the Pakistani tribal zones. It's like a sieve! It's the Pakistanis who settled the score for Dr. Najib;[6] that's an open secret. Yes, Najib was a KGB agent, but he was not a bad sort. Pakistan still wants to go on meddling in our politics, with the Americans' blessing."

Although he never took any active role in the resistance, Hamid was close to the forces of Ahmed Shah Massoud. In September 2001, when the commander was assassinated and the attacks on American soil were perpetrated—leading to the invasion of Afghanistan—he found himself in China, commissioned by the leadership of the Northern Alliance to purchase a radio and television station. By the time he returned to Afghanistan, Kabul was liberated.

The engineer gives his explanation for the Taliban's rise to power: "The mujahideen, who had become the Taliban, used bin Laden as a bank: the Saudi financed Rabbani and other fundamentalists, such as Gulbuddin Hekmatyar,[7] who at the time was the best friend of the United States and of Pakistan. At first, no one was afraid of the Taliban; they were actually rather popular given the chaos wreaked by the mujahideen. But they used religion as an instrument to frighten people, which few people in the West know. You see, those seminarians were not the good, true, pure religious people they proclaimed to be, and their laws set us back to the Middle Ages. Their leaders didn't even care about those laws, but they applied them to set an example and to wreak terror. They set the different factions of society against one another: teachers against students, mujahideen against Islamic authorities, etc., so that the West could find an excuse to invade us. I recently asked an American civilian posted in the region what he thought of the situation. He compared the Taliban to the daughter you educate for years, then she leaves you to get married. That's exactly what happened here: the United States educated and nurtured the Taliban, and then they —they're also called 'seminarians'—exerted their autonomy. The local ex-Taliban have only one regret: they're no longer in power. They still don't realize they've been used by people stronger than they are. They've gone back to being imams, chauffeurs, or government workers; they hide and are much less aggressive. The Taliban of Badakhshān are not ethnic Pashtuns, but they've all lived in Pakistan."

What future does he see for his only daughter, who is six years old? He reflects but appears calm: "Under the Taliban, I was very afraid; they could easily have killed me. Today it's different: I want my daughter to go to school and to be able to work in the field she's chosen. In a year she'll start primary school. I'll protect her from the social pressure that imposes marriage on girls under the age of twenty in the belief that the younger the woman is, the better the husband fares. Men often have two wives; plural marriages are particularly common among the wealthier people—drug runners, for example, or those who deal in precious stones."

Hamid denounces the wearing of the burka as primarily an urban phenomenon. In the villages where everyone knows everyone else, where all the families are connected by blood, and where most of the women work in the fields, the full veil does not exist. He recalls that under Dr. Najib women did not wear burkas. According to Hamid, it was created "so that no one could see whom you're taking home." At that time, he insists, women were like jealously guarded secrets, and every man considered—still considers, it seems to me—his wife or sister his private property. In Pashtun society, he adds, sometimes the husband's brother does not have the right to see his sister-in-law's face! "That's to prevent a man from falling in love too often," he concludes in an about-turn.

As an engineer, Hamid has never wanted to leave his country to seek refuge in Pakistan, as many others have done. It's a very aggressive country, in his view. He has always felt more useful at home, relentlessly pursuing his activities under the Taliban, even when most of his colleagues had taken off. Hamid recalls that he spent seven years abroad (in the Soviet Union, an entity that no longer exists, he points out), and that seven years was quite enough for him. "In Pakistan, I'd just be a second-class citizen, condemned to work illegally to survive. Since I don't know anyone, I couldn't live a normal life, so I'm not interested in leaving, even though, technically and financially, I have the ability to do so." In September 1988, the Taliban forces reached Kichma, fewer than sixty-two miles from Faizābād, where they were stopped by Massoud's troops. It was then that Hamid began to build the only maternity hospital in the region, now run by his elder sister.

In 1996 he created the Association des Ingénieurs du Badakhstan (Badakhshān Engineers' Association), assembling four specialists who worked under contract for the major international agencies such as the United Nations, UNICEF, and the World Food Program, which had never ceased operations in Badakhshān. In fact, that daily collaboration in the field marked the beginning of his anger at them. He accuses them, at best, of not being efficient, and at worst of diverting the funds received for reconstruction for the personal profit of the expatriate wage earners.[8]

In 1978 Hamid, the eldest son in a family of eleven children (six girls and five boys), built this eight-room house, where the tribe lives permanently with the elderly parents. His father, a former military pharmacist under King Zahir Shah,[9] was the first to open a private pharmacy in Faizābād in the 1960s, at a time when the region did not even have a doctor. His grandfather and great-grandfather were both provincial governors under the king. His wife is currently in Kabul, where she works as a UNICEF doctor. One of his brothers went to study in Ukraine in the 1980s and has remained there, and the youngest is a renowned ophthalmologist in Mazār-e-Sharif. The other two brothers live in the family home with wives and children; each couple has a room of their own and a bed. The other rooms (such as the one I spent a week in) are unfurnished; we live and sleep on *kurpachi*. The bathroom is small, for the most part independent of the house proper, with a mud floor and no windows; in the center of the room stands a wood-fueled water heater. You have to compose the mixture of hot and cold water in large buckets. The kitchen is in the yard, under an awning, and the women are always there, squatting near steaming pots placed on powerful gas burners.

In 1980, when the Soviets had just invaded his country and the Communist Babrak Karmal was in power, the twenty-year-old Hamid left to study civil engineering in Baku, Soviet Azerbaijan. He stayed there for seven years, returning home once a year, during the school holidays. "In 1979, when the Soviets arrived in Afghanistan,[10] they were rather well received, at least in the north, since people were afraid of the Afghan fanatics preaching the Communist ideology. Although no one in my family ever took up arms against the Soviets, we did support the resistance. For ten years, until the Soviets left Afghanistan, the mujahideen received money from the United States, probably as much as what that country is now giving Iraq!"

It's Friday and time for the midday prayer, but Hamid has no intention of going to the mosque. So that his neighbors and acquaintances will not notice his breach of the religious rule, the engineer holes up in his house and waits for at least an hour and a half before going out. He is nevertheless eager to show me the hospital he has built. The plaque at the entrance reads: "Hospital of the Transitional Islamic Government of Afghanistan." As we leave the old city, not far from the "new" bridge built by Hamid in 2000, we get stuck behind a wedding convoy of seventeen vehicles, both Soviet ZIL trucks and Toyota minivans. There are many more weddings than usual just before Ramadan, during which time they are forbidden. For this one, it's the "men's day"; Hamid was invited but did not go. The "women's day" took place three days ago, he explains. This evening, during the final ceremony, the mullah will pronounce the couple husband and wife in the groom's home. Tomorrow the men will be able to visit him, their arms loaded down with gifts; then it will be the women's turn. Banquets and dances are also organized separately.

Hamid has the idea of introducing me to the director of the local television station of Badakhshān, a branch of the central station in Kabul that never stopped broadcasting under the Taliban, since they did not control the region. Today that state station is under the control of the region's governor, named by the new Kabul regime. The young director, who began as a film editor twenty years ago, remembers proudly: "Surrounded by the Taliban, we worked very freely: our wives could appear on-screen. I had convinced the mullahs that was necessary and had even gone to visit Rabbani in his village to explain that if we banned women from television, the public would figure out how to access channels by satellite regardless, and that would take away our audience and be particularly harmful to our society. In addition, that ban would contribute toward bringing us closer ideologically to the Taliban, which had to be avoided at all cost. I finally convinced everyone, but I received a number of death threats from local Taliban, who were up in arms at that revolt."

How is the station functioning now? Poorly. He launches into the usual litany, deploring the lack of funds, of transmitters, the decrepit technology. But, above all, the director seems to regret that the central television station jealously keeps its few training positions with foreign NGO specialists for itself. As a result, the provincial journalists feel "cut off from the world." "For the moment," he explains, "none of the television stations has been privatized" (with the exception of the new television station based in Sheberghān, in the domain of the warlord Rashid Dostum; see chapter 22).

The fictional films are shot in Kabul and as such are subject to the norms of the Afghan audience, "whereas even three months ago we were freer." Since the formation of the new government, he has been asked to respect the policy of the central television station, which, for example, bans women singing on-screen.[11] The local television station of Badakhshān disregards that policy. But, according to the director, it is clear that in Kabul those who control culture are being accused of laxity by ultraconservative groups, in other words, by those close to the Taliban, who are still on the prowl behind the scenes of political power.

Uman, one of Hamid's nephews, the son of one of his sisters, is nineteen and is getting ready to live with an uncle in Kabul and attend university there. He confesses to me that school was nothing but a bore for him, that the teaching level has fallen very low. In addition, he criticizes the school for turning into a place of debauchery: "The students drink alcohol and smoke hashish. Even the girls from the school next door drink!" He would like to enroll in the journalism department, but Hamid insists he become an engineer like himself. "As soon as I've finished school, I'll leave this goddamned country, which has had nothing but wars and has no future," mutters the lanky, beardless young man with unmanageable hair. "I'll leave for Australia. I saw a film about that country; it's beautiful there, very quiet. America doesn't appeal to me at all." He is speaking in broken but comprehensible English, acquired after two years of private lessons with a young professor now in Kabul (who works there as an interpreter for the ISAF). Only one other young man in his class shares his dream of exile, but in his case it's in Canada. The others are "no longer even capable of thought," according to the disabused Uman, who would have preferred good math teachers (math is his favorite subject) rather than teachers in geology, Pashtun, Dari, chemistry, history, and *hadith*—short texts reporting the words, counsel, and acts of the prophet Muhammad during his lifetime, studied alongside the Koran—all subjects that don't interest him. As for the Americans, the adolescent hopes they'll leave after finishing their mission. He appreciates American films on video, and they're also good for learning the language better, but, he concedes, "I'd probably need to listen to the radio more, especially the BBC, if I want to become a journalist."

In fact, one of Uman's great worries, typical of his age, is his physical appearance, especially how he dresses. He hates wearing the *shalwar kameez,* the traditional Pakistani tunic, which he cannot avoid doing in his neighborhood if he doesn't want people to gossip about him. "That's how you can recognize a country that's not free; that's the influence of Pakistan!" he shouts. The possibility of avoiding that constraint when he goes to Kabul is a further motivation, since, he thinks, "at least at the university I'll be able to dress as I please."

20

A GYNECOLOGIST

The next morning I witness the triumphant return of Hamid's elder sister to the family home. Dr. Hajira is forty-eight years old and has just spent more than a month in the United States. She was invited by Johns Hopkins University in Baltimore to receive an award for her work as director of the maternity hospital in Faizābād. During the first four months of 2003, without heat or electricity and relying solely on oil lamps, Hajira and her eight colleagues delivered more than four hundred babies, earning a salary of thirty-six dollars per month. This in Afghanistan, where the infant mortality rate is one of the highest in the world, and where 90 percent of women in the region are without medical care.

All morning long, her female colleagues from the maternity hospital waited for her at the Faizābād airport, their arms laden with plastic flowers. When they finally arrived outside her house, the blue chadors could come off, and the women broke into ululations as tears flowed.

I'm invited to go with the women to the main room of the house, where the patriarch lives, confined to his bed on account of illness. Like most Afghan interiors, the room, though rather large, has no furnishings other than the television glowing in a corner and the usual *kurpachi* unrolled along the walls and accented with multicolor cushions. They are all sitting on the floor waiting for tea. Hamid's mother is wearing a long white scarf, looking serious and deeply moved. Doors bang as people bustle about the kitchen. One of the sisters has a degree from the Kabul Law School but had to interrupt her studies in 1992 when the "events" started, as she explains with a sigh.

We are waiting for Hajira, who had barely gotten home when she put her scarf back on to meet a patient waiting for her in her office, near the entrance to the house. She has been anticipating this moment for three months. The news that the chief gynecologist of Faizābād has returned has quickly made the rounds of the city, and patients are already lining up for visits. A beaming Hajira returns to sit with us, announcing that a patient treated for infertility before Hajira left is now pregnant! Nothing could make Hajira happier. Someone brings in four thermoses of tea accompanied by long strings of candy arranged in small porcelain dishes. Most of the sweets available at local street stalls are imported from the United Arab Emirates. Here, they are accompanied by homemade cookies and fresh almonds.

Hamid has joined us and takes out a small video camera from a bag brought in by one of the young people. The reunion must be filmed! Stocky, his face weather-beaten, with blue-green eyes and a thick mustache, Hamid does not look at all like his sister, a tall brunette with green eyes. She is alarmingly pale, probably due to the fatigue of the journey. Hajira is wearing a long black-and-gold-striped wool skirt with a matching black embroidered vest buttoned to the neck. She is constantly fiddling with her fine gold necklace while attempting to respond to the barrage of questions her family and friends are asking. "Many people I met during the trip were astonished that I wanted so much to return home, when I could easily have stayed in the United States. But I felt a real need to come back here, where I feel more useful," she declares in a sweet, steady voice. One of the sisters listening to Hajira is nursing her youngest daughter, born twenty days ago. The account of Hajira's trip sometimes makes her audience laugh; they are amused, for example, to learn that her flight from Dubai to New York on the eve of September 11, 2001, was delayed for several hours for fear of a terrorist attack.

Because the United States has no consulate in Afghanistan, Hajira had to go to Islamabad, the capital of Pakistan, for her visa. She obtained it in only two days, to the astonishment of her brother Hamid. After her travels, Hajira is more resolute than ever: it is right here in Badakhshān that she will continue to practice; she even balks at going

to Kabul, where "the air is more polluted" and where she would necessarily feel "less independent" at a large hospital. Here, in Faizābād, it's
easier and more efficient for her to train a larger number of doctors,
which is the chief aim of her practice.

"A maternity hospital was my dream for so long," she begins.
"UNICEF offered us most of the equipment, and for the last five years
the French organization Doctors without Borders has regularly provided us with medication. Year in, year out, we now have twenty beds,
one operation room, and one labor room, but our main problem is a lack
of qualified staff. And to think of all the Afghan doctors I met in the
United States who are working as taxi drivers or shopkeepers—what a
waste! We need them here. But it's much too late!"

She shows us the photo albums from her trip, which are passed solemnly from hand to hand. Finally, we're served the *och,* an oily spaghetti
soup with meatballs added to it. The younger people ask their aunt the
price of cassettes, DVDs, and various electronic games and are astonished to learn how expensive they are (they are used to the extremely
low prices for pirated imports of computer software and music at the
local markets).

Hajira agrees to tell me the "major episodes" of her life in her office
at the hospital, where "we'll be more at peace." It's a spacious room,
where the gynecologist sees her patients dressed in a white smock and
stockings and a scarf over her shoulders. She lifts the scarf quickly over
her jet-black hair when necessary, that is, in the presence of a man. Her
blue rayon burka hangs modestly from the sill of the open window. She
will not put it on until she leaves the office and returns home.

Her imposing desk is pushed to the back of the room, into a corner.
On it she has set up an enormous computer with a monitor, which looks
like an antique (in any case, it doesn't work since there's no electricity),
a plastic Afghan flag, and the trophy, an odd transparent structure, that
she received in the United States. About fifteen yellow, red, and green
plastic chairs are lined up against the walls. We sit down on two of
them.

"I'm the eldest of eleven children. My mother was seventeen when
I was born, and now she's sixty-five; my father, who suffers from hy-

pertension, is seventy-eight. I was barely a year old when my parents, who'd been living in Kabul, returned to the village of Bahorak, Badakhshān, where our family comes from. It's forty kilometers [twenty-five miles] from Faizābād. I was the first female student there. I was seven when we moved to Faizābād, the capital of the province (this was under King Zahir Shah). My father had agreed I'd go to school with the boys, and there was no question of my wearing the burka. I'm also the first provincial girl to complete high school and to go to university. In Kabul I lived with one of my uncles and his wife, who had just come back from the Soviet Union. They helped me a great deal during my seven years of study. I received my degree from the school of medicine in 1979, just as the Soviet invasion was occurring. At the time, classes were packed: in my year, there were 180 students! In 1978 and 1979, a large number of boys around us began to disappear. We didn't know why they were arrested one after the other, and we were constantly crying. None of us could concentrate on our studies anymore. The previous year, the whole family had joined us in Kabul because the situation in Badakhshān was rapidly deteriorating. The uncle I was living with was arrested; he survived in the end, but four of my other uncles were killed.

"I'd gotten my first job as a gynecologist-obstetrician at the Malalai Hospital, the largest in the capital. All my colleagues at the time had already fled abroad, and the atmosphere was toxic. In 1985 I agreed to go to a medical school in Moscow for two and a half years of training. It was not easy to adapt to a society so different from ours, especially since there was a language barrier. The professors were kind and professional, of course, but I had no friends, and Russian life bored me. Fortunately, my scholarship was generous and allowed me to go to the movies and watch French and Indian films, which I adored and which were not available in Kabul. In mid-1988 I returned to my job at the Malalai Hospital. I was young and pretty, I had many admirers, but they all wanted to leave the country, and that didn't suit me. Nothing could have made me leave. So I've never married and have no children, but I have all my brothers' and sisters' children, and that's quite enough! I had the privilege of going abroad, but I've never had that of touching a man's hand! It's not important; I don't regret it because I love my life, which is devoted primarily to others. My only worry is what will happen when my parents are gone. I may feel differently then. So as not to distress my father, we didn't tell him I'd gone to America— he thought I was traveling to Kabul. This morning, when I showed him the photos of the trip, he couldn't hold back his tears.

"Even with the Soviet bombs falling, I never stopped working. Under Zahir Shah, women were more highly regarded than they are today: each province had at least one clinic responsible for family planning and contraception. That system fell apart during the different conflicts, and today it all has to be rebuilt. The worst times were in autumn 1992, when the different mujahideen factions were constantly bombing Kabul. Nonetheless, I practiced my profession until the very last moment. The last day was one of the most significant in my life because one of my colleagues, who had already had six miscarriages, was now almost to term and was about to give birth, but she needed a cesarean section. That day, at least ten thousand bombs fell on Kabul. I took her in a taxi from hospital to hospital, finding all the doors closed, even at the private clinics. I even asked for help at the military hospital, which was staggering under the number of wounded; blood was flowing like a river in the hallways. I was hoping to find an operation table free. But it was no use. Then I turned to a private Indian clinic in the new part of town, where I begged for a doctor's help, explaining to her I had an emergency cesarean to perform on a high-risk patient. She agreed, provided that I managed to find my own anesthesia, which I did, and my friend is now living in Germany with her eleven-year-old son.

"The blocks of our 'microrayon'* were constantly being bombed, since the mujahideen considered the neighborhood 'Communist' and hence not 'Muslim.' Every day when I came home from work at the hospital, I learned that one neighbor or another had died. That firestorm lasted about two weeks, during which we were literally crawling

*A residential neighborhood in Kabul composed of four-story buildings erected by the Soviets. Microrayons exist in all cities of the Russian Federation and the former Soviet empire.

around our apartment. A five-day cease-fire was finally declared. We took advantage of it to flee to our beloved mountains of Badakhshān, with only one piece of luggage! After we arrived by bus in Mazār-e-Sharif, we were able to get a plane to Faizābād. It was October 6, 1992. Our large house had been requisitioned by an influential mujahideen, and I immediately sought refuge in Bahorak. For two months we had to make do with a single room at the far end of a garden, but it was infinitely more peaceful than the hell of Kabul.

"In January 1993, I started to work at the hospital in Faizābād, where only one room with six beds was set aside for women. My colleagues had no experience, and everyone I worked so hard to train immediately left the country. It was as if we were hemorrhaging to death, but we had to stand firm and constantly train new ones. We had no modern anesthesia, and for four years I had to do without it during operations. Finally, as a result of an earthquake that claimed several thousand victims in 1995, we were able to get aid from foreign medical organizations, who were appalled when they saw our primitive working conditions. Nine years later, we still don't have an adequate supply of oxygen, even though we own the proper equipment.

"People feared that the Taliban would reach our mountain wilderness; at the same time they were hoping that, like the cholera epidemic, they would never get to us. We were right. In my view, those scoundrels were created by the United States, which has every interest in seeing our country torn apart. In fact, with or without the Taliban, nothing has been settled and all our problems remain. During that trip to America, I was able to observe that even though everyone works like robots on that other planet, daily life is clearly more comfortable than our own. The state imposes a tax on every food product and commodity sold and uses the money raised for the good of the community . . . or else to make war on other defenseless countries! [She laughs.] What organization! America as a country seemed to me more comfortable than the Soviet Union in the 1980s, the only other foreign country I've been to. In the United States, I never saw anyone fall down drunk in the street, whereas in Russia alcohol is still wreaking havoc. In Moscow people looked askance at head scarves, but in New York nobody pays them any mind;

there's total freedom, everything's allowed. I don't know if the Americans will carry through their plan in Afghanistan; they'd have to spend more time here than the English and the Russians did, our previous colonizers. Everyone's afraid that if the ISAF leaves the country now, there'll be another war, proof that no one can bring peace here, not even God Almighty!"

As we are leaving for Bahorak, where Uman's parents now live (his mother is one of Hamid's younger sisters), I see that the adolescent has changed his clothes. In black jeans, a long-sleeved Nike T-shirt, and sunglasses, he is barely recognizable. As soon as we're alone in the taxi, he pounces on the driver's tape player and slips in a cassette. He complains that the only modern music cassettes available at the Faizābād market come from Iran or India, when he would like to listen to American hip-hop, available only in Kabul and hard to find even there. Or in Pakistan. He's settled for Indian pop. The road is so bad it takes us three hours to go twenty-eight miles.

In the center of the village, more than a dozen donkeys are smugly gulping down their feed, their long heads buried in nose bags, their tethers attached to rotted debris from the Soviet tanks that seem to be part of the landscape. The small street stalls at the bazaar sell loose goods: plastic sandals, buckets of paint, men's vests with lots of pockets, piece goods, all sorts of kitchen utensils, tinware, prayer rugs. Many men's tailors are hard at work in the dust raised by the constant vehicles going by; their passengers don't pay the slightest attention. Most of the trucks are Soviet-made ZILs and Kamazes; their enormous grilles often boast a triangular colored scarf attached as an ornament. The handlebars of many bicycles, all ridden by men, are also decorated with red plastic flowers.

"Since we're incapable of achieving peace, it's as if a new, more insidious war has begun." Uman's father's gives this keen analysis as he holds his youngest son in his arms. The boy is vision impaired, a malformation due to inbreeding. The father has thrown open the window, which looks out on a magnificent orchard surrounded by high stone walls. The tribe as a whole sometimes gets together for a picnic there, when the summer heat impels the residents of Faizābād to seek out a little coolness. "If the Americans think that our different political parties are going to organize around a central unifying idea, namely, the Afghan state, they're on the wrong track. In fact, they're rushing us, everything's happening too quickly, and it's all going badly. In addition, every party is more or less financed by a foreign power, so the show's only starting! Take the example of the Loya Jirga, our so-called popular assembly: one of my friends was selected to be a representative by the three hundred residents of his village, since he was the best educated. He was immediately summoned by one of the local 'commanders,' who enjoined him to turn over his authority to him in exchange for money. If he'd refused, the 'commander' would have killed him."

According to our host, the main problem is the lack of education and the absence of information on individuals' rights. "Concretely, it's not too difficult to rebuild a country, but culturally and psychologically it's another matter, especially when the elites of the country in question are still busy fighting for power!" he laments. "Obviously, the Americans didn't bring us democracy: looking at our society is as sad as watching a child die without being able to help. As for demilitarization, they'd have to go from house to house in search of weapons, but no one will do that. I've thought a great deal about this: they ought to set a good price and make it public. In any case, right now it doesn't work. Why, when we know where ten thousand weapons can be found, do only five hundred reappear? The refusal to turn in weapons is not due solely to the security issues. It's because, for its owner, a weapon symbolizes much more than money. Some people, after they'd lost one or two members of their families during the jihad or under the Taliban, went to Pakistan and slaved away just so they could procure one. A weapon is also a little piece of power! For the unemployed, holding on to a weapon means holding on to their status. If they turned it in, it would mean accepting they're nothing now. You'd have to convince people it's not so difficult to find work, that everything isn't based on violence. But no political leader dares say such a thing; everyone's too preoccupied with holding on to his little piece of power. Can our gov-

ernors, mayors, police officers, and other government workers, all former mujahideen, really conceive of turning in their weapons? I'm not
so much surprised by what the Americans are doing than by what
they're not doing. They could, for example, start by quite simply en-
listing local leaders to hold meetings that would really inform people."

Uman's bedroom has been assigned to me. It's painted light green
and is next to the room belonging to his parents and two sisters. Two
little niches finessed in the wall hold his schoolbag, along with stuffed
animals and other children's toys. On the windowsill I find his sisters'
Barbie dolls jumbled together with a few Indian pop music laser discs
and photos of his aunt taken in Bishkek, the capital of Kyrgyzstan, in
the former Soviet region of central Asia, where she lives. On the wall is
a political map of the world in English and two posters of the Indian
singer Rani. She is never veiled: on one of them she is holding a guitar,
and on the other she wears makeup and is looking lascivious in the arms
of a man.

Last night I chatted with Uman's mother and several neighbors,
who were on their way back from a wedding, the last one before Ramadan. Ramadan is supposed to begin today, but no one is sure since it
depends on the visibility of the moon. One of the neighbors, a smiling
twenty-eight-year old who had her beautiful hair pulled back, had just
gotten engaged to a thirty-four-year-old man she doesn't know. She
seemed both terrified and excited.

Returning to Faizābād, I observe that a delivery of food aid has just been
distributed on the outskirts of the city: many little girls are returning
home with a heavy load on their heads or in their arms. They are carrying eleven-pound cans of cooking oil, on which is inscribed "USA"
in large red-and-blue letters. There are also 110-pound sacks of flour,
which they make their donkeys carry. In the following days, many disappointed young people will be rolling the empty "USA" cans with
a stick.

Hamid is about to leave: he has to be with his wife and daughter in
Kabul, but it is with regret that he is abandoning his work as an engi-

neer in Faizābād. After a single conversation with the new regional governor, he won't hear of staying any longer, since the governor did not
seem serious. Instead of thinking about projects that would improve
the lives of his fellow citizens, the governor merely mentioned the possibility of building more little street stalls, which are already numerous, along the main road of the city. Thanks to an informal tax system,
each of stall would bring in money for him personally. "The mujahideen are brutes with only four things on their minds: business, women,
buzkachi [a game involving horses, particularly popular in central Asia
and northern Afghanistan], horses, and cars!" he tells me, even more
cynical than usual. Hamid laments the fact that most of the factories
built by the Soviets have been destroyed: "We're not producing anything anymore, no one thinks of creating jobs, and everything that
could be stolen has long since disappeared already, sold to Pakistan. It
seems that even the bones of our dead have been desecrated and sold to
the peasants there, who feed them to the chickens!"

I will take the long return trip to Kundūz by car with twenty-five-year-
old Munir, who is related to Hamid's family via his sister and considers them his "adopted family." Munir is a young man with a good head
on his shoulders; he speaks very good English, which he practices daily
in his work as a logistician for Doctors without Borders in Faizābād. He
is more than a little proud that two and a half years ago he was hired by
a renowned international organization. He is taking advantage of his
month off, coinciding with Ramadan, to play the tourist in his own
country, which he admits he knows poorly. He has been to the large
Tajik cities in the north, as well as Kabul, but never to the southern
Pashtun region.

Munir is impatiently awaiting an e-mail from his employer in Geneva, which is supposed to announce a decision regarding his future
within the organization. His superiors have dangled the lure of training in Europe, then a mission to another country. He's ready to go
anywhere, "even Africa." Nevertheless, if he doesn't get the reply he's
hoping for, next month he'll return to his studies in Anglo-Saxon phi-
lology at the University of Kabul. But it will be an enormous disap-

pointment. Recently, two of his colleagues took advantage of a similar training to go into exile. Because of them, complains Munir, "the bosses are suspicious and reluctant to let us leave, even though we deserve it. I'm ready to give them all the guarantees necessary so they'll agree to let me take that training class. For example, I'll leave them all my savings—several thousand dollars—as security." The idea of being able to leave the inhospitable and uncivilized region of Badakhshān has him walking on air. Here, he says, he might have come to a bad end because there's so much pressure to go into the drug business.[1]

"Here, a kilo [2.2 pounds] of uncut opium costs barely three hundred dollars. Turned into heroin, it's resold for fifteen hundred dollars—it's very lucrative," Munir insists. "Let's be frank: there's not a single person in this country who has not been tempted to get involved in that nasty business. During the six months I was unemployed, I myself was this close to doing it."

The terrible drug chain begins with the peasant who grows poppies. Of all the links, it is the weakest and the one that earns the least money; even so, it's a great deal better than growing wheat or other traditional crops. Then the middleman "in town" controls day laborers, who will take care of the harvesting. He pays them so well that the "traditional" farmer sees his entire labor force slip away from him. Higher up in the hierarchy, the local "commanders" are in charge of processing labs (there are seven in all of Badakhshān). And finally, the high "commanders" control the most dangerous, but also the most lucrative, link in the chain: the borders, in other words, access to the foreign market. At each level, everyone is perfectly aware of being engaged in an illicit trade that is dangerous for other people's health, but it's difficult for them to imagine concretely the evil engendered by the consumption of drugs in unfamiliar societies. "Here at home, no one takes drugs," Munir assures me, adding lucidly that that might change in the future. "In fact, if it is our fate to move closer to those notorious Western societies that are presented as models, why would we not also succumb to the attraction of those artificial paradises? To get back to the drug trade, it's easy here to devote yourself to that business, since the state imposes no penalty on it, whereas for our two neighbors, Iran and Pakistan, there are terrible sanctions. Representatives of the new central power have certainly tried to talk to the peasants, the first links in the chain, but they have no substitute solution to propose (in any case, they're not the ones who ought to be blamed), and to be effective it's really the last link they'd have to take on, meaning, in the end, themselves. . . . So how are we going to get away from it?"

"In my adopted family," Munir confides, "all the important decisions are made in common by the men of the house, and not only by my grandfather, though he's the oldest. I'll go along with their views, even if I don't agree; that's just how it is. For example, when it comes to my marriage, I'll have to accept their choice. Dr. Hajira is the person I respect the most, since she has literally sacrificed her life for others, and that's rare." He won't say anything more about the men, even though he truly worships them.

Munir is more talkative about the different social categories in Faizābād. He divides the residents into three groups: the first group, in the minority, is the wealthiest and in need of nothing; the second group is not really rich but is not in want; and finally, there's the third group, considered poor. In Munir's family (in the second group), the women no longer do their laundry down by the river on Friday: their men have bought them washing machines. Another sign of social status is satellite television, which allows them to receive more than three hundred channels from around the world, including CNN, BBC, and Euronews, for a price that beats all competition: two hundred dollars, the price of the antenna and the decoder.

These three social categories rub shoulders, but do not mix, in the bazaar or at the minuscule street stalls with wooden doors, which at night are simply padlocked. Each person engages in the activities corresponding to a particular category. In the first category are money changers, "all linked by necessity to the opium trade." Equipped with Thuraya satellite phones (the regular telephone system was destroyed by the wars, and wireless phones have not yet arrived here), they are kept informed of the slightest fluctuations on the exchange market, especially in the price of opium and heroin. The second category includes both pharmacists and vendors of stereos, electronic equipment, and various fancy goods. The poorest are the fruit and vegetable vendors, the only ones who don't keep their savings in dollars. "Some of them do not even manage to pay for their electricity, a utility that's just begun charging for its services. If you don't pay, they cut you off; so most of them have opted for weak generators made in China," Munir explains.

During the first day of Ramadan, all the men I've met during the trip stop their vehicles near the river to perform ablutions before their prayer. If I am to believe Munir, who only half respects the annual fast, it is closer to a challenge to oneself than a truly religious act. One must at all cost "take up" that challenge so that neighbors and friends can see you're capable of it. It has almost become a social act.

2 1

EN ROUTE TO
MAZĀR-E-SHARIF

Along the vast plain bordering Uzbekistan, which is almost desert-like in places, one cob village is followed by another. All were completely destroyed in the autumn of 2001 by the Taliban fighters, during their battles against the Northern Alliance forces linked to the Western coalition. In this zone populated primarily by Tajiks and Uzbeks, the Taliban regime conducted a systematic ethnic cleansing policy and imposed its Pashtun "colonists."

We have to register our vehicle—little more than a symbolic gesture—every time we enter or leave a city or province. Often at the checkpoint, which is less a booth than an ordinary chair with an Afghan "police representative" slumped in it, mischievous children amuse themselves by "pulling on the barrier" (sometimes nothing but a rope strung across the road, supposedly to stop vehicles, or a piece of rubber track from an old Soviet tank). Only then does an orderly equipped with a piece of paper and a pencil approach and note the number on the license plate, if there is one.

Often at a curve in the sand-covered road, a group of ragged old men and children, their faces so dirty that the features can barely be discerned, suddenly appear. They stand without saying a word, almost paralyzed. Not one holds out a hand, and yet they are begging. Without even stopping, our driver throws them a few crumpled bills. The boldest ones pounce on them. With that paltry sum, they'll be able to buy either two pieces of chewing gum or two cigarettes, perhaps a box of matches, or an envelope and a piece of paper. We pass a caravan of heavily laden camels. A donkey presses against the wall of a house to get some shade. A long-haired goat with impish eyes scampers on the low walls separating the dwellings.

In post-Taliban Afghanistan, almost all cars (the sole exception being the antique Soviet makes) have their steering wheel on the right, even though Afghans drive on the right. This results in an infinite number of accidents. But the automobile market, which is enjoying a boom, takes no notice. The used cars are mainly Japanese (the Toyota is by far the most highly valued), that is, from a country where people drive on the left.

As soon as a long-enough portion of asphalt appears (sometimes only twenty yards or so), the driver, as if he'd gone mad, starts accelerating dangerously, honking his horn at every opportunity to warn any bicyclist or vehicle that might impede him. The rearview mirror inside the car is often adjusted to face the driver almost directly; he uses it to groom his mustache or comb his hair, a very natural gesture among Afghans.

On both sides of the uneven road stretch drained rice fields. The rice has just been harvested and must now be husked. In anticipation of that process, which is done by hand, enormous conical piles have been arranged on either side of the street. The villages we pass through are almost invisible, since the color of the cob is indistinguishable from the earth. Each year before winter, the men carefully restore the tops of the house walls, which have become crenellated, to keep them from being eaten away by the elements.

Strangely enough, at dusk gas stations and mosques boast the same electrical decorations, the ultimate in modernity; colored neon lights (blue, yellow, red, green) accentuate the roundness of the minarets and embellish every fuel pump. Between Samāngan and Balkh, the pylons are still standing alongside the road, but their electrical cables have long since been cut, stolen in some cases. The wires hanging from them make them look rather sad.

2 2

A WAR CHIEF

Faizullah Zaki, spokesman for General Rashid Dostum, is an Uzbek who divides his time between Mazār-e-Sharif and Shibarghān, the warlord's fief. He invites me to a party to celebrate a Turkish national holiday. The festivities are to take place in a very chic (by local standards) hotel restaurant in Mazār-e-Sharif, built exactly a year ago by a Turkish business to celebrate October 29, the day of Turkish independence. At first glance, I seem to be the only woman in a group of more than three hundred. We are seated at rectangular tables set up for the banquet in the hall usually reserved for weddings. There are few turbans here; instead, there are ordinary suits and ties, as in the West.

Standing in front of the Turkish and Afghan flags, Zaki speaks first, in Dari and in English. Everyone stands up for the Turkish national anthem, punctuated by the polyphonic rings of cell phones. The young Turkish consul posted in Mazār-e-Sharif gets up on the "nuptial" rostrum. The political, economic, and intellectual elites of the province of Balkh, whose capital is Mazār-e-Sharif, seem to hang on his every word. Then it's time for the number-two man in the Jumbesh-e Melli-e Islami (National Islamic Movement) Party to read a letter of congratulations from Dostum. A series of endless and grandiloquent speeches review at length the "historic" and "very ancient" friendly relations between Turks and Afghans. In his letter, Dostum praises Turkish aid to the national Afghan army and the recent creation of an Afghan-Turkish high school. At the end, the recently named governor of the Balkh region takes the floor. He's a very distinguished Pashtun, a former university rector who studied chemistry in Moscow.

At the back of the hall, about eighty duly armed soldiers in camouflage are sitting quietly. Perfectly calibrated for Ramadan, the speeches
have the length needed to last until nightfall, when the mullah sounds
the famous signal for evening prayer, breaking the fast (iftar). At the
first notes from the muezzin, everyone rushes toward the mounds of rice
pilaf, the grilled meat, the salads, and the fresh nonalcoholic drinks.
Nearly three quarters of an hour later, when the feast is in full swing,
Dostum arrives in person, preceded by an impressive number of guards.
A former buzkachi player well respected for his strength and agility, he
is a gruff giant with a broad face and close-cropped hair. Despite his
conspicuous arrival, Dostum takes his place almost furtively, and the
assembly, now serene, continues to eat noisily.

Suddenly there's a great racket caused by chairs being pushed back:
Dostum has stood up and the others at the gathering have imitated
him. The chieftain is retiring! The guards' Kalashnikovs, thrown hastily over their shoulders, knock against one another while drivers run to
their vehicles. Within a few minutes, everyone has disappeared.

Considered one of the most powerful Afghan warlords, Dostum now
heads the politico-military movement of Jumbesh-e Melli-e Islami,
heir to a mostly Uzbek pro-Communist militia reputed for its ferocity
under the Soviet occupation and now in control of a large portion of
northern Afghanistan.[1] Dostum began as vice minister of defense to
President Karzai and was named his "special adviser" for northern Afghanistan in mid-2002. He is now asking to be named to a ministerial
post, particularly at defense, or as general chief of staff.

In the autumn of 2003, the battles between Dostum and Mohammad Atta, a commander of the Jamiyat-i-Islami (Islamic Society) Party
of Burhanuddin Rabbani and the late Commander Massoud,[2] were raging in the northern provinces. It reached the point of persistent rumors,
since proved false, that the central government had named them, re-
spectively, minister of energy and water and minister of mines and in-
dustries, in an attempt to ease matters and end the fighting.

In April 2004 I will learn that relations became seriously strained
between General Dostum and the central government when the warlord's militias took control of part of the northeastern province of Far-

yab, expelling the progovernment forces and the governor. Since then, the central government has reestablished order in the provincial capital of Meymaneh, sending in about seven hundred men from the new Afghan army. After these incidents, Dostum condescended to go to Kabul, where he met President Hamid Karzai and Zalmay Khalilzad, the very powerful U.S. ambassador.

For the time being, I walk around Mazār-e-Sharif. Not far from what is believed to be the mausoleum of Imam Ali, around which the city has been built, enormous portraits of Commander Massoud have appeared. One of them is accompanied by this caption: "A country where the population eats its fill, has enough water, and lives under normal economic conditions is not worthy of the name if it is under occupation. We will continue to fight for our freedom—Signed: Massoud." A warning to the Americans! On every street corner and on most windshields, the delicate features of the proud Tajik's profile are displayed. After his death, the spectacular commemorations of his memory and his effigies multiplied.

Behind another poster of Massoud, near the mausoleum, stands the discreet white building of the Ministry of Foreign Affairs in Kabul.[3] Its representative, a member of Dostum's Jumbesh Party, is a friend of Zaki Faizullah, which explains why the latter is on the premises almost constantly. The inside of the building, more or less air-conditioned, greatly resembles a Soviet administration building, with its massive couches in the corners and its heavy, plush draperies on the windows. The only orderly is deeply absorbed in a three-dimensional video game. He doesn't care what is happening around him: manning the levers, he is now just an American soldier, weapon in hand, moving step by step through an urban jungle where a virtual nuclear war against the Russians is being waged. The waiting room's walls are decorated with posters showing General Dostum in the field, wearing his uniform and combat helmet and surrounded by U.S. noncommissioned officers during the special operation conducted in northern Afghanistan after the terrorist attacks of September 11, 2001.

I accept Zaki's suggestion to go to Sheberghān, a large industrial

city in the northwest, the headquarters and residence of the warlord and
the only place where the general receives guests. Zaki speaks both English and Russian well. He claims to have learned Russian "on the job."
He says he is Uzbek on his father's side and Tajik on his mother's (his
mother's mother spoke only Persian). His four children (the oldest is
nineteen, the youngest eight) are safe in Tashkent, the capital of neighboring Uzbekistan. Zaki is a public relations specialist and has been in
Dostum's service since the fall of the Taliban regime and the general's
return to Afghanistan after spending a short period of time in exile in
Turkey.

We make rapid progress in a Soviet jeep bearing the general's effigy.
It eats up the ninety-four miles between the two cities: the road is completely paved and free of potholes (a first for me!). A gas pipeline that
seems to be well maintained runs alongside us. "That gas comes from
Sheberghān, where the first complete gas complex in the country is located, built by the Soviets in the 1980s and restored by the general,"
Zaki explains. "It also supplies the city of Mazār-e-Sharif, thanks entirely to the general." Nevertheless, "the complex is far from operating
at full power, because there's a lack of potential investors, who still base
their decision on feasibility studies. But these studies are being held up
because the Russians, who possess key documents concerning the factory's operation, claim they provided copies of them to the Afghan engineers at the time of construction, but the engineers supposedly lost
them in the series of wars.... So now the Russians make their future
collaboration and hence their financial investment contingent on the
return of these documents to Afghan territory. For the moment, negotiations are at an impasse!"

Whether he is truly being ironic or simply wants to display his
knowledge of Western films, Zaki proposes this metaphor regarding
the state of his country: "In the American film *The Matrix,* at one
point the hero wonders if he's really dead. No, he hears himself reply,
you're still far from it. That, in a word, is the state in which we now
find ourselves!"

I arrive in Sheberghān, which I've been told is much less dirty and
dusty than many other cities, and find that it's true. In Mazār-e-Sharif

my only fear was that the wind would come up suddenly and blind us all. Sand and dust prevailed. This morning, a street vendor from whom I bought two bottles of Pepsi—during the day, it's impossible to find anything else to drink or, of course, any food at all during Ramadan —immersed them in a tub of water for a long time before giving them to me.

Here everything is clean. Zaki announces that I have the tremendous honor of staying at the hotel complex reserved for Dostum's distinguished guests. Built by the Soviets a dozen years ago, just before they withdrew from the country, the various large buildings are not without a certain charm. A concrete frame contrasts with the majority of the houses surrounding it, which are painted cob. Three buildings face the swimming pool with its central fountain. Attached to that pool is a rectangular wading pool with three fountains and two smaller circular wading pools. The large all-male staff, which has placed a few white plastic garden tables and pastel green chairs on the attractive tiles, get down to work each morning cleaning the pool, turning the dry soil, and working to restore the outbuildings. Dostum likes to take long walks in the garden to smell the flowers, and on his personal order an army of gardeners in turbans and light sandals takes very special care of the thousands of yellow, red, and pink roses adorning the grounds—quite a feat in these arid regions! The garden paths are cement; there are shaded arbors and, at the back of the garden, a small mosque. According to Zaki, even when the property was occupied by the Taliban, Dostum regularly phoned caretakers from his foreign refuge, giving long and precise instructions for maintaining that Eden.

The two-story hotel where I'm staying was recently repainted a peach color. It is complemented by a pale green villa with yellow colonnades and many glass walls, which will supposedly house a gymnastics room. The third building, beige and single-storied, seems more subtle. It is Dostum's favorite: its dining room windows look out on the famous rose garden.

Zaki presents the Jumbesh Party's position on the different political systems that might govern post-Taliban Afghanistan. The Uzbek minority is tired of being excluded from power, and this time, through

Dostum, it certainly intends to participate in the process of political re-
structuring. To that end, it must first undertake a tedious information
campaign about Dostum's party, which is misunderstood and suffers
from a negative image. "We know that the southern part of our country is in favor of a constitutional monarchy, whereas the north would
prefer a federalist regime. There are also many who would like to live
in a so-called Islamist republic. As for us, we want power to be shared.
Hence a parliamentary regime seems preferable to a presidential regime, which would be a catastrophe, given Karzai's authoritarian tendencies. We'd be headed straight for a dictatorship," he fumes, "but no
one wants to hear that!"

"According to the Jumbesh, the Tajik community is getting weaker
because its political leaders have become hostages to the Jamiyat's fundamentalists, who have taken a more radical turn since Massoud died.
Its chief leader, Rabbani, will undoubtedly run in the presidential election, and the monarchists in the south, who don't support Karzai, are
looking for allies. The Tajiks have no clear strategy and are forced to
keep wavering, which is dangerous. It's impossible to convert them to
federalism; we know that. We'd just be happy if they came out in favor
of parliamentarianism."

The next day we leave for Andkhui, an ethnically Uzbek locality in the
northwest, about nineteen miles from the border with Turkmenistan.
The official buildings in the city are inevitably decorated with the separate portraits of Karzai, an astrakhan hat on his head and a *chapan* (a
heavy cotton coat worn by central Asian men) on his shoulders, and
General Dostum in his military uniform. "They have to cooperate,"
comments Zaki, half amused, confirming that Dostum's being named
to the Ministry of Energy and Water was a joke, pure disinformation.
He reminds me that the general is soliciting a post as minister of interior or of defense, nothing else.

To begin our visit, Zaki wants to take me to the television station
Aïna, the first private station in Afghanistan and the property of a local import-export business. It claims to be independent, but some of its
ties to the general are undeniable. In fact, at the station I find the team

of Turkish engineers who are staying with me at the state residence and with whom I share my meals. They are responsible for making the hertz relay system work. One of the engineers, a Tatar Russian citizen from Kazan who studied in Turkey, is delighted to be able to exchange a few words with me in his native language. Zaki is a skillful spokesman and has an answer for everything. It's clear that "Dostum has aided Aïna technologically, so it could get its license and its supply of electricity from Turkmenistan, but ideologically the television station will be independent."

Out on the road, he is eager to show me the recent memorial erected in honor of the "martyrs of freedom," the 212 Afghan soldiers who fought Al-Qaeda and the Taliban beside the Northern Alliance and the international coalition (more specifically, the U.S. Special Forces) in the autumn of 2001. Every tomb is wrapped in an Afghan flag and bears a photo of the "martyr."[4] Continuing toward Turkmenistan, we go past an enormous rectangular building with a half-destroyed cupola —a madrasa built by the Taliban, says Zaki. The scorching desert air, filled with gas, blasts us in the face. Yesterday, in the official Soviet jeep, we were listening to cassettes of traditional Indian music—Zaki adores these melodies, which were a big part of his adolescence—but today the sound system of our late-model 4x4 Toyota is sputtering Russian pop. We have borrowed the vehicle from the general's thirty-four-year-old nephew, who was raised by Dostum after his parents' death and lives in Tashkent. The Russian group's hit, strangely enough, is called "With You, Saddam Hussein." Thanks to Indian music, Zaki understands Hindi. He assures me that for Afghans of his generation, the large neighboring country of India is a real model: "Such a vast population living in a perfect democracy in such a large country, and with so many different ethnic groups—that commands respect." He is obviously impressed.

It is Friday afternoon, the weekly day of rest and siesta time in Andkhui. But the news of our arrival rapidly spreads around the city, and the provincial governor finally makes an appearance. Intimidated by Zaki's presence, he praises General Dostum and his regional policy: thanks to the general, the difficult disarmament is said to be practically complete and more than fifteen hundred weapons have been stored safely away in depots, the idea being that the population could easily reclaim them if needed. "The UN can come verify if it wishes; everything is in order."

Allegiance to the central power is far from being achieved. The governor complains that he often receives "stupid" orders from Kabul: "Only a month ago, our students could study the Turkic language and the Uzbek language if they wished. We've recently received a directive ordering the replacement of these subjects with the Pashtun language, even though that language has not been taught in the region for the last ten years. We had to comply." The governor also declares he is in favor of electing on a local level regional government workers currently named by Kabul: "If you get people voting, you get them involved in the affairs of their region. Otherwise, they remain indifferent." He was chosen by the local population, which was dissatisfied with the previous governor, but the Ministry of the Interior has not yet endorsed anything. The district also wishes to be attached administratively to the nearby province, whose capital, Sheberghān, is connected to Andkhui by a road in good condition. Despite the steps taken by their delegates in Kabul and a delegation sent from the ministry to make an evaluation, which appeared favorable, the district was finally attached to Meymaneh. For the governor, that is proof that Kabul does not respect the famous democratic rules and is little concerned with what the people want and need. "No one's helping us except General Dostum, whom I regularly explain my problems to and who does understand us," he concludes.

On the return trip, something reddish brown darts across the road. A fox with mischievous eyes, safe on the shoulder, briefly interrupts his run to watch us pass.

It would appear that in the territories controlled by the general, women have more rights than elsewhere. I am hardly noticed as I go through the streets of Sheberghān, since burkas, though present, are not predominant. Even though most of the women still wear the full veil to get around downtown—"So long as the disarmament is not complete, it's better to protect oneself," one of them explains—their participation in local associations and political life is beyond doubt, and more of them are going to school. (None of the girls' schools were blown up in the north.) The "women's" branch of the Jumbesh Party holds evening classes that are always full, where volunteers can study Turkish, English, or computers at no cost. The male professor of "computer sciences" is a young Turk who is very much at ease in front of the thirty-some women of all ages who share fifteen computers. He teaches them the rudiments of word processing as well as bookkeeping programs. The teachers do not necessarily speak Dari, but the students, most of them Uzbeks and Turkomans, are already Turkish speakers (I have also seen Tajik and Pashtun women). When they leave their classes, most of these women doctors, engineers, or simply students cover their clothes with an ample black or gray buttoned coat that matches their head scarf.

After patiently waiting for the general to finish his many interviews— today he received a few bigwigs from his party; the European Union reporter covering Afghanistan, who is completing a tour of the major cities in the country; an American friend and former UN mediator who has become one of his advisers; the new head of the provincial reconstruction team (PRT); and the village tribes from the surrounding area who always have something to request of him—I am finally allowed to ask him a few questions. The interview will take place in Uzbek, since Dostum is not fond of speaking Russian. Calm and focused, sitting comfortably on a couch in the lounge of the beige residence, the general begins with a long statement—the matter is obviously close to his heart—reminding me of the collaboration between his two thousand men and the U.S. Special Forces during their November 2001 offensive. His slow manner of speaking and his grave voice remind me of another general who brought people together, the Russian Aleksandr Lebed, who managed to get a peace accord signed between the Russian federal army and the Chechen independence fighters in 1996, but who has since died in a helicopter accident.

Even while displaying enormous admiration for the U.S. soldiers, Dostum launches into a series of criticisms directed at the coalition and the central Afghan government, which he believes have forgotten him. When I ask about terrorism in his country today, he doesn't evade the question: "We don't know anything more today about Osama bin Laden. Is he dead or alive? No one knows. And there's the same uncertainty about Mullah Omar and Gulbuddin Hekmatyar,[5] a supporter of the fundamentalist hard line. Nevertheless, those three men are terrorists, and they must be arrested. Obviously, in the south, the situation is deteriorating day by day! The Taliban are regrouping and are harassing the UN agencies and other foreign NGOs as much as they can, taking their vehicles and their headquarters as targets. At night they don't hesitate to kidnap people on the Kabul-Kandahar road [see chapter 25]. Along with the Al-Qaeda agents, they're the chief ones responsible for the lack of security, but I would go even further: fundamentalist elements close to Karzai's cabinet, or even in it, are themselves involved!" While making this revelation, Dostum assumes a look of consternation and continues solemnly: "I wish to remind the Western powers that although Al-Qaeda and the Taliban have always been a danger to the world, today their Afghan base of support has broadened, since they have won the favor of the fundamentalists who infiltrated the Afghan government. The current situation is therefore much worse than it was at the fall of the regime."

Aware of his negative image in the West, the general tries to be reassuring and points to the successful experiment in collaboration with the Americans in the autumn of 2001: "The West must not confuse their friends with their enemies. I'm the only nonfundamentalist leader in Afghanistan, where I do my utmost to defend democratic values. I'm still the friend of the Western powers and am ready to help them today as I did in 2001, even if the central government of Kabul is trying to isolate me. Of course, I don't have the fine education of most Afghan politicians; I'm a general who rose from the masses and acquired his experience in the mountains, the villages, and the trenches of this splendid country, but seeking to isolate me is a grave mistake!

"No one seems to realize what my men and I have accomplished: along with Commander Massoud, we first brought down the Najibullah regime, then we eliminated the Taliban regime with its links to Al-

Qaeda, expelling them from the north of the country. Of course, without European, American, and NATO help, it would have been almost impossible to defeat them, but if we hadn't eliminated them, those religious extremists would already have reached central Asia.... We're proud of those successes and are envied by our rivals, who are still trying to connect me to pan-Turkism and Greater Turkey because I'm Uzbek!"

As for his country's future political system, Dostum claims to be the first to have championed federalism, and he was supported by a petition that supposedly drew four million signatures. In his final statement, he does not conceal his great ambition: to be recognized, to be named to a very high post in the government he so criticizes. "I know Afghanistan better than anyone. I dare hope that if people in high places think of me, it will be for minister of defense, to create the new national army. I will agree to leave Sheberghān for Kabul only on that condition. Then I could fight effectively against terrorism throughout our country's territory, and not only in the north. And our populations here will have more confidence in the government, since the ethnic composition of the country will have been respected."

23

EN ROUTE TO KABUL

South of the town of Pul-e-Khumri, the landscape changes: we leave the plain and move deep into an arid mountain pass, a sign that we are approaching the Salang Tunnel, which reaches an altitude of eleven hundred feet at its highest point. It cuts through the mountain chain of Hindu Kush and symbolizes the real separation between north and south. The tunnel, built by the Soviets and opened in 1964, was blown up and blocked by anti-Taliban resistance forces to prevent the troops of the Islamist regime in Kabul from reaching the northern part of the country.

The road is fairly good, and traffic—primarily freight trucks, often elaborately decorated—is heavy in both directions. The Mercedes-Benz and Japanese Hino tanker trucks are always the most richly colored. There are different motifs, but one often comes across variations on a single theme: a peaceful mountain landscape with a large lake, an enormous building that is supposed to represent modernity, or a concrete luxury hotel in the shade of palm trees, next to a pool from which two or three brown heads are emerging. Sometimes the artist also chooses two heavily made-up woman's eyes. Female eyes, often visible only in the space between veils, are well represented. Or you'll sometimes see a galloping white horse or a bleeding heart pierced by an arrow.

At the end of the winding road, we finally arrive at the mouth of the tunnel, where a long line has formed. It is still officially closed for renovation work,[1] and vehicles are allowed to go through only at certain hours. Finally cleared in early 2002, the tunnel remains very dangerous, unlighted and unventilated, and in the winter the waters that seeped through its walls turned into a sort of black ice, causing frequent accidents. It is 1.5 miles long and constitutes an essential strategic link between Mazār-e-Sharīf, the third largest city of Afghanistan, the central Asian republics of Tajikistan and Uzbekistan, and Kabul.

After we've vociferously insisted, an official of some sort gives us permission to come to the front of the line, but we still have to wait. Suddenly, for no apparent reason, cars start driving around us and are swallowed up by the black hole. Impatiently, our taxi takes off. In the middle of the tunnel, we're stopped again! A machine blocks our way, looking like it's from a different time and swarming with busy workers wearing helmets and welder's masks. The people behind us are impatient, then, like us, resigned.

On the other side of the tunnel, cob has clearly been replaced by stone. The houses clinging to mountain peaks remind me of Albania. Over and over again our driver has played the only cassette he possesses, at least on this trip: Indian music. The songs with their lively rhythm keep him laughing. They all begin with brief spoken scenarios between a man and a woman—a husband and wife or a brother and sister—which present the theme. I find the refrain from one of the rare songs in English particularly amusing: "Let me be veiled, and don't try to open it!"

24

KABUL

At a few minutes after five p.m., just as the sun has disappeared, a clamor rises from every corner of the city. The muezzins are calling people to prayer. But since this is Ramadan, it's the signal for *iftar*. Almost instantaneously, the streets empty and the myriad cars, which moments earlier had seemed caught in traffic jams, vanish, along with the bicycles and their bells. As if by magic, the earthly din has ceased; everyone has sat down on the ground to eat.

Accompanied by Shafiz and his friend Daud, I have climbed to the top of the bare hill holding the ruined mausoleum of King Nadir, father of the former ruler Zahir Shah, who returned from exile in Italy in the spring of 2002. I contemplate the huge megalopolis (more than two million residents). Nestled in the heart of rugged mountains, the city has attacked the flanks of neighboring hills, and masses of little houses, most of them lacking water and electricity, sometimes climb far past the halfway point, clinging to the slightest outcropping. Kabul is also a place of constant pollution, deafening horns, frequent car accidents (I note at least one a day during my stay), and insidious dust occupying even the smallest crevice. Few advertising billboards clutter the main streets of the capital, except those for Rochan (a cell phone company owned by Aga Khan) and the ubiquitous FedEx. I also see countless signs in Arabic, translated into broken English, praising doctors, pharmacists, photocopy centers, or some other street business.

The notorious stadium where executions were held during the Taliban regime once more hosts soccer games under the stern gaze of three giant figures that—is it by accident?—form a sort of founding triad of the Afghan state. President Hamid Karzai is next to Commander Massoud (at the bottom of his portrait is inscribed: "We grieve your loss, but respect the course of your life"), who himself stands beside former king Ahmad Shāh Durrāni,[1] one of the founders of the modern Afghan nation.

Behind the royal tomb, an enormous cemetery stretches out into the arid land. In a state of neglect, it lies exposed to the elements, like all sepulchres in Afghanistan (a wall would keep the souls of the dead from moving about as they wish). Shafiz's brother, a Communist who fought against the mujahideen in the 1980s, is buried there. We pass in front of a cracked marble platform where the "eternal flame" went out long ago. The graves have been plundered: some are still wide open, their tombstones upended. Rumor has it that Pakistanis, taking advantage of the chaos, have come to dig up Kabul's dead in search of some metal or piece of jewelry to sell. In times of trouble, it's always the "stranger" who's blamed. It's because of the "filthy Communists," as they say in his circle, that Daud, who has recently returned from exile in the United States, lost his father. "None of it makes any sense; Shafiz and I are dumbfounded," explains the Afghan American in an expressionless voice. "My father and his brother both died for a cause they truly believed in, whereas now, Shafiz and I don't know what our lives mean."

To take their minds off such things, and because it's Friday, the two men decide to take me to a *buzkachi* game. The sport, played for the most part in the northern provinces such as Kundūz, Badakhshān, Baghlān, and Balkh, each of which has its champions, idols, and regional pride, was theoretically banned under the Taliban. In Zahir Shah's time, the "spring *buzkachi*" opened the celebrations of the Afghan New Year every March 21, the day of *Nawruz*. Currently, the games are played on a weekly basis in October and November, in the stadium of a military garrison in town. Mohammad Qasim Fahim, minister of defense, a great lover of this national sport, owns thirty-five horses specially raised for buzkachi. It's a sort of joust in which two teams of about twenty or thirty players—the *chapendoz**—violently

---

*Horsemen paid by the owners of horses selected for their strength and agility. The number of horsemen is not limited and, in the Tajik part of the Fergana Valley in central Asia, I have seen several hundred participate.

fight over the carcass of a decapitated goat weighing nearly 220 pounds. The melees are brutal and dangerous, both for the horsemen and for their mounts, the most skillful of which have learned to place their front hooves on the carcass to immobilize it until the *chapendoz* has grabbed it and to bow down to help their horseman get hold of it.

Not far from us, children are limbering up the horses, keeping them active on the field while a tanker truck pours out a little water to moisten the dry soil. An old man draws in the goals with white chalk; a one-legged man, taking his time, crosses the entire field. The huge crowd —all men, or nearly so—stand shoulder to shoulder on a tier of stone seats, waiting for the chapendoz, most of them former Tajik soldiers. In the VIP space on the rostrum, someone has placed a few dozen plastic chairs and four armchairs, one of which, it is said, is reserved for Marshal Fahim himself. Uniformed French soldiers from the ISAF take their place in the reserved area, soon joined by four Western-looking women in pants and colorful scarves. Someone turns on a crackling microphone, and the master of ceremonies, the commentator of the joust, asks the horsemen to get ready. Girded in their *chapan,* a traditional padded coat drawn in at the waist by a fabric belt, they generally wear a fur hat with ear flaps—some sport a military cap—along with high boots. Since their hands are occupied with the reins, the riding crop is usually held between their teeth. As Shafiz, who comes from a former Communist family, moves off for a moment to pray at the appointed time, Daud, though he is anti-Communist and closer to the mujahideen, jokes about what a "bad Muslim" he is, since he does not pray or practice his religion.

There are now constant melees, sometimes so dense that they give the impression that nothing is happening. The horsemen, lying on their mounts and bracing themselves in an effort to pick up the bloody animal, concentrate their attention. Then suddenly a horse breaks free, his horseman brandishing the carcass he has pulled off the ground, and gallops toward the goal as the crowd roars. Before our eyes, a horse spitefully allows himself to get trampled—his rider is on the ground— then stands up and moves haughtily away, and the chapendoz who has just scored a goal does a victory lap and pockets the many afghani bills handed to him. After Marshal Fahim arrives and takes his place in the central armchair, the game increases in intensity.

Thanks to the intermediacy of Omar Sharifi, a student employed at the Foundation for Culture and Civil Society (an international organization supporting the development of Afghan culture), I meet Abulhaq, a native Kabuli who wants to talk about his city. He resides in what is now the neighborhood of the Shihlsitun Gardens ("Forty Pillars" in Persian), old fertile lands conserved from generation to generation in a single peasant family (his ancestors) until King Amānollāh appropriated them.[2] "Amānollāh had his heart set on that place; he wanted to build an addition for his children to one of his many palaces. He offered the villagers any of his other properties in Kabul in exchange for the lands. After much equivocation, a council of elders decided on a price, which was verified by the king personally. The monarch came to the site and insisted on asking every villager if he or she was satisfied with the transaction. Everyone was. In an act of largesse befitting a lord, he gave them twice what had been agreed on and distributed other lands to them. That's what I call justice," the man recounted. He looks intelligent, and his voice is soft as he repeats the words of his father, who died last year at the age of ninety-eight. The father was a former peasant who became King Zahir's domestic servant as a way of financing his children's education. "Since then, however, one injustice has followed another," he concludes sadly.

Wearing a Western-style jacket and sweater and a gold watch on his left wrist, forty-eight-year-old Abulhaq has short gray hair and an elegant, apparently very well-cared-for beard. He is the youngest in a family of five children (four boys and one girl). During the Soviet occupation, he graduated from the Polytechnic Institute of Kabul and now teaches there part-time. For the last sixteen years, to earn a little money on the side, he has managed a glazier's shop, which was destroyed several times by the mujahideen. "Zahir Shah was not a bad king," he remembers; "it was under his reign, in fact, that my elder brother was able to study in Germany. After he finished school, he wanted to remain in the host country and wrote to our father, who ordered him to return, furious that his son was taking unfair advantage of a favor the Afghan Ministry of Education had granted him. My brother came back and established himself as a teacher but had to flee under the Communists, since they did not particularly appreciate people who had studied in Western countries. If he'd stayed, the pressure on him would have become insurmountable. Without giving us any warning, he fled to Quetta, Pakistan. Six months after he left, he married a German woman."

Abulhaq declares he does not remember flagrant injustices committed by the state under Zahir Shah or under the republican Daud Khan. "We felt safe, free to move around. There was little crime," he recalls. "Afghanistan began to fall apart during the coup d'état of April 1978.[3] People became afraid of their own shadows, started speaking only in whispers. Then came the war with the USSR." How did he imagine his future at the age of twenty-three? "I didn't understand the Communists, who repudiated all our customs. The slogan they invented, "Those Who Are Not with Us Are against Us," terrified me. I felt oppressed in a society that didn't offer any opportunities. But did I have a choice? I had to give in. There was strong pressure to join the Communist Party. I remember the questions they asked me to try to better determine my personality and to convince me: "You must choose between becoming a Muslim extremist and becoming a modern Afghan. Opt for modernity, become a card-carrying member!" I didn't know how to reply. Now that the question of Afghan identity is again being raised, the answer, unfortunately, is that being Afghan means consciously displaying indifference toward ethnic or religious problems. Before the civil war, the different ethnic communities intermarried and traded with one another. Today it's different; things are tense. I've personally never made any distinctions between Pashtuns, Tajiks, Hazara, and Uzbeks, but I realize that the many years of war and intolerance have embittered relations between communities. The Communists were the first to turn us against one another by drawing sharp ethnic lines. For example, they purposely appealed to the Uzbek warlord Rashid Dostum to fight the Pashtuns in the south. It must be said that the seeds of that hatred were sown by the British; the Russians only had to irrigate it and the Taliban to harvest the fruit! Being an Afghan may simply mean having made the choice to stay."

Abulhaq has little confidence in the current rulers, who are unconcerned with morality and conduct only a short-term policy. "Whom did the Americans put in power? The 'commanders,' that is, the former mujahideen, in other words, their old associates! I have the greatest respect for Hamid Karzai, but you must admit that with almost permanent fighting in the north and south, our country is still far from 'secured,' and I wonder what would happen if the ISAF abandoned us. That military organization is still playing a preponderant role. In any case, here in Kabul, no one's ready as yet to put hatred and tension aside, to forgive. But as I tell my students at the Polytechnic Institute, although my generation has lost nearly everything, they have a chance to escape, thanks to education, continous learning, and knowledge. The international community may have disarmed our militias, but it's pointless if they're not offered work. It will be a huge sham, since giving someone who turns in a weapon [only] two hundred dollars fuels resentment. All those colossal sums of international aid ought to be used more efficiently, by starting at the base, creating jobs in businesses that still produce something. Otherwise, we'll keep begging for money. We're too used to expecting everything from the West. That makes me ashamed! Let's identify the wound and analyze how deep it is before swallowing the medicine!"

Nevertheless, anxious at the thought that his country will fall back into its former madness, he approves of the return to legality. "A country without basic laws is like a family that's lost its patriarch. I pray to God that our constitution will be applied as soon as possible, in the hope that it will serve as a safeguard against the all-powerful will of those bloodthirsty 'commanders.'" He is very familiar with the Taliban period, since—though at first he sought refuge in Pakistan with his family and his father (as the youngest child, the latter was his responsibility)—he returned in 1998 because the old man was tormented by the idea of not dying in his native land. "So I had to resign myself to teaching while wearing a black turban after letting my beard grow in. The situation had worsened under the mujahideen, but the Taliban led us into total madness, barring girls from going to school and establishing a vice squad, as in Iran! In fact, neither the Taliban nor the mujahideen were fit to hold power," he admits with a smile.

Abulhaq's wife is illiterate. She's his first cousin, whom he married after his mother's death because he needed a wife to run the house. The couple were unable to have children and took in and adopted the daughter of one of Abulhaq's brothers-in-law, who was killed during the jihad against the Soviets. The child is now fourteen, and Abulhaq has dreams that some day she'll be a doctor or engineer. She is currently studying in a school that he played a role in creating. After his father died, he rented out the house the old man had built to an international organization, which turned it into a school for girls, the first to reopen in Kabul after the fall of the Taliban. He is proud that things are back to how they were, since in the 1970s, in Kabul precisely, he went to school side by side with girls in miniskirts.

Abulhaq loves every stone of his native city of Kabul, even if it's a ruin, just as he is delighted with each new house under construction. But he would like his city to recover its former glory. It had a reputation for always giving priority to education and for its hospitality. Unfortunately, the latter is disappearing. "There are fewer and fewer native Kabuli in Kabul and more and more people who have migrated from the northern and southern provinces. We must coexist with them, and sometimes they impose their way of life. An authentic Kabuli woman would never have worn the chador! Forty years ago, my mother moved about the city freely, without a veil, since everyone knew everyone else. That practice, which has intensified with the decrease in security, has been imposed on us in the last ten years."

On a sidewalk of the city center, two armored U.S. vehicles have taken up their positions. Eight helmeted soldiers wearing munitions belts across their upper bodies and hunched up in their bullet-resistant vests are posted on both sides of a restaurant entrance. In the alleyway sit numerous cars. The soldiers are staring straight ahead, and the tension is palpable. With their weapons in hand and fingers on the trigger, they clearly seem to feel they're in hostile territory. The reason for the deployment of forces? The newly named U.S. ambassador to Afghanistan, the Afghan American Zalmay Khalilzad (his former title was special envoy of the president of the United States in Afghanistan, and he is currently the U.S. ambassador to Iraq), is having dinner in town.

Every day but Friday, between eight in the morning and four in the afternoon, navigating the traffic in Kabul is a gamble. The stoplights aren't working, and if by chance one is operational, no one respects it. To remedy that, the state has placed a police officer in a fancy dress uniform at the center of every important intersection. Perched on a circular platform and armed only with his whistle, he spends his time on his feet, wildly waving his white-gloved arms. Sometimes overwhelmed, even demoralized, he sits down on his chair and lets the traffic sink into chaos. The vehicles entering the intersection pay no attention to the basic rules of right of way. The goal is to get through at any cost, especially if you're at the wheel of a late-model 4×4 with tinted windows. Sometimes the tension mounts, as when a wobbly minibus stops right in the middle of the intersection, blocking everyone and disregarding the officer's scolding. Exasperated and humiliated, the police officer gets off his platform and heads toward the minibus. Opening the driver's side door, he grabs hold of the driver to make him pay for the affront. The man is nimble, and he flees, pursued by the officer, who struggles to run after him. Because nature abhors a vacuum, a sympathetic passerby plants himself in the policeman's place and takes over his job. The flow resumes.

In a villa of the beautiful Share Naw neighborhoods ("the new city"), I meet Ahmed Wali Massoud, one of Commander Massoud's two younger brothers. He is ambassador to London and is spending time in his native country to observe Ramadan. He is amused when I report Dostum's ostentatious declarations and sighs pleasantly as soon as I mention the "federalism" that is so dear to the general. Ahmed Massoud was received by President Karzai as soon as he arrived, but he turned down the ministerial position the president offered him, lamenting that "confidence"—a word I also heard a great deal in the north—has still not been reestablished. "Two years have gone by already," he mutters, as if speaking to himself, "and in the end, nothing has happened. Karzai himself is a good man, but I wouldn't say so much for those around him, and I'm very afraid he's giving in to some of their pernicious demands. During our interview, I advised him not to lose sight of the famous 'vision' he's supposed to be harboring for his country, the 'great plan' we are so lacking and which seems to me more important than defining the structures of power and the legal framework for exercising it. Those elements ought to be set in place afterward, of course, but we're doing everything backward here! Afghanistan is at the crossroads and has not yet decided which path to take. I'm very sorry about that." He smiles slightly but still looks worried.

25

EN ROUTE TO KANDAHĀR

At dawn—the temperature is just thirty-seven degrees Fahrenheit—
we take our first taxi to the bus station located in the western part of
the capital, the most devastated area. The cars awaiting their turn are
shaded by an enormous silo riddled with marks from exploded shells.
There are four of us in the taxi, which will transport us to the south of
the country. We're going to travel via the notorious highway I have
been strongly advised against using; it is known as "the highway of
every danger" in the local press, and even high officials don't dare take
it. It's three hundred miles long and connects Kabul to Kandahār, the
former imperial capital, along a path destroyed by twenty-three years
of war and by U.S. bombs. This highway is the first major public works
project of Afghan reconstruction, sponsored by the international community and largely financed by the United States (at a cost of $270 mil-
lion), but also by Saudi Arabia and Japan.

The driver of our Toyota Corolla, a Pashtun like my two traveling
companions, is bundled up in a cream-colored *patu* that highlights his
brown skin, his Roman nose, and his dark, sparkling eyes. To keep
warmer on this cold morning, the man has pulled that essential attri-
bute of male Afghan dress over his turban, almost like a woman's veil.
We leave Kabul. The settlements become sparser, but now and again
we still go past high baked clay walls enclosing empty spaces, which
serve to mark the boundaries of the property. As someone explains to
me, when the walls are built, no one else has the right to claim the land.

Most of the signs planted on either side of the new road are in Turkish. The constitutional Loya Jirga planned for mid-December 2003 is

approaching, and the digging is proceeding apace.[1] The work site is huge: more than a thousand workers from five foreign businesses (three Turkish, one Indian, and one Afghan American) labor night and day. Here and there a few sharp stones have been placed on strips of fresh asphalt to dissuade the occasional cars from driving over it. The road, running alongside a grandiose desert landscape, is by far the most beautiful of any I have taken up to now. There is not a tree or bush on the horizon, only the bare stony hills standing under an immaculate blue sky.

The few travelers who brave the danger (many people have been kidnapped during the five months of construction work, including Turkish engineers) actually relish the five-hour trip (the trip took fifteen hours before the renovations!). Sometimes men walk slowly along the black ribbon of highway. We run into a few tractors, bicycles, and trucks from Herāt with goods imported from Iran and Turkmenistan, including a minesweeping convoy. Shortly before we reach Ghaznī, we stop for gas. Once again, I am surprised that none of the drivers turns off the engine when the vehicle is stopped, not even at the gas pump.

In the taxi, I peek out from under the netting of my burka, slipped on as a precaution as soon as we left the capital, and discern huge quantities of dry wood stacked for winter. Sometimes the asphalt peters out into a trail, then reappears, as our car radio broadcasts traditional Kandahār music, as monotonous as a long prayer.

Our driver, a veteran of this route, shares his memories of the battles that took place here between the Soviets and mujahideen commanders. Simultaneously, he skillfully maneuvers the steering wheel, since we sometimes have to drive through sand.

We are stopped by the government police. At the entrance to Qalat, the capital of Zabul Province, still unofficially in the Taliban's hands, we go past a checkpoint, a common occurrence near U.S. army bases. None of the police officers pays any attention to us, and the driver goes by without stopping, though he does slow to a snail's pace.

"Hey, you there, stop!" a uniformed man behind us calls out suddenly. "Since when do you just go by like that?"

"The chain was down . . ."

"I was busy with another motorist; couldn't you see that?"

"All right, do your job, search the car!"

"No, no, not necessary. Just give me twenty afghanis."[2]

Our driver, unreceptive and irritated by the police officer's behavior, finally hands him a ten-afghani bill.

As the black ribbon of highway continues to unfurl in the yellow desert, our driver admits that he misses the Taliban, at least for the security they guaranteed on this thoroughfare.

I note that the road sounds different: we're now on the old surface, installed in the 1960s by the Soviets. The sheets of concrete lined up the length of the highway make me think of landing strips.

Things are unsafe everywhere, the driver continues, here and even more so on the three hundred miles of still-unbuilt roads in the northwest, between Kandahār and Herāt. Armed men ambush travelers, rob them, and beat them badly. One of the other passengers confirms this: "Last week, I took a taxi with my mother on this very road. There were already three passengers, but the driver took on a fourth to earn a little more money. He put him in the front seat next to him. The man had barely gotten in when he started looking preoccupied, turning around constantly as if to spot something or someone who wasn't showing up. In fact, he was waiting for his accomplice to rob us. The accomplice finally appeared on a moped and came up alongside the taxi. We all understood what they were up to. I was afraid for my mother—she has a weak heart and looked terrified. Ten minutes later, the 'bogus fare' ordered the driver to stop and let him out, having undoubtedly decided we weren't worth the trouble. The driver got an earful from us, believe me!"

We start talking freely in our communal taxi. According to another passenger—a regional village chief returning from the capital—despite the launch of "Operation Enduring Freedom" in the autumn of 2001 in response to the September 11 attacks, the United States hasn't the slightest chance of eradicating the Taliban presence, which is too well rooted locally. Although no one in Qalat dares openly criticize the installation of U.S. troops in the city, everyone thinks "it will end the way it did with the Russians; they'll have to leave." Our companion continues: "According to the ancestral laws of our region, any Pashtun worthy of the name must, in every circumstance, offer hospitality to anyone who asks for it, even the Taliban. They are, in some sense, protected by our villagers. In addition, they're armed and could kill us if we don't comply." In fact, he concludes bizarrely (his is a very common view in Kabul), "It's not the fault of those poor 'seminarians' if this road, which they've continually attacked, is still not finished. The blame lies with their Pakistani financial backers, who refuse to let our country become stabilized!"

Like a number of his compatriots, the driver is persuaded that the goal of the U.S. soldiers is not to fight the Taliban or Al-Qaeda but to strip the country of its natural resources, such as gold and uranium. He assures us that although no one dares criticize the Americans, it's only because they don't want to be accused of being pro-Al-Qaeda or to be arrested. The result is a code of silence: no one denounces the Taliban to the Americans.

26

A Former Taliban

The mythical Kandahār was formerly an imperial capital, then the temporary capital of the Taliban after Mullah Omar established himself there (he was from a nearby village). It's an oasis that produces the juiciest pomegranates in the country. It's also the birthplace of the Afghan nation, the original home of Pashtun rulers such as Ahmad Shāh Durrāni, affectionately nicknamed Ahmad Shāh Baba ("Grandpa Ahmad") by the people of the country. In 1747 he was elected by popular consent to head the first Afghan federation and was in some sense the first major figure of modern Afghanistan.

Besmellah, my guide, first wants to show me Shelzinaw, one of the most bewildering monuments from the Mogul period. It consists of forty-two tall and irregular steps carved into the rock of one of the spiky peaks that surround the vast plain, at whose center the city was established. At the summit, in a commanding recess guarded by two lions —now mutilated—Bābur the Conqueror had a list of his victories engraved,[1] accompanied by those of his grandson Akbar. From the top of that sumptuous stone throne, a pocket of life in the midst of a hostile environment, the sight of the great flowing Arghandab River greets our eyes.

Also clearly visible are the four monumental gates to the city of Kandahār. An impressive dome stands out in the distance: it's the giant Blue Mosque, designed by Mullah Omar as one of the largest madrasas in the world and left unfinished in the autumn of 2001 when he fled the city. Not far away is the mullah's residence, which contains several private mosques. Besmellah went to visit it when that was still possible. The interior is in the worst possible taste: across from the entrance stands an artificial mountain with fake palm trees. Today the mullah is one of the most wanted figures in the world, and his residence is occupied by the CIA and the FBI, which have barricaded themselves inside because they fear attacks.

On August 15, 2003, Yusuf Pashtun, an engineer who had long worked for Western humanitarian organizations, was named governor of Kandahār Province. He replaced Gul Agha Sherzai, who was recalled to Kabul and assigned to the Ministry of Rural Development. Agha Sherzai was a former "commander" and, like many warlords under the Taliban, took refuge in the neighboring city of Quetta in Baluchistan, Pakistan. Scandalmongers believe that from there he supported the fundamentalist Gulbuddin Hekmatyar. He nevertheless managed to become popular in the southern capital by rebuilding the city after Mullah Omar's disappearance. Many roads, official buildings, and historical monuments were renovated at the time. But according to Besmellah, who supported King Zahir Shah, Agha Sherzai was called back to Kabul because he had supported, rather too actively, a demonstration in favor of the monarchy's return.

Armed with a letter of introduction from an Afghan diplomat in Moscow and accompanied by Besmellah, I attempt to meet with the new governor. In the waiting room, I note a portrait of none other than the former king Zahir Shah still in place. Just a moment before on the road from Herāt, we saw a huge construction site for a private luxury hotel "built with opium money." According to Besmellah, opium is pouring into Kandahār, and local high officials are by necessity involved in the trafficking. It's this subject I would like to discuss with Yusuf Pashtun, as well as another matter the city is still buzzing about. On September 12, 2003, as a result of various kinds of collusion, a bribe of seven hundred thousand dollars, and a thirty-two-yard tunnel, a group of forty Taliban prisoners are said to have made a bid for freedom. The chains on their feet posed no problem: they had arranged to be issued different ones, which they slipped on to put the jailers on the false scent if necessary. A mullah, the brother of the former minister of defense, was among the escapees. Since the start of the investigation, only minor suspects have been arrested. The embarrassed police officers justify themselves as best they can: lack of training on the jailers' part, a change of the supervising ministry, and so on.

We wait two and a half hours in the governor's antechamber under the watchful gaze of his young "press secretary," who is wearing jeans and a baseball cap and is conspicuously chewing gum. Is he purposely making us cool our heels? I lose patience and give up on the interview. My companion picks up the thread of his interesting reflections: "The Americans, for example, astonished everyone by releasing Waqil Ahmad Muttawakil, the Taliban's former minister of foreign affairs, and no doubt intend to use him."

He skewers the republic that the Westerners are trying to establish: "Applied to us, it's a system that consists of turning the tribes against one another. In a monarchy, that's impossible." For the moment, former king Zahir is also still under U.S. pressure. "Our hope is that he'll designate his successor. Everyone's thinking of his grandson Mustapha, the current Afghan ambassador to Italy," adds Besmellah. "We'd be happy to hear him express his views, but he doesn't say anything. During the first Loya Jirga in 2002, most of the delegates favored a monarchy, but the Americans didn't let them have their say. A monarchy doesn't fit with their plans! In short, there's such dissatisfaction that it won't be long before intellectuals, tribal chiefs, and ordinary citizens start collaborating with the Taliban simply to sabotage the work of the central government," he predicts.

Besmellah also harshly criticizes the pressures emanating from the center to get the tribal chiefs from the regions of Helmand, Zabul, and Uruzgān to support Hamid Karzai in the coming presidential elections, and he is outraged that villages that will vote "the right way" openly receive financial and material aid.

Besmellah takes me to see Mullah Abdullah Fayaz, head of the regional Council of Ulema (twelve hundred members), who is considered a religious moderate. The mullah receives us in the guest room. Its floor is covered with sumptuous carpets, and three of its walls are hidden be-

hind a large bookcase. Like most Afghans, Abdullah Fayaz begins the
conversation by alluding to his forebears:

"Like me, my father was religious, which got him arrested and
killed by the Communists; my grandfather was a close friend of Ahmad Shāh Durrāni [an Afghan monarch; see note 1 of chapter 24].
All these books belonged to them. Today I take ideas from them to
solve the problems my visitors present to me. There are scientific, literary, and religious works in Pashto, Dari, Arabic, and sometimes English. Some are manuscripts from two hundred years ago. The most
frequently asked questions right now are related to rules of inheritance regarding the different wives of the same man and his children." Under the Communists, property rights were simpler. With the
Taliban, Islamic law as it is taught in books was applied. "During
Ramadan I also do my utmost to educate the common people in particular about the hadith and the Koran, which are still not well enough
known."

We speak of the Taliban period. At the time, Abdullah went to the
mosque to pray but refused to preach on Friday for fear that the "seminarians" would realize he disagreed with them. He has a very firm position on these "religious men." "The Taliban are not religious scholars
but impostors who have destroyed the value of the Sharia, and, more seriously, its image. They have managed to use Islam's appeal to achieve
their ends, namely, power. I detected their duplicity as early as the jihad against the Soviets, and when some of them invited me to their
madrasa in Pakistan on various occasions. I always refused to be associated with them, discerning that behind the religious facade were concealed diabolical paramilitary groups financed by foreign powers. This
movement did not come about naturally; it was created by disruptive
foreign elements who wanted to destabilize our country. As a religious
leader, I'm able to make a judgment about their authenticity: they
never had any real credibility for me."

And what do they represent today? Abdullah Fayaz acknowledges
that although they have not completely disappeared, they'll find it impossible to return to power, since the people have come to understand
who they really are.

The assembly he leads has issued two fatwas[*] on important subjects: the first rejects the jihad desired by the extremist Taliban groups
against U.S. soldiers occupying Afghanistan; the second expresses the
ulema's support for the government in place in Kabul, one of whose
chief aims is the struggle against these very Taliban.

"It's because of that second fatwa that they recently tried to kill me
for the third time. They put a small grenade in the sleeve of a jacket I
left at the mosque. I was severely wounded, as were twenty-eight other
people," the *mulawi* calmly recounts. "We don't want the new government to collaborate in any way whatsoever with the Taliban,[2] whom we
judge harmful to society as a whole. As for the thorny question of the
relationship between religion and the state, we think that in Afghanistan the religious leaders ought to be able to go on pursuing their activities freely. I explained that in person to Karzai when I met with him,
and I hope he'll take it into account. The majority of the Afghan population are practicing Muslims—we are, for example, much more religious than the Turks—a fact that ought to argue for a political regime
in which the rulers cooperate with the people of religion." Last, he admits he's in contact with the ulema in neighboring Pakistan, which he
divides into three categories: "Those who are close to the ideas of Al-
Qaeda, those who are close to us, and those who are still neutral."

Having cast a furtive look at his watch, the old man gets up suddenly and leaves the room to deliver a course in his madrasa, where 250
students are waiting for him.

Now we stand before the impressive mosque of Mullah Omar, the one
that was to welcome Muslims the world over for the feast of *Īd* celebrating the end of Ramadan. It sits on rocky ground in the city's northern foothills. Construction work has recently resumed under the aegis
of the central government, with Pakistani and Arabic workers being re-

---

*Responses given to a legal question by a jurist charged with presenting an inter-
pretation that facilitates the application of the law. See Janine Sourdel and Dominique
Sourdel, *Dictionnaire historique de l'islam* (Paris: PUF, 1996; repr. coll., "Quadrige,"
2004), 288.

placed by their Turkish counterparts. One of the three dormitories next to the religious building, covered in a layer of fresh paint, is getting ready to welcome students from the University of Kandahār.

The round, completely empty space of the mosque immediately echoes back every word, even if it's only whispered. The Koran is very visible, set on a lectern and open to a different page every day. Around its entire circumference, the dome above its glass base still has the murals that artists "decorated" it with on the orders of the Taliban masters: a long string of octagonal vignettes depicting an Afghan landscape considered typical, each in a colorful and naive style. For example, there's the Intercontinental Hotel of Kabul, the Friday Mosque in Herāt, and many mountainous and bucolic landscapes with seemingly endless torrents flowing into them. The white flag of the Taliban inscribed with "Allah Is Great" is waving over an official building of Kandahār, and the black stone of the Kaaba, the Muslims' sanctuary in Mecca, is also represented.

As we are preparing to get into the car and head toward the city's center, I hear a loud explosion and a thick black cloud forms above the rooftops. We return to the center. Access to the neighborhood of the NGOs is denied: a booby-trapped car has exploded outside the building of a local UN agency. Apparently no one was wounded.

We rush through labyrinthine alleyways to reach Besmellah's house, sheltered behind high stone walls, in time for *iftar*. We signal our presence by knocking on the wooden door with its iron ring, duck our heads under the lintel, and enter the courtyard. At thirty-eight, Besmellah lives with his mother, his wife, and his four daughters, aged seven, six, five, and three and a half. Right now, he has no sons—a serious disadvantage according to Pashtun protocols. To cap it off, Besmellah has four sisters but no brothers, which is also a problem.

His wife, Laīli, ten years his junior and married for ten years, rushes around to bring us plates of instantly seeded pomegranates, which we have just purchased from one of the many itinerant vendors who laboriously pull their carts around town. Laīli is enveloped in her veils, and I have trouble making out her face. In the evening, however, she'll dare look directly at me, and I'll observe that the almond green of her magnificent eyes matches her chador and baggy pants. How elegant! Besmellah's mother, who is considered "old," is no more than fifty. She has just finished her prayer and puts away her rug as we are sitting down. Besmellah and his tribe moved into this house in the eastern section of the city about three weeks ago. They rent it for a little less than a hundred dollars a month from a businessman living in exile in Quetta. Since the fall of the religious regime, the city has become the center of Taliban activities, "without anyone hiding the fact or taking offense," Besmellah declares.

A little later, in a burst of laughter, Besmellah admits that in 1996 he was part of the Taliban government. For several months he worked in Kabul as head of the investigations department at the Ministry of the Interior and served several times as interim minister to Mullah Khaksar. He immediately defends himself: "But I'm primarily a nationalist and not a religious fundamentalist." He was also fooled by the Taliban. "Like many people, I took the Taliban to be supporters of Zahir Shah, then was disappointed and disgusted to realize that they were in fact financed by the United States via Saudi Arabia and the Pakistani ISI [Inter Services Intelligence]. Some time later, they arrested me and imprisoned me for three months, accusing me of being a monarchist, of speaking against Pakistan and against the fundamentalist ulema, which was true. Their director of intelligence services was particularly fundamentalist and insisted I denounce 'my group.' I realized that they were obsessed with the notion of a conspiracy." Having been bamboozled, Besmellah still feels some bitterness toward the Taliban. He knows that Mullah Khaksar (to whom President Karzai offered the position of provincial governor of Paktīā) now lives quietly in Kabul. According to Besmellah, he's a traitor who trembles in fear at the idea of returning to his lands and thinks only of saving his own hide.

Besmellah is cautious when he goes to Kabul, shaving off his beautiful brown beard fringe, removing his turban, and stuffing one of his many passports into his pocket, "just in case." He again speaks scathingly of the "Taliban imposture": "When the Taliban appeared, they represented such a great hope for change that everyone wanted to help them. The euphoria quickly dissolved; a year later, we'd all changed our

minds. One of my missions at the Ministry of the Interior was to in-
terrogate prisoners of war. One day we learned through the Pakistanis
that representatives of a French NGO were holding a party with alcohol and music. Afghan women were supposedly going to take part,
which was strictly forbidden. In accordance with the Taliban laws in
force, I was obliged to arrest two Frenchmen and five Afghans. The next
day I received a letter from Mullah Omar enjoining us to torture them
savagely, which I never allowed. Yet the minister of the interior drove
around in a Land Rover and listened to forbidden music! At the ministry, he asked us to speak English with him! When Taliban groups arrived in Kandahār, they received logistical support from Abdul Rasul
Sayyaf,[3] as well as financial aid from Burhanuddin Rabbani [see note
5 of chapter 2]. Even the Tajik Massoud supported them militarily,
thinking that these young madmen were going to oust the 'warlords'
in the south, especially Gulbuddin Hekmatyar. We went from one disappointment to another. When Karzai was appointed, we all wanted to
help him as well, and now we realize it's not worth the trouble."

Our conversation now takes a more personal turn. Besmellah confides concerns that, for him, are far more important than Karzai's in-
tegrity or his cronies. As the father of four daughters and with no
brothers of his own, his advancement on the local social scene is considered stalled. "According to tradition, I should marry a second wife
who might be able to give me a son, but I have no desire to do so, since
I love my wife and know that bringing another woman into our home
would create insurmountable problems. Maybe I don't have a boy with
Laīli precisely because I love her?" He smiles. "I've noticed that all the
men who don't love their wives and shamelessly cheat on them have
boys, whereas those who are faithful have girls. . . . Maybe I should love
her less?"

At the mention of that strange possibility, his delicately featured
face goes hard. It's a grave problem, since the "shame" of not having
male progeny weighs heavily on Besmellah and his wife, and the consequences are severe. "Above all, I mustn't become wealthy in too obvious a manner, otherwise one of my cousins might get the idea to kill
me so as to claim my inheritance, and according to our *pashtunwali* laws,

our code of honor, he would not be condemned for that act," he explains to me, showing no emotion.

The fact is, in Pashtun regions the technological modernity of cell phones and DVDs coexists with the assertion of a specific identity, which still includes respect for that ancient code. Hence, for example, a murder can be "redeemed" if the criminal's family gives their young women in marriage to the family of the victim. As for questions of inheritance, the *pashtunwali* is in clear opposition to the Koran, which is more equitable toward women and in no case authorizes the death of a member of the family to claim its wealth. "If I were to die tomorrow," Besmellah continues, giving a forced laugh, "each of my daughters would be 'claimed' by one of my cousins, who would take Laīli as his second wife. According to our traditions, no other solution is conceivable. In our tribe, without sons I have no real existence. How can I get out of it?" he asks, looking to me as if I had the answer. "My wife is scared to death about getting pregnant again. Our whole family is obsessed about it! My mother thinks only of getting me another wife, and my wife is pressuring me just as much! She's already asked me several times for permission to begin a search for the one we need. . . . My wife is covered in shame and is ready to do anything to rid herself of the moral burden and get back to a normal life."

It is then that he begins to tell me the conditions surrounding the birth of their fourth daughter, the very one he has on his knee at the moment. At age three and a half, she still can't talk, and Besmellah is reluctant to take her to a specialist in Pakistan, hoping she'll say something more than "yes" and "no," or sometimes "papa" and "mama," in Pashto. "When it was clear that the baby was another girl, it was as if we'd had a death in the family. My wife was so shocked that her milk didn't come in; she abandoned her baby for nearly a week. You heard nothing but weeping in the house. The three sisters were also crying in imitation. Could that be one of the causes of her behavior today? We made serious mistakes, I've instinctively understood that, even if I never discuss it with my wife or mother, and I try to give her much more love than her sisters at the same age!" the anxious father declares. He presses the little girl against his enormous torso after giving her a

spoonful of pomegranate, red like her cheeks, and planting a noisy kiss
on her forehead. "My wife has warned me that if it's another girl next
time, she'll let herself die. She's asked me not to announce the child's
sex immediately after she gives birth, in order to protect her." Reluc-
tantly, Besmellah is considering taking a second wife if the fifth child
is also a girl.

To reach the neighborhood of the chief of the influential Popalzaī tribe,
to which Besmellah (like President Hamid Karzai) belongs, we must
go through the "Arab" neighborhood, so named because under the Taliban the very large retinue of Osama bin Laden's extended family resided there. Since the "Arabs" fled, just before the U.S. attack in the
autumn of 2001, the houses have been reclaimed by their true Kan-
dahārī owners, who themselves returned from Pakistan where they had
sought refuge. One group replaced the other.

When we arrive, Sheikh Abdullah is paying a visit to neighbors; he
receives us in their guest room. He is the leader of the largest tribe in
Kandahār, numbering eighty thousand people out of an overall population of six hundred thousand. Sitting cross-legged, looking roguish
behind his long beard, which trembles in rhythm to his words, Abdullah proudly explains to me that for five generations his ancestors have
always served as representatives to the state institutions existing at the
time, whether that was the Royal Senate or the post-Taliban Loya Jirga.
He claims to be eighty-two, but I have my doubts; for once I'm faced
with an Afghan who looks younger than his years. The sheikh married
only one woman, who died ten years ago and who had two sons with
him. The elder son was killed by the Russians, for whom he has har-
bored an inexpiable hatred ever since. Like Besmellah, he is suspicious
of democracy: "Now that it's Ramadan, I read the Holy Book daily and
pray for the return of our king, whom I support over Karzai, the other
native of our region," he begins. "If Zahir were to reign, he would stand
above the fray and would bar the different ethnic groups that compose
our people from being placed in competition. Karzai certainly has very
honorable plans, such as disarming the militias and establishing a national army, but what does he intend to do about 'Baba'? We are, I'm

told, in a democracy, which obliges us to hold elections. The problem is that in this system, politics is a real joke and everything involves money. The Loya Jirga is a farce, and the presidential elections will be so as well. The constitution, which they say is democratic, was not the occasion for any debate. How can you say you're a democrat when almost our whole population is illiterate? When a man gets sick, you take care of him with treatments familiar to him, to avoid any unexpected reactions. Today our country is sick, and we're the only ones capable of taking care of it with the remedies we know; the return to the monarchy is one. I don't understand why the United States opposes it when they're allies with England, one of the most respected constitutional monarchies in the world. Zahir as king and Karzai in the government —that would be the ideal thing!"

While driving to a wedding recently, Abdullah was the victim of an assassination attempt. It's not the first time. He imputes the act to frictions between tribes, which are common. He also admits he was duped by the Taliban: "In 1996, soon after he'd established himself in Kandahār, Mullah Omar paid me a visit and swore on the Koran that his movement had only one aim: to battle the 'warlords' and the anarchy they had caused. He lied to me. We were really had!" he now laments. In exchange for his pledge, Mullah Omar obtained the support of several thousand men from the sheikh. "I know where one of his hiding places is: in the mountains of Shah Wali Kot District, not far from my native village. There he's protected by the villagers, but if the Americans wanted to, they could arrest him. But they don't give me the impression that they're really fighting the Taliban. Rather, they're quietly establishing themselves here. They claim they want to bring peace, but in fact they're pursuing their own interests and are manipulating Karzai to that end. Like the Soviets in their time, they intend, but in their own way, to destroy our culture."

In place of Massoud's posters, which are found in the north and in Kabul, photos of the former king Zahir Shah at the time of his glory, posing in ceremonial dress of different kinds, cover Kandahār. Young men go past them proudly, holding hands.

We enter a new cemetery containing the graves of the "Arabs" killed by U.S. bombs in the autumn of 2001 as they were fleeing toward the border city of Spin Buldak. Their names are not even inscribed on the tombs. The worship of martyred saints goes against the strict prescriptions of Islam, but it is still very popular in Pashtun culture, and this cemetery has immediately turned into a pilgrimage site. Black and green oriflammes tied to the tops of poles indicate the martyrs' graves, and the thickets around them are covered with ex-votos made of various rags. Men and women who have come on foot, by bicycle, by car, or even by minibus from the neighboring cities meditate there in the hope that the visit to these "innocent martyrs" will heal them or make their women fertile. During my own visit, I count about sixty people, including paraplegics in wheelchairs. On Fridays, Besmellah whispers to me, the crowd is even larger. At this moment, not far away, two U.S. military convoys flanked by Toyota pickups from the Afghan police pass amid general indifference. According to rumors, when they were living in Kandahār the "Arabs" owned several dozen horses, which vanished with them. They are reportedly still using them to move about between the Afghan provinces. In Pakistan, where their chiefs are hiding, small fundamentalist groups attached to the Pakistani secret service and financed by bin Laden make cars available to them.

Clusters of women in soiled burkas beg on the steps outside the mausoleum of Ahmad Shāh Durrrāni and the neighboring mosque, where for centuries a brown piece of fabric, identified by the region's faithful as the Prophet's holy cape, is housed. It is that cape that Mullah Omar symbolically and hysterically seized during one of his rare public appearances, on April 4, 1996, before proclaiming himself "emir of all believers," a caliphal title. Inside Ahmad Shāh's mausoleum, a man holds his infant tightly in his arms. With his right hand, one by one, he lightly touches the walls of the tomb and the baby's head, as if he wanted to communicate some mysterious power to it.

Across from a small playground built under the aegis of the previous governor stands the central tribunal of Kandahār, where we are to meet with the presiding judge. Abdul Basir, impressive under his immaculate white turban, which makes him look even taller than he already is, is a prizewinner from the law school in Kabul and a specialist in Islamic law. He was named to that post by the central government just after the Bonn accords. For me, the respect commanded by his long gray beard combines with the bewildering impression produced by his painted toenails, which are very visible through his *shapli,* men's high-heeled leather sandals. "Whether we are officially living under a Taliban regime or not hardly matters," Abdul declares, maintaining the ambiguity, "because the Afghans are Muslims, true Muslims, which is to say, very devout. We administer justice today as we did before the fall of the regime, because for Afghans the Sharia is the only equitable means for settling lawsuits. The Taliban did not create the Sharia; it preceded them. It seems to me our society is not ready for, shall we say, a more modern and Western evolution of its justice system."

The judge admits he has not read the proposed constitution, but he hopes it will be founded on the precepts of communal life, in keeping with Islam and its laws, which are derived from the Holy Book. "We don't intend to convert Bush," he tells me, ironic and full of contempt at the same time, "but we demand that the American president let us practice our religion as we choose. The Americans won't dare attempt to reproduce what the Soviets imposed, that is, make the country secular or even atheist by modifying its legal code, among other things. The majority of them support capital punishment in their own country: how, then, do they expect to prevent us from practicing it, publicly or not? I'm sorry capital punishment is no longer in force here since the fall of the Taliban. But, above all, I'm sorry our people are not educated enough to understand the benefits of the Sharia."

Profoundly hostile to any foreign element, he continues: "Everyone knows that Hamid Karzai is a puppet set up by the Americans and that the real strongman here is Zalmay Khalilzad, Bush's envoy to Afghanistan. We ought categorically to reject all foreign aid because, in helping us, foreigners take advantage to 'Westernize' our society, to secularize it, and that does not correspond at all to our way of thinking. But I'm still optimistic, since foreign aid won't last forever, and then again, haven't we already driven out the British, followed by the Russians? So those Americans won't last long here. Only a minority working with them, especially the many charitable organizations, are drawing a significant material advantage and accept their meddling. All other Afghans reject it."

Even though it's Ramadan, during our entire conversation Judge Basir furtively but regularly digs out of his tunic pocket pinches of *naswar,* a sort of spiced tobacco, which he chews on briefly and spits out. Besmellah will later admit to me that he was shocked by that gesture, which breaks one of the most sacred rules of the fast: not to bring anything to one's lips between dawn and dusk. According to him, the *naswar* had even gone to the fasting judge's head. That was supposedly the reason for certain contradictions, even certain exaggerations in his extremist talk. For myself, I think the judge is an extremist who declares his views with an easy mind.

"Who are the Taliban?" At that question, he stares at me in surprise. The U.S. propaganda against them is intense, he says, even though for the most part they're just young, inexperienced religion students, manipulated by these very same Americans. His theory is that during the Cold War, the Americans, who did not have an ideology as powerful as the Soviets', invented Islamic fundamentalism and went in search of individuals to implement it. "The Taliban are human beings like everyone else and deserve to be treated as such. Hence we disapprove of America's attitude toward its prisoners in Guantánamo Bay. As for Al-Qaeda, it's an organization created by anti-Islamic conspirators," he fires back in a single breath.

From the windows of his shabby and frigid office, where not a book, not a piece of paper, even less a computer, is visible, you can see a large multicolor Ferris wheel on the playground. After leaving the tribunal, we finally manage to drive by the place of this morning's explosion, outside the United Nations building. Afghan workers are busy setting blocks of concrete in place to make cars slow down. Amid them, CIA agents in civilian clothes photograph the site; one of them has spotted us and takes a photo of our car. Besmellah couldn't care less about the CIA, knowing how poorly it infiltrated the Taliban network and the nebulous Al-Qaeda and that it was not even able to prevent the September 11 attacks.

Two blocks later Besmellah shows me the garrison house of Pres-

ident Karzai's brother (his personal but not official representative in
Kandahār). Then he takes me to see a female delegate to the December 2003 Loya Jirga. Shaheeda Hussein, the mother of five sons and
three daughters between the ages of eight and thirty, is forty-eight years
old. She also participated in the first Loya Jirga, in June 2002. After studying for fifteen years at the Kandahār Medical School, she left
the country in 1981 following the Soviet invasion and took refuge in
Quetta, Pakistan, for fifteen years. There she collaborated with different international medical aid agencies active in the refugee camps of
Baluchistan.

She begins by explaining the selection process for the second Loya
Jirga: "In Kandahār two women, one from Kabul, the other from Farāh
Province, were appointed by fiat; neither one was Kandahāri. United
Nations agents in charge of the selection process tried to argue with me,
saying that since those two had already been selected, an election was
out of the question. But it was no use. I replied that if that was the case,
several hundred women would demonstrate for me outside their building!" Supported by four hundred women from Kandahār, Shaheeda did
appear more credible. Once she had collected the signatures of about a
hundred of these women, she managed to register as a delegate, furious
that "the government had no hesitation in selecting the delegates in our
place, with the sole aim of protecting the interests of the Karzai clan."

Shaheeda denounces that process, which, according to her, demon-
strates the absence of democracy in Afghanistan. "I truly have doubts
about our capacity to become a democratic society," she says. "What
are we to think, for example, of Ahmad Wali Karzai, the president's
brother, who has no official function but does not hesitate to resort to
blackmail if he judges it necessary? And everything that was debated
at the first Loya Jirga has remained moot." Shaheeda gives an example
close to her heart: there was a proposal that former members of the royal
family might run for the presidency, but there has been no follow-up.

As for the strong presidential regime favored by the future constitution, Shaheeda disapproves of it: "The Afghans know nothing about
the democratic and republican system, which was in some sense imposed on us after Daud Khan's coup d'état. The best political regime

for Afghanistan is a constitutional monarchy, which we already have experience with. We have lived under communism, under the muja-hideen, and under the Taliban; we've had ample opportunity to compare. No one today has the courage to work for national unity. Our leaders remain under the influence of foreign countries: Pakistan, Russia, the United States, Iraq, even Saudi Arabia. Unfortunately, since our king returned from exile, we haven't really had access to him. Yet Commander Gul Agha Serzai, former governor of Kandahār, promised to bring him to the region. We don't know anything about his reaction to the regime established by the Americans or to Karzai. We haven't heard him express his views. The Americans are playing one funny game: they support both the former war chiefs Marshal Fahim, Ismail Khan, and Rashid Dostum, who ruined our country, and a presidential system that, though strong, won't work!"

Is she still afraid of the Taliban, or does she believe that politically they have been definitively thrust aside in Afghanistan? "It's still dangerous to go out into the rural areas north of Kandahār and to the eastern part of the country, which are regions under Taliban control. We have one fear: that the Americans will decide to give Mullah Mut-tawakil a second chance.[4] It's even said he's already gotten out of prison and is offering to collaborate with the central government. If that's the case, how can we speak of eradicating the Taliban? People hoped that, thanks to the Americans, the Taliban would disappear, that the new strongmen of the country would bring us peace, stability, and prosperity and would rebuild our country. Yet I've never felt so unsafe. . . . On that subject, let's talk a little about the veil. Under the monarchy, the order was given to quit wearing the veil, which, for many of us, was unnatural. With the Taliban, the order was reversed: walking in the streets without a burka was strictly forbidden. Now, oddly enough, it's more or less the same thing. We, the women of Kandahār, would not for the world go into town without our full veil, which has become the passport we need to move around. Strangely, the burka is now in some sense the guarantor of our freedom! But I'm sure we'd have less of a tendency to veil ourselves if we felt safe!"

How do the men of her household react to her political activities?

"One of my sons-in-law, a high school teacher, is proud of me; as for my husband, a former officer under Zahir Shah, he just lets me be."

Then she mentions her experience in the Pakistani camps, which she was well acquainted with between 1982 and 1997: "In the refugee camps in Pakistan, the portrait of Hekmatyar is everywhere. Justice is subject to the Sharia. Those camps are the refuge of modern-day terrorists and a breeding ground for future terrorists who work for Al-Qaeda and the ISI. Taliban have threatened me to get me to stop collaborating with the international aid agencies. They did not hesitate to beat us if we acted 'contrary' to their primitive and decadent vision of Islam. We came back to Afghanistan when some of the Taliban presented themselves as supporters of the monarchy, ready to establish peace, and lured us with bright prospects. But in fact, they only claimed all that because they knew that here, in the south, the announcement of a return to that political system would help them win support. The Americans didn't do anything different: they used the king's return to establish Karzai's legitimacy. The Taliban changed under Osama bin Laden's bad influence: they turned us against one another. Where the Russians divided us politically, the Taliban divided us ethnically. All of us, even the Americans, know that most of the Taliban are in Pakistan and not in Afghan territory. So why don't the Americans attack Pakistan?" How many times have I heard that view expressed?

Now Shaheeda goes on endlessly about the malfunction of foreign nongovernment organizations: "Did anyone ask our population if they needed that aid? No! If they'd been allowed to express themselves, 95 percent would have given a negative response, since that aid disappointed everyone. Up to this point, the reconstruction projects have not been completed. Worse, they haven't been adopted, and the staff responsible for them are paid royally to conduct 'preliminary inquiries' and then disappear. The NGOs serve no purpose; it's our own people who need to be given work. But before anything else, we must show them that national unity is possible. Instead, explosions and ambushes are multiplying, proof of the intense activity of the Taliban, Al-Qaeda, and the mujahideen. I'm very afraid the situation will fester, as it did between Israel and Palestine.

"With or without elections, Karzai is in the Americans' hands. He was unknown just a short time ago; they pulled him out of their hat for us at the Bonn conference. Or rather, if they shaved off Mullah Omar's beard, replaced his blind eye, dressed him in Western clothes, and put him in Karzai's place, no one would be offended! Anything is possible here," she exclaims finally. We laugh at that grotesque possibility.

The murky past of Mullah Naquib(ullah), chief of the all-powerful Alokozai tribe, whom we are now going to visit, reflects all the complexity of the alliances in Afghan territory. Allegiances change constantly, as a function of the interests of the moment. The mullah certainly took care of his own interests: his various dealings in the last twenty-three years have made him rich. Some say he has fifty million dollars in foreign bank accounts.

Naquib became supreme commander of Kandahār in 1992 after the mujahideen took power, having fought alongside Massoud against the Soviets and their Afghan allies in the 1980s. Curiously enough, in 1994 he handed the city over to the Taliban groups from Pakistan without firing a shot. He then collaborated fully with their leaders, providing weapons and men against the anti-Taliban "commanders." Contacted in autumn 2001 by Hamid Karzai to oust the "seminarians," he managed to waver until December, then negotiated their surrender. On December 6, 2001, however, Mullah Omar and his cronies managed to flee to the east.

Hungry for power, Mullah Naquib and his more than two thousand troops then attempted to take control of the city, fighting against Commander Gul Agha Sherzai's men, who prevailed in the end. It was thus Sherzai, Naquib's sworn enemy, who was named governor of the province by President Karzai. Naquib, annoyed and mortified, turned down the position of commander in chief of the city's military garrison.[5] Officially, Naquib withdrew from the local political scene; in reality, he continues to pull strings behind the scenes.

Besmellah had warned me: the mullah is a very busy man. When he's away from his vast home in Kandahār, he can surely be found "in his gardens" outside the city, where, it is said, he has increased his production of opium. He is pudgy and, though he looks cunning, is actually affable. Wearing large plastic eyeglasses, he never looks directly at me. At our arrival, and then again when we leave, Besmellah will kiss his hand several times as a sign of great deference ("I'm obliged to," he'll subsequently explain to me).

The mullah sets forth a very personal version of the latest events that have ruined his country. "I was shocked by the cruelty of the Russians, who ransacked our villages and our traditions with the same insane fury. I fought them and have many wounds to show for it. But fortunately, we were supported in our jihad by foreign countries that have now come to help us rebuild. Ever since the Taliban have given up power, the central government has every interest in dealing with them, not so they'll participate in the central government but so they'll finally be able to come back to live peacefully on their lands, once they've turned in their weapons. In fact, I went to Kabul to suggest that compromise to Karzai. The president assured me that the possibility was being studied, since the Taliban are, after all, also Afghans!" The mullah is obviously well informed because that's what happened a few months later.

Although he prides himself on having almost daily contact with the representatives of U.S. troops in his region, he claims not to know anything precise, retreating behind the fact that he holds no official position. When I report Rashid Dostum's desire to be named minister of defense in place of Tajik Fahim, he is piqued by the general's effrontery. He shouts aggressively: "As of tomorrow, I'm prepared to send three thousand men to fight Dostum on his own lands if Karzai authorizes me to do so!" Proof, if any were needed, that the mullah has not yet lowered his guard or disarmed.

Five local journalists, barely twenty-five years old, who claim to be "Taliban who have not taken up arms," insisted on seeing "the Western journalist." So here we are, sitting in a circle of chairs in the garden of a house in the center of the city. I'm wearing a Pakistani outfit that veils my hair but leaves my face uncovered. Across from me are five identical turbans and five long black beards, which make these young faces, all similarly impenetrable, look older than they are. We are con-

versing just before *iftar,* and I sense on both sides a certain tension due
to the fast. For them, no doubt, it artificially reinforces the bitterness
of their words.

"We're worried and hurt that the Western media always send out
the same image of Islam as 'the cradle of terrorism,' " one of them begins in a reproachful tone. "According to the Koran, which is our ultimate point of reference, Islam is a way of life. Just because you're
Pashtun doesn't necessarily mean you're Taliban, and being Taliban
doesn't inevitably make you a terrorist." What is a Taliban? "A man of
faith, so not necessarily a bad person, but certainly somebody different,
someone who doesn't allow certain Western ways of life to be imported
into Afghanistan. It must be said that sometimes what is considered
'normal' there produces stupefaction here, and vice versa. Why not try
to understand these differences instead of demonizing them? I remember, by the way, that some Taliban pronounced themselves in favor of a
democratic system, but they were not heeded because they were not at
the top of the Taliban hierarchy. In the end, the Taliban failed because
there were too many wolves mixed in among the sheep."

The question of the nation is what preoccupies another: "The people in the north (the Tajiks and Uzbeks) accuse us of every kind of evil
because we're Pashtuns, the chief ethnic group from which the Taliban
emerged, but we reject such reductively nationalist views. When these
same people in the north point to the lack of security reigning in the
south, and especially here in Kandahār, I might very well reply that
when I go to Kabul, it's my turn not to feel safe." His four companions
signal their assent. "My physical appearance is immediately assimilated
to that of a Taliban, hence an enemy. Some want to change the name
of our country, but why? Why insist on the divisions? All the ethnic
groups that compose this country ought to be part of the construction
process of the Afghan nation. We are pleased that negotiations between
Karzai and the Taliban hierarchy have begun, since they mark the first
signs of the reconciliation that has been anticipated for so long."

Besmellah, my companion and guide, constantly intrigues me. Seductive, affable, scintillating, and the author of long poems in Pashto when

he's in the mood, who is this former Taliban really? At home, where his mother, wife, and daughters live in seclusion, time is clearly demarcated: there are the times when he is there and times when he is gone. As soon as he has crossed the threshold, I hear the tinkling of the many bracelets on Laïli's wrists; she's not far away, she's coming toward us. Now she shadows her husband, on the lookout for the slightest gesture, the slightest word expressing a wish she could fulfill. As for the little girls, they come running to embrace their father one after the other. Then they sit down, pressed up against one another, both joyful and intimidated by my presence, while we settle onto the *kurpachi* to relax.

This evening Besmellah is upset: his eldest daughter says she was beaten a few days ago by her schoolteacher, on the pretext that she hadn't finished her homework. The teacher grabbed her long hair and hit her in the head several times in front of the other students. Besmellah will call him to account, but he knows his efforts will be in vain: "In our society, that sort of violence toward girls is altogether common. The worst of it is that I can already hear the teacher telling me: 'Don't send her back to school if you don't want it to happen again!' "

Feeling sated after *iftar,* we go out again at nightfall. Before we leave, Besmellah, for the first time, takes off his turban in front of me to tie it tighter. I get a glimpse of the first signs of baldness and say to myself that the impressive turban is sometimes a real advantage! Still looking in the mirror, Besmellah, unruffled, now rolls enormous strips of fabric around his skull until it is covered completely, then he passes the last strip behind his left ear and lets it fall to his shoulder. He's ready, we can go. Has Besmellah decided not to hide anything of his life from this Western woman before him?

In any case, he wants me to meet the woman he may choose for his second wife, his niece Fatima. So we go to see the family, which is related by marriage. Respecting the rule, a young woman stands near the entryway to better serve us, behind her mother and her two elder brothers. She is dressed in turquoise, which is very becoming to her dark complexion, her long and heavy braided hair, and her jet-black eyes. According to Besmellah, she's already in love with him, a passion she's been able to express in the very rare and brief moments—a few seconds—when they've found themselves alone, by kissing him. For several months, in an agreement known only to them, they've been communicating with brief messages that Besmellah finds or leaves behind on each of his visits, under the quilt on which he has seated himself. "Fatima learned to read and write Pashto in order to communicate with me," the suitor explains, flattered by the achievement, "whereas my wife is illiterate and doesn't even understand Dari!"

All six of us are seated in the small room off the back yard, and we look at the music videos that the family was watching when we came in, as they do every evening. Without allowing her eyes to rest on her uncle for an instant, the young woman serves us from a tray containing the usual thermos of green tea, accompanied by pistachio nuts. Even when I ask her questions, it's her brothers who answer for her. She must remain discreet and silent. Across from us, the elder brother, a tradesman at the bazaar, holds the VCR's remote control in his right hand. When he gets up for a few minutes to rummage through a wooden chest in search of a new video, I see Besmellah, defying etiquette and decorum, look intently at Fatima. She is embarrassed and can hardly stand to have his eyes on her.

The elder brother, honored by my presence, insists on showing me the "best clips" of Afghan music. He begins with traditional pieces played at weddings within the expatriate Afghan community of the United States. These cassettes circulated under the counter during the "no music" regime of the Taliban. Back then, you could listen to male and female singers who had fled the country during the previous ten years, including a very beautiful Kandahāri woman. Her hair skillfully coiffed in the style of the 1970s, her eyebrows carefully plucked, lipstick on her mouth, her eyes heavy, she looks like an Afghan, brunette Brigitte Bardot. The singer is accompanied by male dancers, who circle around her lasciviously, in rhythm to the music, and clasp her tighter and tighter, the height of provocation by Afghan standards, even post-Taliban ones.[6] We go on to a potpourri of Arabic videos, obviously among the most popular pirated Afghan cassettes on the market at the moment. A magnificent Egyptian woman, followed by a

sumptuous Lebanese one, sways her hips in front of us without restraint. No one in the group seems embarrassed or shocked. And I discover the huge gap between men's and women's behavior in public and
the reality of private life at home with the family. The elder son declares
he bought the video under the Taliban regime, in neighboring Pakistan. It's now for sale on both sides of the border. Glancing at Fatima,
I observe that she knows by heart the words of the songs in Arabic, and
her lips move in silence, her eyes riveted to the screen, the empty tray
in her hand.

Besmellah says that all the Taliban officials, with Mullah Omar in
the lead, were mad about this type of music, which they listened to with
the windows closed in their fast-driving cars so that it wouldn't be noticed. "The prohibitions were for the poor, the common people, the
plebs!" he says excitedly. "The leaders did what they liked." Later, when
we're alone again, Besmellah will tell me he once caught a high digni-
tary of the regime with Kabul prostitutes. "He begged me on his knees
not to denounce him." He still laughs about it.

After three electrical outages, it's time for the Indian dance and music videos the Afghans are so fond of. "Indian women are the best
dancers in the world," says Fatima's elder brother, though he's not very
loquacious. It's true, the tune is very lively.

There's another electrical outage, and we take advantage of it to
leave. "Come back soon" are the only words Fatima managed to slip to
Besmellah—so he tells me—when her mother and brothers escorted us
to the door by the light of an oil lamp.

"In my opinion, her parents would not be against my marrying her,
even as a second wife. I think five thousand dollars would manage
to convince them," mutters Besmellah as we head for his car. "But it
would be better to wait at least another year, which will allow me to
have another child with my wife, and if it's a boy . . . then there'll be
no more reason for Fatima to come into my life. Otherwise, I'll marry
her! But they [the two women] won't live together. I plan on putting
Fatima in a cottage I'll buy on the other side of the city. Then I'll have
to divide my time between the two households." He sighs into the
darkness.

The next day we drop by to see a landowner friend who recently returned from Holland and has empty lots to sell. "Fifteen thousand dollars for 240 square yards; that's too expensive," says Besmellah. "Too bad."

That night, while we're conversing in the large whitewashed guest room with vaulted walls where I sleep, Besmellah will reveal a bit more of himself to me, unpacking the photos from the different periods of his tumultuous life. From a niche he pulls large padlocked athletic bags. From them he takes plastic sacks containing piles of yellowing envelopes. I had not noticed that niche, which is veiled by a strip of cloth; as in all Afghan interiors, no personal effects are apparent, especially in the room reserved for guests. Carpets, mattresses, and quilts are only temporary "furnishings." A bed is never left visible during the day. Its linen is folded, set aside, and stacked in a corner.

I take a look at the snapshots. The mujahideen photos taken in the 1980s during the Soviet invasion are amusing: wearing no turban and sporting long hair, the young man poses and flaunts himself with malicious pleasure. He's in great physical shape. He stands near a river, sporting munitions belts, his "Kalash" in his hand. I've seen the same photos of fighters among the Chechens, carefully preserved in plastic albums. The groups of mujahideen in long hair remind me of peaceniks, except these are armed. "Everyone had long hair at the time," explains Besmellah; "it was the fashion, and it also scared off the Russians!"

Then there are photos of Pakistan, where, Besmellah says, he spent many years in different refugee camps. In them he appears with a beard and mustache, like today, but his head is completely shaved. Rummaging through the envelopes, I come across a photo of his father. A former *quazi* (judge) of the city and a much respected tribal chief, he was "murdered by the Communists" when Besmellah was ten years old. He has the same square jaw, the same mouth with sharply drawn lips, and the same large brown eyes and high forehead. His face is framed by a beard. The resemblance between father and son is striking. Besmellah was barely an adolescent when he had to take his father's place, and he gradually came to identify with him.

Finally, there are photos of the official Taliban period in Kabul. His eyes are dark, his beard full, the top of his head concealed by the famous black turban, skillfully tied. Today he speaks of those years with amusement, even detachment: "I'm not ashamed to say I was a Taliban, because I have no blood on my hands and I never hurt anyone. My only regret is that I made a mistake. The Taliban were not the people I thought they were." Of his Taliban past, he relates this last anecdote: "One of my Algerian friends, who probably worked for an organization close to Al-Qaeda, asked me on several occasions to help him set up training camps in Azerbaijan. I refused, since I did not share his fundamentalist, purist, even backward-looking vision of Islam, especially in terms of women's condition."

Besmellah speaks Pashto, Dari, Urdu, Hindi, Arabic, and English fluently (the Afghans are born linguists) and dreams of becoming a diplomat in Morocco and Libya, but certainly not in a Western country, where he's afraid he won't feel comfortable. He admits, however, that he's been to Turkey—but is that really a Western country?—and has excellent memories of it. What does he think of the Americans? Not very much. "I suspect they're putting their spies in the political parties, in the government, among the former warlords, so that they can pull the strings in our politics for as long as they decide. But they're not the only ones who are the masters in this region: China is silent right now, but it's waiting for its moment."

How does Besmellah earn his living, now that he's no longer a Taliban? Of his current activities he'll say only that he's in the car import-export business. He prefers to turn the conversation back to his family. When he was very young, he was responsible for his four sisters, hence for the heavy responsibility of marrying them off. Following tradition, he sought out the suitors and proceeded to make preliminary inquiries about their families, their social group, their level of education, as well as their physical health (a factor taken into account like all the others). But, he tells me, contrary to tradition, he refused each time to take the money that in-laws customarily give the bride's parents for the "purchase" of their daughter. Instead, he proposed that the money be used for wedding gifts for the young couple, especially jewelry for each of his sisters. Although they are still grateful to him for his generosity, his mother, who is more traditionalist, did not approve of that "liberal" attitude. But she had to fall in with the decision of the man of the house.

"And I truly intend to do the same thing with my daughters," declares Besmellah. "I imagine them as doctors, nurses, or teachers, professions that are perfectly acceptable for women." When parents of young boys visit him for preliminary discussions—this has already happened—"I tell it like it is: none of them will be married before nineteen, twenty, or even twenty-one, and they'll all have finished their education." Proof that, in spite of everything, Afghan society is evolving.

On these cold autumn days, the men of Kandahār bundle themselves up in their *patu*. Sometimes, sitting back on their heels and looking sullen, they collapse into themselves. Besmellah never does this. He is always tall and dignified in his enormous shawl, his hands unfailingly crossed behind his back.

27

EN ROUTE TO KHOST

Once again I've taken a communal taxi. From Kabul I head for Khost, ninety-four miles southeast of the capital, in a province bordering Pakistan, where training camps established by Al-Qaeda were bombed by the United States in November 2001. I have slipped on my burka so as not to attract attention. All things considered, it is my best protection because I can work without being seen and even take notes under it. Between Kabul and Gardēz (a city located about sixty miles from Khost), we drive past snow-covered mountain passes lined with fir trees, the only forests in the whole country.

Kuchi women (a nomadic Pashtun tribe), dressed in long, full, multicolored skirts, walk single file along the road to rejoin their encampment, heavy bundles on their heads. They don't hide their faces as we pass. Once we've gone by the wall of white-crested mountains, the settlements change. The houses, still in harmony with the color of the soil, seem to have gotten bigger. Surrounded by high cob walls, the properties are very impressive closed rectangles, sometimes as large as a hundred yards long and twenty-five yards wide. A single wooden door, the entrance to the *qala* (a giant cob house typical in the Pashtun south, with high walls and turrets, like a fortress), is painted in bright colors. No wonder that behind these walls the minds of Pashtun families are not very flexible, for these societies are very closed.

Everywhere, hundreds of piles of wood sit alongside the river that is used to transport it. The approaching winter is the best time to supply the markets in Kabul and in other large cities of Afghanistan with construction materials and firewood. Apparently, the Karzai government's ban on cutting down trees that are growing wild so as to save the few forests left in the country has not been heard.

At a bend in the road, just before we head down toward the vast plain of Khost and Pakistan, our car is suddenly stopped by three armed men wearing beards and turbans and looking placid. One of them hands a tract to our driver, who has lowered his window as if he's been expecting it. No words are exchanged. The car sets off again. Barely have I grasped that these are Taliban warriors than they have disappeared behind the rocks. I have had no time for fear. In our vehicle, no one seems surprised or comments on the "incident." The tract passes from hand to hand. I hold on to it to get it translated, since it's in Pashto.

The top half consists of a color photograph that could not be more explicit. In a rural landscape, an African American GI is crouching in front of an Afghan woman, searching her body. The woman's face is turned toward him, and she has apparently lifted up her burka to make the task easier for him. Behind her, as if waiting her turn, a second veiled woman clasps a young child in her arms. The commentary also couldn't be clearer: "In the above photograph, you may observe that the soldiers with the most advanced technologies have decided to terrorize our population; and these technologies clearly show the kind of democracy and freedom championed by America. Under the banner of that so-called freedom, the Americans have annihilated the freedom of many small and poor nations. Oh, brave Afghan, mujahideen fighter, Afghan youth, take your fate into your own hands. It is up to you to follow in the footsteps of your courageous fathers and grandfathers . . . or to embrace that bad, virtual democracy! Take a good look at the photo and make your choice!"

This tract mentions a mysterious publishing house called Al Omar. So Taliban propagandists have decided to use photography and its evocative power to call for a jihad.[1]

28

A GOVERNOR AND
FORMER COMMANDER

During the years of the Taliban's reign, Khost Province took advantage of its key geographic position on Pakistan's border to weave the maximum number of commercial ties with the rare countries that recognized the regime, such as Saudi Arabia and the United Arab Emirates. Khost, the capital of the province, survives mostly thanks to its trade with neighboring Pakistan. Its central bazaar is very well stocked. There you run into old men in turbans with henna-tinted orangish hair and a few women in bright orange burkas, a dazzling sight in the grayness surrounding it. Despite a ban by the provincial governor, gasoline and most food products are paid for in Pakistani rupees because they cost less that way.[1]

Today I am received in the guesthouse of the central city by the governor himself. Hakim Taniwal is an educated man who completed his studies in Germany, then lived in Pakistan for seventeen years. After that, he and his family lived in exile in Australia until the fall of the Taliban persuaded him to return to Afghanistan. He was named governor in May 2003.[2] He is nice enough but seems rather overwhelmed by events. He does not seem very comfortable. Could it be the combination of his turban and his elegant gray Western suit?

"My work is so hard; I'm having trouble carrying it out suitably." Taniwal at least has the merit of recognizing this, with a sincerity that is disarming and unusual in a high official. "My position involves enormous responsibilities. For example, I'm having a terrible time settling the constant disputes that erupt between the people I govern, whether fights over land or businesses, or mere disagreements between tribes.

After twenty-three years of war, everyone is demanding something, and there is obviously not enough land to go around. Values have changed: a boy who was seven at the beginning of the Communist revolution is now a thirty-year-old man. During all those years, he did not really go to school, he probably fled to Pakistan with his family, and he was dragged from one refugee camp to another. The tribal structure used to be better respected. The elders possessed real authority over the young people, and the young listened to them. Today their influence has diminished. There's the same development going on in the government: it's no longer credible. It's weak and has no revenues, even though the least it could do is prove itself capable of levying taxes! But most of the war chiefs who control the financial windfall of border revenues still fail to transfer these enormous sums into the central coffers."

I ask him about the U.S. presence: "What are the American soldiers based here and in Gardez doing?"

"They're fighting Al-Qaeda."

"Are you sure? No one out on the street believes it. . . ."

"Well, let's say that's what they're supposed to be doing. . . ."

"But does the local population accept it? Those Americans don't seem to have good relationships with the local people."

"That may be true in the neighboring villages, but not in Khost. Here we're close to the border with Pakistan, and the Americans are training our border guards so that they'll at least know how to respond in case of an Al-Qaeda attack!"

"But there's no Al-Qaeda in Khost?"

"No, not really. A little . . . probably a few individuals. . . ."

"How do you recognize the members of Al-Qaeda, and how do you distinguish between them and the Taliban?"

"For us it's very simple: any individual who fights against us belongs to Al-Qaeda. If the Americans were to leave Afghanistan tomorrow, the population would feel less safe, since everything would become fuzzier. . . . For the moment, it's good they're there, particularly because of the Pakistani factor. (Everyone knows the Pakistanis armed the Taliban and still haven't given up on the idea of conquering Afghanistan. Their country is a headquarters for regrouping Al-Qaeda members.) Then, when the National Afghan Army is in place, along with our police and other state institutions, perhaps we'll be able to manage alone."

Displaying a rare honesty, the governor confesses his sins regarding the Taliban phenomenon, admitting he was also fooled: "At first, the people seemed to accept the Taliban. I myself felt close to that movement; I supported it. Why? Because the mujahideen had no morals, they were poorly organized, incapable of forming a government. I thought all those religious men who had come out of the madrasa, who arrived barefoot and empty-handed, were really going to keep their promises, that is, improve the security of our country. Like many people, I believed in providential men who would get our country on the right path, without having any political ambitions."

How did he come to realize his mistake?

"Because they formed their own government, started to drive around in fancy cars, and because, once they'd come to power, they became aggressive. They didn't know how to manage that power; they were lacking in intelligence. People need space: when there are no media, no cassette machines, no television, no music, no secular schools but only madrasas, and when you don't even have the right to shave . . . society suffocates! You can't prohibit everything. They didn't understand that."

Hakim Taniwal doesn't think these "stupid" limits on freedom were dictated to the Afghan Taliban by Pakistan, or even by Al-Qaeda. "In a certain way, Afghans are naive and stupid. . . . I'm the first to regret it, but I have to acknowledge it. Especially the Pashtuns, who claim to do everything better than other people: nobody can be better Muslims or better warriors than they are. In friendship as well, they're the best, and in political fervor. If they were Communists, they'd kill their fathers and mothers to achieve ideological purity. We are a radical and maximalist people."

As in Kandahār, a *mazar* (holy site) was recently built at the entrance to the city, in memory of the thirty-nine Arabs who lost their lives to U.S. bombs in the autumn of 2001 while meditating in the Matachina Mosque. For lack of names, the thirty-nine tombs, arranged between high earthen walls, include inscriptions of the fallen Arabs' place of origin in Arabic—"from Karachi," "from Yemen," "from Quetta"—and are heavily decorated with garlands, scarves, ribbons, and other pieces of colored fabric. Women wanting to have babies have often tied knots in the cloth as a symbol of their wish. Once dedicated to the great men of the past, to the Muslim conquerors, and to local sages, these modern *mazar* are the new holy sites of Islam, objects of real veneration, something that is not well regarded by everyone, however.

"Get knowledge, even in China": these words, inscribed in chalk on the wall of a classroom belonging to Hafizullah, a professor of English at the University of Khost, supposedly constitute a Pashto proverb emphasizing the importance of education. The University of Khost was created in 1996, the year the Taliban came to power, and was very quickly closed and exiled to Peshawar, Pakistan. Now it's trying to reorganize. As we are chatting outside under the autumnal sun, surrounded by a half-dozen students listening silently to their teacher, Hafizullah insists on the priority to be granted to education. The young men (there are no women) seem more curious about my presence—they observe my every movement—than about how the discussion is proceeding. "Under the Taliban, one of my students was the lieutenant governor and head of customs, proof that some understood the importance of English. Others came out against teaching it on the pretext that, as Muslims, we should be learning Arabic, not English. These same Taliban commanders came to ask for my help when they had to write letters to the U.S. troops during the attack of 2001." He finds this amusing.

Pasha Khan Zadran is a former member of the mujahideen and a figure in the jihad against the Soviet occupier (1979–1989) and in the resistance movement against the Taliban (1996–2001). He briefly occupied the post of provincial governor of Paktīa at the fall of the fundamentalist regime, before being thrust aside by Kabul, which preferred the moderate Taniwal. The former local commander, having in the meantime taken refuge in his native village, is still reluctant to accept the authority of the central government and that of the new governor of Khost.[3]

In addition, he still controls about twelve miles (and two checkpoints) on the winding road from Gardez, just before Khost. It's enough to prevent Governor Taniwal from taking that route, even though it's the only one to Kabul that's close to being suitable for motor vehicles. Taniwal is forced to take long and dangerous detours along back roads. (The governor has not mentioned this problem during our interview, no doubt wanting to minimize its import.)

Neither a Taliban nor a member of Al-Qaeda, but a war chief and veteran of the jihad against the Soviets, Pasha Khan is stubbornly demanding his share of power and challenging Taniwal. That quarrel, which drags on interminably, illustrates the many difficulties the central power has and its lack of credibility among the local population.[4] Pasha Khan is an ambiguous figure; nevertheless, he is far from unpopular in his country even now. During the first Loya Jirga in 2002, he is said to have prevented opposing tribal chiefs and other local delegates from taking "his" road and even reported them to the U.S. forces stationed nearby, denouncing them as "Taliban" and close to Al-Qaeda. The counterattack was not long in coming: their villages were bombed by U.S. planes.

Amir Bahir, a local correspondent for Radio Free Europe, provided me with details regarding Pasha Khan's importance on the local political scene: "When the United States finally arrived with Massoud's Northern Alliance, Pasha Khan controlled the Khost airport. It was total chaos; the four hundred Arabs in bin Laden's entourage wanted to flee to Pakistan. Mullah Khakani, a former member of the mujahideen who had become a Taliban, enjoined Pasha Khan to abandon the airport. He refused and the fighting began. Aided by the United States, Pasha Khan emerged the winner, whereas Mullah Khakani crossed the border and took refuge in Miranshah. On the first day of the emergency session of the Loya Jirga called in June 2002, Pasha Khan nevertheless came out against the Northern Alliance, refusing to let the 'Tajiks' take power in our region. Karzai had been incautious enough to give him a paper signed by him stipulating that he was de facto commander of

the three border regions in the east: Paktīa, Paktika, and Khost." For a
year and a half, the fighting between the Northern Alliance and Pasha
Khan's men was fierce. The city of Khost lived under a dual regime:
Pasha Khan's and the one the central government tried to impose. "Today, Taniwal, and hence Kabul, seems to have taken the upper hand,
but that's surely temporary," the journalist explains.

To meet with Pasha Khan, I start out on the road he controls. As I am
leaving Khost, I note the presence of portraits of Karzai and of Taniwal
above the brick gate built by the Taliban. In the absence of his father,
it is twenty-eight-year-old Abdul Waki, one of Pasha Khan's sons, who
receives me in a shack protected by antique Soviet cannons. The Americans have just visited him to verify that there are no Taliban or Al-
Qaeda agents hiding in this mountain pass. Pasha Khan's men have
given their word. So long as they're there, neither group will be able to
use that corridor.

A few months ago, in June 2003, these same U.S. troops arrested
Abdul Waki, who spent a month in prison at the Bagram airport, not
far from Kabul, in the company of about a hundred other prisoners,
who, he asserted, were all "innocent" like him. "They had taken us for
Al-Qaeda," he mutters by way of explanation, a confusion that Pasha
Khan's son seems to forgive them, however. How did he get away? They
admitted their mistake, but at the same time Hamid Karzai intervened,
concerned to maintain good relations with the Zadran tribe.

As for the "truce" with Governor Taniwal, it's at a standstill. Pasha
Khan would like to be done with it and sign an accord with the central
government, but the latter is not responding. Might his conditions be
exorbitant? "My father wants only two things," Abdul emphasizes, "to
defend the rights of the Pashtun nation and to be named to a post with
the central government." He bitterly points out the excessive power
of the former Northern Alliance, and hence of the Tajiks within the
government, especially at the Department of Defense. "The Americans
were happy to find us when they needed to fight the Taliban locally, but
in the conflict between my father and the central government they refuse to get involved. No one is helping us anymore," laments the young

man. "Frankly, we just don't understand those Americans. The Taliban often cross the border to hand tracts to travelers, even on the highway. They brave the soldiers barricaded inside their base, just a few steps away! In Miranshah, just the other side of the border, many collaborators of Al-Qaeda live undisturbed. I know it, my whole family lives there! The Americans would only have to cross the border to finish their mission! No, theirs is a strange strategy: they let the situation bog down. Yet in the autumn of 2001, when we helped them retake the country, they showed us what they could do. We members of the Zadran tribe desire only one thing: stability. The overactive presence of the Northern Alliance does not please us, and Karzai is too symbolic a president. Only the former king, Zahir Shah, is there to settle disputes; all the others just divert the money entrusted to them by the foreign powers to their own ends. Commander Massoud, for his part, is a true strategist as well as a diplomat. He was just as good at softening up the Russians, from whom he received weapons, as he is at working with the Americans. Massoud may be the only one who really wanted our country's independence, and that's the reason he was eliminated, maybe even by the Americans."

He lowers his head and won't say anything more.

Mina is twenty-eight years old, has been married for six years, and has given birth to a child. Originally from Logar Province, she has lived in Khost for four years. Under the Communists, she resided in Mazār-e-Sharif and Kabul, when her father, a government employee, was working in those two cities. Dressed entirely in red with matching nail polish, the young woman receives me in the family home. Mina is a teacher at the girls' school in the neighborhood. Her family are former Communists: the eldest son was sent to study at the police academy of Ryazan' in the USSR in the late 1980s, and the second son died in 1994 fighting Hekmatyar's mujahideen. They have now become completely pro-American, as if what counted for them was collaboration with the invader, whoever it might be. We touch on the subject of Chechnya. The battle for independence there leaves them perplexed: why would such a small and weak country want to leave the bosom of mighty Russia? It's always better to be on the strongest side.

Only two women, including Mina, were chosen for the Loya Jirga in Khost Province, since Pashtun families do not exactly encourage women's political activities. Mina has plans: to fight for greater rights for women, especially the right to education. This right is often violated in the southeast, where the number of girls' schools being blown up continues to mount. Nevertheless, she seems a bit bewildered by the method of "conducting a campaign" and declares she has not received any instructions at all about it. Of course, she would like to hold a dialogue with the women of the region, but she would need to find transportation. Mina is very sensitive to the issue of domestic violence because her elder sister is married to a man who regularly beats her (and promises never to do it again). That sort of behavior is not rare in Pashtun marriages. Will Mina be listened to? She doubts it, but she embraces her sister's cause. "For us, her husband is Al-Qaeda," she says without humor, and the group bursts into laughter.

On Friday afternoon, I leave Khost for the village of Chovay, on a neighboring mountain. Yunas, who is accompanying me, wants me to meet his family. We leave the asphalt and take a trail, which turns into a road running alongside a stony, dry riverbed. A few austere *qala* appear out of nowhere on the hills, their doors stubbornly closed. Our taxi climbs to the last house in the village, "the highest of all," Yunas proudly declares. It's also the oldest, built fifty years ago by his paternal grandfather. Today the families of Yunas's four brothers live there, as well as his mother. His five sisters have been living with their in-laws for a long time. Yunas is twenty-five, the youngest. Three of his brothers have settled in Dubai, where they work as taxi drivers and shopkeepers. The eldest has lived there for twenty years. Every month, the brothers contribute between eight hundred and a thousand dollars to the family.

Every year, ever since she made her pilgrimage to Mecca, Yunas's mother has isolated herself in one room of the house for the last ten days of Ramadan, "as it is said in the Koran," her son points out with the greatest respect. He is therefore not sure whether she wants me to greet her. When we arrive, just before *iftar*, he nevertheless leads me straight to her quarters. Dressed all in white and bowing toward the setting sun, the old woman is saying her last afternoon prayer. She feebly shakes the hand I hold out to her but does not make any gesture to leave. Her hands and feet are painted with henna motifs. The fifteen or so children in the household gather at our side and look at us, their eyes big. When she's finished her prayer, Yunas's mother begins to read aloud a few pages from the Koran that one of her granddaughters hands her, a reading interrupted by domestic orders given rapidly to anyone who pokes a nose through the doorway. Finally, she recites holy words under her breath, telling her beads and sometimes joining in the conversation whispered by her granddaughters, only to resume her psalmody even more quickly, not the least concerned with my presence. The pilgrimage she completed five years ago, at a cost of twelve hundred dollars, paid by her sons, changed her social status in the village: today Yunas's mother is a respected hajji.

Yunas's father died of hepatitis B when Yunas was five. The eldest son, then fifteen, had to take charge of the household and left for Dubai. "My father traded in wood between Pakistan and Afghanistan," Yunas says. "I remember long lines of camels staggering under their loads of wood and gifts he brought back to us from the cities of Pakistan. He worked very hard, but we still ate rice cakes three meals a day. I spent more than fifteen years in Pakistan. I did my studies there at the encouragement of my brothers, even though it cost them money. My dream would be to go to India for two years to study to become an engineer. I'd leave my wife and daughter here. But for the moment that's not feasible."

Yunas, his mother, and I are eating while sitting cross-legged on the edge of the *dastakhan,* with about ten other people watching us. The food, served in small tin bowls, is spicy like Indian food, combining beef and curry, fried spinach, fried eggs, and fried potatoes with tomato. It is delicious. Yunas's mother does not speak much except to complain that her sons do not say their prayers at the proper time. Under our very eyes, Yunas corrects this lapse.

Later, in the room shared by Yunas and his wife, who have gone to sleep elsewhere, I am visited by two of Yunas's cousins. They are happy to speak to me openly. One of them knows Arabic perfectly, having learned it at the madrasa, and has read the Old and New Testaments. After studying religious science for sixteen years, he has returned to the village and is devoting himself to writing a book on the relations between Christianity, Judaism, Hinduism, Buddhism, and Islam. His point of view on the current situation is interesting:

"We have nothing against the presence of the Americans if they prove to us that they will really establish democracy and leave. If that's not the case, we're against it; they have methods we don't appreciate. For example, they wrongly accuse an individual of belonging to Al-Qaeda and force him to flee to the mountains. Once he's in the underground, he'll most certainly become a member of the international terrorist organization! When the Taliban took power, I sought refuge in Germany, where I pursued my religious studies. In such an observant society as the Afghan one, and with the low education level we have here, it was easy for the Taliban to dupe everyone. Terrorism is a response to the unilateral and arrogant behavior of the major—non-Muslim—powers against the Muslims, and we are outraged that the United States continues to support Israel so overtly and so blindly. But we are also shocked by the ambivalent attitude of Saudi Arabia, which insists on remaining the friend of the United States so that it can continue to sell them its oil. While the Saudi government pursues its financial interests, the average Saudi, who is by nature very devout, hates the United States. For our part, we must do everything to modify the false view the Western countries have of our relationship to terrorism, which reflects on every Muslim on this planet.

"When I arrived in Germany, I thought I'd be well received, but people saw me only as a Muslim, a potentially dangerous person, a terrorist. We all ought to keep in mind the verse from the Koran that exhorts us to get to know one another better and to get along. The misunderstandings between the different worlds, the different civilizations —even though we live in a 'global village'—are such that when I returned to Afghanistan, everyone bombarded me with questions: how had I been able to practice our religion in a Western country? Were our laws respected in non-Muslim lands? When I explained to them that freedom of religion was almost greater there than it is here, they were surprised and distraught. It's that ignorance gap we must try to fill. The money in our military budget ought to be used for an information campaign on Islam as it is perceived in the West and on the way to modify its image. Or else our opinion makers ought to be sent to take 'Western studies training' and to grasp the reality on their own. In that way, we would cut the ground out from under the feet of the terrorist networks, which can only benefit from the preconceived media images on both sides and from the absence of real information and mutual curiosity."

In his view, the religious education he received, primarily in Pakistan, is solid, but he regrets that certain subjects are not better adapted to the modern world, such as, for example, the teaching of English. He believes it ought to be systematic, like Arabic and computer studies. "Ideally, an engineer could be a graduate of a madrasa," he suggests, at the same time refuting the idea that bin Laden and his entourage graduated from religious schools. Of the Taliban around them, 10 percent—no more—were experts in religion. "It was a gang of impostors." Conversely, he does not believe the conspiracy theories insinuating that Osama bin Laden is a U.S. agent. "That's impossible, since his rage comes from the presence of U.S. troops in the holy land of Saudi Arabia. The reason he still hasn't been found is that many are prepared to sacrifice themselves for him, and because his network is not based solely on money—another factor the West refuses to admit when it puts a price on Osama's head—more proof of the gulf of misunderstanding that separates us!"

My interlocutor calmly considers the consequences of September 11. He quickly understood that the terrorist attacks would produce serious tensions between the Christian and Muslim worlds. For him, following the attack on Iraq and the failure of the U.S. occupation, world terrorism can only gain in strength: "The mind-set of the September 11 martyrs corresponds to that of the Palestinians who are driven to suicide. The pro-Israel policy of the United States sows seeds of terrorism throughout the Arab world. Osama lived in Afghanistan among his Taliban 'hosts' for only six years, but the men chosen for the suicide mission piloting the three planes had been mentally preparing for their act for the previous fifteen to twenty years."

29

THE MINOR HOLIDAYS

With the approach of the Īd holidays,* celebrated when the new moon appears, I sense an excitement rising in the population, a combination of anticipation and true joy at the idea of being close to loved ones or young wives again. It's the only thing people talk about, and the only thing they think about; it's impossible to make any plans before the famous celebrations—"We'll see after Īd" is the invariable response. I'm amused that no one knows exactly when the holiday begins, and there was the same uncertainty a month ago in Badakhshān about the official beginning of the month of fasting. This is all a result of the complexity of the lunar calendar. In the rural areas, I'm told, when the elders in the mountain villages catch sight of the moon or, more prosaically, hear about it on the radio, they order the youngsters to climb to nearby mountaintops, the highest they can manage, and light enormous fires. Thanks to these orange lights in the darkness, the solitary traveler savoring his last *iftar* is informed that the holiday begins the next day.

Īd-al-fitr is also called feast of the breaking of the fast. According to Janine Sourdel and Dominique Sourdel in *Dictionnaire historique de l'islam* (Paris: PUF, 1996; repr. coll., "Quadrige," 2004), it is "one of the two canonical holidays that punctuate the Muslim year at fixed times, based on the lunar calendar in use since the era of the prophet Muhammad. It is characterized by participation in a solemn prayer and in marks of devotion—such as visits to gravesites—that often become occasions for enjoyment and family reunions accompanied by the exchange of presents. Despite its name, it arouses far more interest than the feast of sacrifice."

———

One morning before Īd, I find the two employees at the reception desk of my guesthouse in Kabul unwrapping packages with the impatient joy of Christmas morning. In anticipation of the holiday, the management has bought them new suits and shoes. These two young Afghans are very elegant, proud to be wearing Western clothes. One of the two, Arrash, a twenty-one-year-old Pashtun educated entirely in Pakistan, recently returned to Kabul because his uncle, a professor of medicine in Lyon, is planning to have him go to Europe once Arrash has set aside the money by working for a few months as a receptionist in this guesthouse. Arrash lived in Peshawar, then in Islamabad, the capital of Pakistan, which is both spurned and envied by the Afghans for being architecturally more beautiful than its Afghan counterpart and, above all, cleaner and more modern. He looks on Afghan customs with vague disgust; although they constitute an important part of his identity, they also repulse him and make him feel ashamed. Nothing of what is happening in Kabul seems to interest him, not the daily efforts at reconstruction or the failures of the new government, even less the relations between the center and the regional warlords. According to Arrash, all these factors serve only to place his country among the "backward" and "uncivilized" countries.

Arrash acquits himself of his duties with a certain contempt. Why continue to work here? "Because of that girl," he replies, nodding toward a very beautiful Afghan woman in a black coat, jeans, and a blood-red head scarf, sitting up straight in front of her computer in the Internet room recently opened to the public. They met; he talked about marriage and offered jewelry. She just presented him with a talking greeting card, in which a recorded voice tirelessly repeats, *"Assalam alaykum, Īd mubarak!"* (May the Lord be with you, best wishes for Īd)—which he cannot resign himself to putting away. But when the organization for which she works (a local humanitarian group) is connected to the World Wide Web—it's only a question of days—they will have less of a chance to see each other because she will have no more reason to come over.

I meet Rahmatullah in Khost, where he lives to be close to his job. He has been married for a year to a young woman from his native village far away—in the central mountains of Wardak—and had to leave his wife behind. The mention of their first meeting makes him visibly redden. In Afghan society, it's the kind of subject one approaches only with great modesty. Similarly, a Pashtun man will never utter the first name of his wife or of his sister to a man who has asked him for it unless the latter is a medical doctor. Rahmatullah's first meeting with his wife took place at least ten years ago (she was fifteen and he thirteen) on a hill not far from the village. His wife, following the Pashtun tradition, is in fact one of his many cousins. The family ties and the holidays allowed him to see her several times and to get to know her somewhat before the engagement. Then the wedding took place.

In passing, Rahmatullah wants to provide me with a few prosaic details on the subject. His marriage cost him a great deal: four thousand dollars in Pakistani rupees were paid to his in-laws, and some three thousand dollars were spent to hold the banquet and purchase the bride's trousseau, including the many pieces of jewelry—gold rings, bracelets, earrings, and necklaces (but he got them at a discount, since one of Rahmatullah's uncles was working in Dubai at the time and had them "set aside" for him)—seven thousand dollars in all, a large sum for the average Afghan. But every young man applies himself for years to save such a sum for himself or for his elder brother in anticipation of the big day, which is considered the most important in the couple's life.

Rahmatullah, who was not the only suitor, was thus the one chosen. Another candidate, mortified at being refused, finally accepted the "compromise" of marrying one of the bride's sisters, but he remained bitter. "Six months after my wedding, in an act of revenge," Rahmatullah recounts, "members of his family opened fire on our house." The young man shows me photographs of the bullet holes he keeps in the memory of his digital camera, which he's never without. "My father was alone, he took his only hunting rifle down from the living room wall, and he fired. He couldn't let it go; that would have brought shame on our family! It was unfair, four against one, but the exchange of gunfire lasted for several minutes nonetheless. Fortunately, nobody was wounded. But the problem's still the same: we were attacked and must respond to save our honor. The village elders will find a solution to our conflict; that's their role. We hope to have news from them after the Īd holidays, *insh Allah.*"

At the Khost bazaar, prices have risen significantly on the eve of the largest family gathering of the year. Nevertheless, the men spend their days there and buy for the entire household. Rahmatullah has chosen a ring with a faux amethyst for his wife, who is already wearing three rings. Before he offers it to her, he puts it on his own little finger. In the greatest secrecy, Rahmatullah agrees to show me photos of the young woman, taken with the digital camera and kept safe from prying eyes on a disk in a locked desk drawer. He always keeps the key on his person.

Like many Afghans—whether they are war chiefs, governors, police officers, journalists, or ordinary laborers—Rahmatullah not only knows many poems by heart but also writes them. For the most part, they are *landay,* short poems consisting of nine iambs in the first line and thirteen in the second that illustrate various themes of daily life or, more precisely, the relationship between husband and wife. According to Rahmatullah, "a Pashtun worthy of the name must know at least a hundred *landay* by heart!" (There's the same romanticism, it seems to me, in the traditional songs, which often have melodious tunes and exalt the anticipation of being loved in a distant village or a couple's reunion on a hilltop in a fine mist.)

What's nice about Rahmatullah is his sincere desire to open his illiterate partner to the modern world, as much as that is possible. Not only does he want his wife to learn to read and write—he dreams of the time when he'll be able to send her letters and she'll be able to reply on her own—but he also intends personally to teach her to speak rudimentary English and to operate a computer so that she can learn the "technologies of the contemporary world." For the time being, Rahmatullah is thinking of teaching her to use his satellite phone so that they can talk to each other between Wardak and Khost, since he misses her voice "terribly."

Hafizullah, a journalist in Kabul, takes me to celebrate Īd with his loved ones. I wake up in Bumbay in the district of Chak—forty-four miles from the capital and at an altitude of 7,283 feet, facing a circle of mountains with snow-covered peaks. This morning is particularly windy; looking out from the fogged-up windows, I admire hoar frost forming minuscule snow flurries. To mark the holiday, Hafiz's grandmother has put kohl on her old eyelids. Her manner is stiff, and she is wearing a pale pink dress and a matching shawl. She is happy to see this grandson who has made a special trip from the capital, and she takes advantage of the situation to ask him for news of Habibullah, his elder brother. Habibullah is thirty years old and has already lived in Cairo for ten years, where he is finishing his studies at the prestigious Al-Azhar University. Every year, the grandmother expects him to come as he has promised, but the visit is always postponed (it may be next spring, since it's time for him to find a wife—at home, of course).

For the first family breakfast in a month, the women prepare gallons of tea with milk, heated in the tandoor. They are in the kitchen, a very long room separate from the house that faces glacial mountains. Hafizullah has bathed and done his ablutions; wrapped tightly in his brown *patu,* he walks at a good pace on the dusty road, headed to the mosque for a special morning prayer celebrating the end of the fast.

During all this time, the women bustle about. The say little, except to exchange a few comments on the tasks remaining to be completed. In the silence, you hear only the jangle of their delicate bracelets; some have so many of them that the bracelets cover their entire forearms. The women begin by cooking the delicious nan cakes. The balls of dough were prepared the night before. Their gestures are precise and purposeful; nothing is left to chance. One woman flattens the dough with a wooden rolling pin; the second places the dough on a circular mold, then applies it rapidly to a wall of the humming, fiery oven. It comes out cooked after three minutes, and a third woman stacks the delicate, sweet-smelling cakes and carries them "in to the men." There are about fifteen per meal. When the bread is finished, other dishes must be heated. It takes only four branches to block the mouth of the tandoor. Saucepans and other cooking pots are placed on top. One of the women, breaking the silence, asks me if in my country I cook my own bread in a tandoor as they do here, and she is astonished when I say no.

In Hafizullah's absence, his sixty-five-year-old uncle, thirty-year-old cousin, twenty-year-old brother, and another, twelve-year-old cousin (who does the serving between the guest rooms, which are heated by a wood stove, and the kitchen) have the responsibility of receiving the visitors, whether from nearby or far away, who come to express their good wishes. They will make the rounds this afternoon, taking care always to leave two or three men at home, since a stranger never enters an Afghan home when only women are present. The first to come by is a neighbor, who stays for exactly seven minutes, enough time to congratulate those present and to accept and drink the cup of tea offered to him. For the holiday, the oilcloth *dastarkhan* used the night before has been replaced by a colored tablecloth, on which are served steaming pancakes, glasses of fresh milk, eggs cooked in oil, still-warm baked apples, and cakes and cookies prepared for the occasion.

To enter the house belonging to Hafizullah's family, you first have to pass alongside a high ocher wall; then you discover a small wooden gate with a heavy door. Once you've gone through it, you find yourself facing a staircase that runs the length of the large building. Terraces open onto a vast orchard sloping down to an *arek* (a thin stream of water). On the first floor is the library, a rectangular room filled with volumes arranged in cabinets that creak when they're opened. This mountain village holds the only library in the region, a treasure amassed over time by a family of religious men and intellectuals and now consisting of more than five thousand volumes in Dari, Pashto, Arabic, and even English. "Unfortunately, our library suffered a great deal under the Communists, the mujahideen, and the Taliban," says Hafizullah, though he is happy to show it to me. "We even possess a New Testament in Pashto,[1] which we have to hide most of the time." Stashed under sacks of potatoes during the Taliban period, the Holy Book recently returned to the library shelves. But then two days ago, one of Hafizullah's cousins decided to hide it again temporarily for the Īd holidays. Some obtuse guests might not appreciate the sight of the Christian Bible in Muslim territory.

The library Hafizullah is so proud of was conceived by his grandfather, who died in 1997. There was no girls' school in that remote village,[2] where such institutions did not exist under the mujahideen,[3] any more than they did under the Taliban. The grandfather himself educated all the women in the family at home: his wife, his sisters, his daughters, and even his granddaughters, right alongside the boys, who also received lessons at school. "My grandfather was born in this village and studied at the mosque; he and his father were much respected mullahs. Every day we sat in front of the blackboard from seven to nine in the morning. Friday morning was exam day, with different prizes for the girls and for the boys," Hafizullah remembers with emotion. "The boys' school in the village was a madrasa, and during the jihad the level of education was quite low. I learned English here with my grandfather, who went to work for the government under His Majesty Zahir Shah—he was assistant to the prime minister—after completing his religious education. He himself learned English in Kabul, with the help of his friends, no doubt."

That education bore fruit: since mid-2002, Hafiz's three female cousins still living in the village compose, publish, and distribute a review called *Gudar,* thanks to financial aid from a shopkeeper uncle in London. "It's a publication written by women for women," Hafizullah insists. Without getting support of any kind (except for financial aid from his uncle), the review is being published three times a year. Although they are educated, the young women remain withdrawn; they use a camera for their "reporting" but stubbornly refuse to let me take their picture. The mere sight of my camera causes a wave of panic.

The editorial for the first issue of *Gudar,* "the Social and Cultural Magazine of Pashtun Sisters" (its English subtitle), was written in Pashto by Rushna, a twenty-five-year-old aunt of Hafizullah's, then translated into English by a physician uncle living in Peshawar. The authors are not paid for their work. The budget for a thousand copies can be as high as four hundred dollars, primarily for printing costs. Distribution is irregular. It takes place through family networks and friends, covering nearby regions and extending as far as Peshawar.

In this first issue, I find, among other things, an article on "the problems of women's rights," attributed to a former minister of refugees; a reflection on "the responsibilities of men and women in Afghan society," written by a woman; advice on the best way to classify books and publications in one's personal library; an illustrated report on Siamese twins; a poem composed by a Palestinian woman and translated into Urdu; a Pashtun alphabet with Arabic letters and their pronunciation; a model letter of congratulations from a young woman to her friend on the occasion of the birth of a son; the English alphabet; games; and domestic instructions on "how to keep a better house."

The editorial is worth considering at length. I reproduce it in full, translated from Pashto into English.[4]

We are happy to launch this new review, dedicated to women in the rural areas, whose level of education is poor and who are the most neglected group in our male-dominated society, where women are still the object of discriminatory attitudes. We consider it urgent to promote education, consciousness-raising, motivation, and a positive change in men's behavior toward women in this country devastated by war, where the illiteracy rate is very high. For not only does our religion, Islam, clearly emphasize that women and men have the same right to receive an education and to perfect their skills, but we women have already proved ourselves in the respect we have for our cultures and our traditions, and in our zeal for work in the fields and various seasonal tasks. Whether harvesting the crops or taking the animals out to graze, women have always worked alongside the men; there is therefore no reason for them to be deprived of education. This review is the first stage in our emancipation, and we hope that in the future reading it will contribute toward improving the living conditions of women in the rural areas. A library of more than five thousand books, which we are trying to take on the road, is available to the women of the region, and we intend to launch a local radio program to help educate every household in our mountain regions.

We are aware that this effort at education is particularly difficult under current living conditions, but we believe it necessary, especially since our leaders have not seemed to realize the urgency of balanced development between the cities and the rural areas. They certainly opened the door to progress and prosperity in large cities such as Kabul, but they left most of the rural zones in ignorance and poverty. Even though a large number of publications for women exist in Kabul, none corresponds to the needs of the female population living outside the urban zones, even though they are in the majority. Are these "central" journals convinced that our level of education does not even allow us to have such aspirations?

Gudar is a traditional Pashto word designating "the place"— the riverside or a spring—around which mature women, young women, and little girls gather to discuss their concerns while filling their jugs, which they will carry back to the house on their shoulders. We want to concentrate on the most frequent problems our sisters are facing, and at the same time we aspire to be a source of knowledge and entertainment for them. We deeply hope our readers will help us by sharing their suggestions and opinions in writing.

When the magazine first appeared, Hafizullah explains in his soft, calm voice, many people in the region were shocked that some husbands allowed their wives to sign their own names to the articles. "Our goal is precisely to change that mind-set and to urge our neighbors' educated sons to read aloud to their mothers and sisters articles that directly concern them," the editorial continues.

While listening to us with one ear, the old bachelor uncle chews *naswar* and spits it out in copious quantities into a jug beside him. That saves him from having to open the window and quickly expel his quid outdoors, which I have seen people do many times in other houses.

Hafizullah shows me the library, where we take pleasure in slowly opening the five glass doors with shelves filled with books. They are categorized by subject—"Pashtun literature," "history," "religion," and so forth—thanks to nicely calligraphed signs done by Hafizullah himself at his grandfather's request. There are many complete collections of magazines in Pashto and Dari published during the jihad and then under Dr. Najibullah. Hafiz hands me a copy of the June 1986 issue of the political magazine *Al-Mujahideen,* published in Arabic by the Jamiyat-i-Islami Party.

The most precious works are found elsewhere, in a less accessible place, a sort of storage room smelling of overripe apples, at one end containing a padlocked glass cabinet. "We're the only library in the province, and there are those who come from far away to consult a work. Unfortunately, unscrupulous people have stolen too many books from us, and we were obliged to enforce stricter rules. So now, they consult the books exclusively on-site. But we never turn away anyone," explains Hafizullah. The complete list of works, kept up to date by his grandfather, was lost during the jihad. Hafizullah will soon take on the task of establishing another one, this time on computer.

Hafizullah would like to show me the famous copy of the New Testament; he thinks his cousin has hidden it here. He doesn't have the key to the reserve collection on him and sends someone to get it. "Many people don't understand why we want to keep this book," Hafizullah comments sadly. "A minority even think that it's anti-Islamic to keep the Gospels in a Muslim home. And none of our visitors, not even the most religious people, have manifested any curiosity to read it. A very famous mullah even berated us for keeping such a book in our library, referring to the prophet Muhammad, who said that Muslims must study the Koran and not waste their time reading the Bible. Some people will even go so far as to accuse us of proselytizing for the Christian religion. I read the Bible and sometimes even listen to programs on Christianity in Pashto on Radio Free Europe," Hafizullah confides, opening the doors to the cabinet. "There's a mathematical treatise in here that was handwritten a hundred and fifty years ago, and also our Korans rolled up in cloth."

I notice, in fact, piles of dusty books rolled up in different multicolor fabrics. Why are there so many?

"Because we're a large family, and each of us owns his own copy," explains Hafizullah. "We have about fifty in all, including about twenty stored here. These are our oldest Korans in Arabic. Some date from more than a hundred and fifty years ago."

One after another, we unroll the colored cloths to admire the Korans, and, slipped in among them, we discover the New Testament.

At lunch, Sultan, one of the village mullahs, declares that during the *khotba,* the Friday-prayer sermon, there is no question of honoring "this pro-American, hence secular, government that is not implementing the Sharia, which we fought for during the years of jihad and obtained under the Taliban!" The roguish religious man, with his long white beard and squinty eyes, particularly mistrusts the old warlords called on to play a role in the new government: "The Afghans who collaborate with the Americans are not thinking about the future of their country. They live from day to day in relative peace. They forget that these same Americans have wreaked havoc in the various Taliban factions, after financing them for so long. As for the Tajiks in the Northern Alliance, such as Rabbani and Massoud, they really worked only for themselves and their ethnic group; the Taliban never did that!" he exclaims, looking offended.

The mullah does not hide his Taliban opinions—for example, he desires the return of the caliphate—and admits he was chief of security in the neighboring region of Uruzgān during the reign of the "seminarians." The religious differences between them and the mujahideen are slight, and people are grateful to the "seminarians" for at least making a real effort to set up an Islamist government, explains the old man. He has once more become a farmer, but he keeps his ear to the radio receiver every day at regular hours to listen to the news on the BBC and on Radio-Azadi, in Pashto and Dari. "This morning, in fact, I heard the journalist for the Pashto branch of the BBC report Mullah Omar's best wishes for the Īd holidays. He even added that 'as a good Muslim,' none of us ought to agree to participate in the Loya Jirga or in any elections. We will respect his will," he assures me. "The Taliban fighters are not far away; personally, I'll join them as soon as there's less snow."

Sultan misses the time when he was authorized to fight against local farmers to destroy hundreds of hectares of opium crops on the orders of Kabul, which was then in Taliban hands. "Now the state has lost interest, and cultivation has resumed," he laments. As for the girls' school, Sultan denies any direct opposition by the Taliban but insists on the "conditions of security" necessary for their existence, which are supposedly not in place: "Under the mujahideen, there had been many abuses toward women, so we had to restrict the professions in which they could be employed. But if our women agree to wear the hijab, nothing is forbidden to them." He is doing his utmost to convince me.

At about seven o'clock in the morning, Hafiz takes me to the mosque bearing the name of his grandfather, Abdul Hadi, built by his own hands in 1961. On this third morning of Īd, men from the village have gathered here, not to pray but to take tea together between the first morning prayer before the appearance of the sun (salat al-subh) and the noon prayer, after the sun has reached its zenith (salat al-zuhr). In its heyday, the building was used by only three families, including Hafizullah's ancestors; it is tiny. We sit down among about fifty villagers, including about twenty very young boys, who sample cookies while sipping their tea.[5] Thanks to a clever underground wood heating system, the temperature is constant and evenly distributed. Sitting cross-legged on the outer edge of the dastarkhan, people pass the kettles from hand to hand, conversing under their breath. The atmosphere is easygoing, the curiosity directed at me is great but contained, and I am not poorly received.

I recognize the imam, whom I met yesterday at Hafizullah's house. He has officiated within these walls since they were erected. He says that thanks to money from a local man in the import-export business with Pakistan, a madrasa for girls was built in the village last year. Now nearly two hundred girls are learning the Koran by heart. As is often the case, the Rahmatullah madrasa, named after its patron, is not properly certified by the state, which does not pay its teachers (all of whom are women). Momo, another of Hafizullah's uncles, has accompanied us. He rushes to the back of the mosque, where he has spotted a friend. This morning he got up at five o'clock, prayed, then set out for his nephew's house, where he joined us at seven o'clock. Aged forty, he jovially complains of his rheumatism, but I have seen him walk at a good pace in light leather sandals.

In these festive days, tradition dictates that various games of skill, with balls or marbles or on horseback, be held in the village. But the twenty-three years of war, the Soviet bombs, the disorganization under the mujahideen, followed by the Taliban frenzy, have changed people's habits. Now no one knows if the community of about four hundred households[6] will gather together for games in the dirt roads.

When we get home, we are served a second tea, since it's still early. Hafizullah's satellite phone rings: it's his brother, calling from Egypt. Hafizullah, who has asked him if the mosques also invite the faithful to drink tea on the morning of Īd in Egypt, hears him respond with a laugh that in Arab countries, mosques are "places of prayer, not tea-rooms." His brother adds that the doors are even locked between services. That's unthinkable in Afghanistan.

The two brothers of Hafizullah's cousin's wife arrived last evening, and they get up to give their good wishes to their sister before returning to their village. Hafiz immediately informs the women's quarters of their visit so that the men will not run into the other women of the house.

We decide to leave for Hakimkeil, the native village of a cousin of Hafizullah's, where we are expected for an Īd celebration. We drive for three hours straight on rocky footpaths. The austere fortified *qala* cloistered within their clay walls are impressive: to hug the sloping terrain, their walls, with four high corner towers, are often built as stairs. The region used to have many Buddhist archaeological relics. They were destroyed over time by the local population, which had no regard for any religion established prior to Islam. Hence few were saddened or shocked by the Taliban's destruction of the giant Buddhas of Bāmiān.[7]

Majestically clinging to a hillside between Bumbay and Hakimkeil is the monumental "fortress of the infidels," the stone remains of a giant fort. Its origin? No one here seems to know, but they suspect that this military structure was built neither by nor for Muslims. There is also the "*qala* of nine towers," eight on the buttresses, one in the center. We stop to visit it, surrounded by a host of village boys for whom our intrusion, and especially the presence of a foreign woman, represents a real event. Overhanging its giant entryway, made of wood and forged iron and consisting of two doors, is an inscription in Persian, which reveals that the edifice was built in the mid-eighteenth century by a regional prince and that its construction lasted for more than thirteen years. The fort is circular and still has a hammam with vaulted walls decorated by a few faded frescoes, where the villagers store fodder to keep it dry for the winter.

At a detour in the road, a woman sitting on a donkey and escorted on foot by her husband or brother reveals her beautiful bare and frightened face for a moment. Didn't she hear us? Was she thinking about something else? Panic-stricken, she hastily covers it with her hands, then with a corner of her scarf.

Hakimkeil comprises twenty-three clay houses that dissolve into the landscape. There isn't a single tree, not the slightest vegetation. Hafizullah introduces me to one of his cousins, forty-eight-year-old Habib, a former military commander of the region under the jihad, and then under the Taliban. Today he is unemployed. "I lost fourteen years of my life in combat," he admits sadly. "Even today, I curl up in bed with my right hand on my right leg, as if I was still holding my Kalashnikov."

Habib, who certainly loved to fight, has changed his allegiance almost blindly, moving from one group to another. He no longer believes in political leaders. With time and experience, he has become more realistic, less fundamentalist, but he is still very anti-American. The wholly improbable theory of a plot against Ahmed Shah Massoud seems plausible to him. "Massoud may have been eliminated by U.S. intelligence agents, who are also surely behind the September 11 attacks. Because, as if by chance, not a Jew was present in the Twin Towers of the World Trade Center when they were hit," he declares in all seriousness. His hatred of the Americans is such that he has almost come to miss the Soviet adversary. "At least back then, we had a very well-defined enemy, and we knew why we were fighting. Now the enemy has made himself invisible, his ambitions are even more voracious, and no one in the world can stop him," he laments. "During the jihad, I was a member of Gulbuddin Hekmatyar's party, which was all powerful in our region, since it supplied us with weapons from Pakistan. I met bin Laden in 1982. At the time, people knew he was a rich Arab, but mostly he was a fighter like the others. He kindly provided me with four of the latest walkie-talkies. Then I joined Massoud's troops. When the Taliban arrived in our mountains, I was at the head of two thousand heavily armed men. We all surrendered without a fight, since the 'seminarians' had made a good impression on us: we thought they were going to restore order. They named me chief of security, but they had doubts about my loyalty and arrested me once, then a second time, and finally savagely tortured me. Today my torturers are in power; that's why I have no confidence in the Americans, who are behind the phenomenal growth of the extremist Islamic movements they claim to combat."

Hafizullah silently listens to his cousin without flinching.

For the last fourteen months, Habib has fought hard with the village elders to get them to agree to a religious school for girls: "I showed them the suras in the Koran where the Prophet expressly declares that men and women must receive the same education. But it was no use. They had the impression that sending a future woman to school was a subject of shame, not pride. They called me an infidel."

After its first year of operation, thirty-two students of the seventy school-age children in the village attend the school, including Habib's two daughters, and the process to get it certified by the authorities is well under way. "The villagers realized there was nothing reprehensible about what was being taught in that school. On the contrary." Habib smiles: *that* battle he has won!

30

DETOUR THROUGH PESHAWAR

On this already-cold morning at the famous Khyber Pass, the main crossing point between Afghanistan and Pakistan, the flow of pedestrians going into and coming out of Pakistan is uninterrupted. Young people loaded down with heavy athletic bags, not-so-young people helping one another with their canes, women in burkas carrying their kids in their arms over their veils, children pushing light carts with an odd assortment of things in them, all cross the border, oblivious to its very existence. Now that the Īd vacation break is over, all the trading has resumed, and there is a great deal to do.

Forty-two-year-old Gulbuddin has pulled a multipocketed sleeveless jacket over his Pakistani outfit. An Afghan border guard, he does not conceal his aversion to Hamid Karzai, the president in place: "Who is he? We don't even know him here, and some consider him a traitor, since he has totally let us down. Not only is he unconcerned about the border—even though it ought to be one of his priorities—but he lets himself be manipulated by the Americans and Pakistanis. . . . So it's up to us to defend that border!" Gulbuddin declares that every night armed groups of former Afghan mujahideen "defend themselves" against the "hostile" incursions of the Pakistani armed forces violating the famous "Durand line."[1] As for the contraband in drugs, cars, stereo equipment, and even refrigerators, it's very lucrative, he says, pointing out the distant mountain footpaths, used and known by all. Some of them, where his men are posted, bring in five thousand dollars a day in bribes to be shared with the hierarchy. "As for the Pakistanis, we know them well, they don't frighten us. It's rather the possibility of U.S. bombs that could frighten us," he concludes, giving a belly laugh.

With my Adidas knockoff bag on my shoulder over my full veil in blue rayon, I docilely set off behind him, also to cross that border (illegally, since I don't have a Pakistani visa). Fifty yards later, in an incredible mob of automobiles, handcarts, heavily laden donkeys, and motorbikes all thrown together, we're in Pakistan. I didn't see even the inkling of a customs agent. A road sign declares in English: "Welcome to Pakistan, keep to your left." We rush into a taxi. We are headed toward Peshawar, the capital of the northwestern province, a megalopolis that the Afghans have taken to considering "their" city, because so many of them live there.[2]

The steep road descends toward the plain. The mountain landscape is the same as on the Afghan side, but there are many more billboards here, especially for Pepsi, one of the most popular drinks in the region. The road is much better than in Afghanistan and passes fairly close to military forts with meticulously sharp lines, freshly repainted facades, and English names.

Ayad Abad is a neighborhood of stylish houses built over the last twenty years by Afghans who took refuge on this side of the border. We enter one of them, where the family of twenty-year-old Rosa lives, having arrived in Pakistan when Rosa was six.

The family is viewing the video made of the young woman's "engagement party," held in Mazār-e-Sharif in her absence three months ago.[3] Ludwig, the fiancé, has been here visiting for the last few days and has offered them all a copy of the film. Ludwig is a rich Afghan cousin whose father is in the oil business. In keeping with the wishes of both families, the wedding is to take place two years after the engagement, to give Ludwig time to complete his studies.

On the screen, some five hundred women in outrageous makeup dance together in a restaurant booked for the occasion. None of them has a veil, and the youngest wear short, tight-fitting evening gowns that leave their arms and shoulders bare. Ludwig's mother welcomes the guests one after another. She is wearing a long gown, and a heavy necklace of red stones adorns her chest. The only men present this evening are the four singers and the cameraman. Dancing in more or less lively circles, the women shamelessly sway their hips, elegantly gesturing with their arms. Finally, the fiancé makes his appearance, arm in arm with two of his friends, who are dressed in traditional Afghan costume, a necklace of multicolored paper flowers around his neck. He stands in a corner of the room, his father and sister behind him, and receives lengthy congratulations from the guests. Green bills are thrown at him, but no one gathers them up.

Slender and very elegant in her high-heeled sandals, flowing black pants with orange-flowered motifs, and a matching orange hijab, Rosa tenses up when I suggest to her that I've never run into such a "liberated" silhouette in Kabul. Since she lives in Pakistan, the young Afghan woman has never worn a burka, only a head scarf that conceals her beautiful hair, and she knows only by hearsay the customs of dress in her country of origin. Embarrassed, Rosa shuts herself in the kitchen while we look at the film. I would like to collect her impressions, but with her family present in full force, that's impossible. Of Kabul, which she left fourteen years ago, she remembers only the yard of her house and her school. She speaks Dari (her mother tongue), Pashto, Urdu, Arabic, and, with me, English, all perfectly well. Rosa obtained the equivalent of a high school diploma and would like to major in computers at college. Yet she is teaching "Islamic sciences" at the primary school. Why hasn't she enrolled at the Pakistani university? Because, as an Afghan refugee, she can be only an "auditor," and her diploma will not be recognized when she has finished her schooling. Despite her future husband's veto, it is her dream to continue her studies.

"I don't know Ludwig at all, since we never really had a chance to discuss the subjects that count. He's been staying with us for a week, and we haven't had a moment of privacy, not even a conversation, and it wouldn't be good form to force one or the other."

When we go out for a walk to the central bazaar, however, I note that the couple is arm in arm or hand in hand, but he's the one who mostly seeks physical contact.

"The fact that he has come here gives me pleasure and worries me at the same time, since he's insisting that we get married sooner. Myself, I'd like to wait till I'm twenty-two, which is what our families agreed on, in fact. I'm apprehensive, but what can I do? I spent my childhood and adolescence in Pakistan, I don't know what an Afghan wife is, and I'm afraid of becoming one. I can't talk about it to my mother, and even less to my father. The only ones I could share my anguish with are my married sisters, but they both live in London! Ludwig seems like a pretty good man, but I wonder if I can trust him. What if his promises are forgotten as soon as the ceremony's over? I don't want very much, though, only for him to listen to my views and really take my personality into account. Physically, I'm not particularly attracted to him. As a little girl, I dreamed of a Prince Charming who would fulfill my every wish! Now I have to adapt to the reality. My parents want this union because Ludwig is part of the family and his father has a good job. He's what's called a catch. With him, I won't ever do without. If I let this chance pass me by, it probably won't present itself again, and the next one could very well be worse! In any case, I'm obliged to bow to the will of my parents, since everything has already been decided."

She breaks off for a few moments and seems to be thinking.

"Of course that frightens me! The only thing Ludwig's told me is that he doesn't need a 'professor' in the house. What does that mean, except that he doesn't want me to continue my studies or to go on teaching after our marriage? He doesn't understand that I need to do that to develop at a personal level and to be happy, which will also make him happy. But in our society, no one thinks about the individual; only the survival of the clan and the community counts. I knew that one day or another I'd be compelled to return to Afghanistan, and now that day has come," Rosa confides to me, already resigned, in the bus that is taking us back home.

Three seats away, sitting next to one of Rosa's younger brothers, her fiancé periodically casts worried glances at us.

"In any case, he doesn't understand English," she concludes sadly.

Conclusion

The U.S. Senate's intelligence report regarding the real justification for military intervention in Iraq was published in the summer of 2004.[1] In light of that report, and given the absence of weapons of mass destruction, the U.S. government no longer has any legitimate reason for having "gone to war." In retrospect, it seems just as clear that the "invasion/liberation" of Afghanistan, which was supposed to lead to the arrest of Osama bin Laden (the aim of the U.S. military response in the region), was rapidly relegated to the background so that the U.S. general staff could concentrate on attacking Iraq and its leader, Saddam Hussein. The dictator was supposedly linked to Al-Qaeda, but it is now well known how inane that theory is. Even so, President George W. Bush stubbornly continues to hide his head in the sand, claiming that today we live in a more secure world than we did in 2001. Yet the experts are categorical: the terrorist threat in the world is higher now than it was four years ago. In short, not only did the U.S. president's obsession with Iraq end with a proliferation of doubts and questions, but he has also squandered a large part of his initial success in Afghanistan.

The media, subject to enormous pressures, have too often offered undeserved publicity to the sources close to the centers of power, which easily succumbed either to psychological bias and the hype surrounding the war or to very professional government propaganda. The excellence of the choreography, the perfection of the script, and the inevitable spinning of information in the era of global media have left little room for sincere and authentic speech.

In Kabul as in Baghdad, military victories were relatively easy, yet the political process has bogged down. In both countries, the people still suffer and wonder about the intentions of the United States. They suspect that it wants, among other things, to exploit their natural resources, even as their own basic needs go unsatisfied. In both places, ethnic populations consolidated by the dictatorship find themselves once more divided. In their still-tribal culture, notions of honor and vengeance prevail. In Afghanistan and Iraq, the Americans rush to adopt "democratic" constitutions whose content, formulated with their help, does not necessarily square with what the clerics recommend. In Iraq, the Shiites, led by Ayatollah Sistani, accepted the document only because it is provisional. The general elections held in January 2005 have not calmed the resistance; nor have they convinced Iraqis of the benefits of democracy. Extreme violence is a daily affair, and the insurgents attack international military troops, the local police forces that are trained and financed by them, and the representatives of non-government organizations with equal intensity.

Afghanistan, though a year ahead of Iraq and also with an elected president, still does not have the impartial state administrations that are suppoosed to represent the people. Outside the capital, power remains in the hands of experienced commanders who prospered thanks to the American windfall distributed in the years of jihad against the Soviet Union (the 1980s), then during the antiterrorist struggle that began in 2001. As we have seen, some of those who had worked for the Taliban continue to be manipulated by the United States.

The scandal of the torture perpetrated in the Iraqi prison of Abu Ghraib shocked the entire world, particularly the United States; but let us wager that similar acts of barbarism were committed—and are still being committed—in Afghanistan, Guantánamo Bay, and everywhere else the United States' war on "terrorism" incarcerates its prisoners on-site.[2]

In Iraq as in Afghanistan, the arrogant behavior of U.S. troops has created rancor and resentment. Afghans who participated in the war against the Taliban have expressed their surprise to me that the U.S. forces don't bomb the laboratories that process opium to turn it into heroin, whose coordinates they know. They suggested the U.S. forces

did not bomb them because all the drugs go to the European market
—not the American one. That indifference to the resumption of the
opium business in Afghanistan and the looting of major cities in Iraq
have shocked the local populations and tarnished forever the Americans' image as "liberators." The mistakes constantly committed by
U.S. troops have widened the gap between them and the residents. The
offenses against the civilian population feed insurrection by the people of both countries, who feel battered and ridiculed, their dignity
compromised. This is especially true during house searches. According to Afghan and Iraqi men, foreign soldiers show no respect for
women, frisking them and bullying them along with the men, sometimes even stealing their meager family savings. Humiliation gives rise
to vengefulness.

In addition, the astonishing decision of the U.S. forces to install
themselves in the former dictator's palaces throughout Iraq, even in
Baghdad, can only increase the gulf between those who now physically
and symbolically occupy the place of the fallen dictator and the local
population, which continues to survive in devastated neighborhoods
without electricity or the slightest comforts. The population understands that these palaces were intentionally saved from bombing, and
for them one oppressor has quite simply replaced another.

In fact, the Americans are increasingly ensconced inside secure sites
that cut them off from the local population. The U.S. Embassy in Baghdad, inside one of Saddam's former palaces in the notorious green zone,
is the best-guarded building in the world. Finally, relations between
soldiers and the local people are strained and difficult, as if the objective was to have as little as contact as possible with a population considered "hostile" overall. In the cities, heavily armed soldiers on patrol,
dealing with unprotected residents, constantly keep their fingers on the
triggers of their automatic pistols.

But the most serious issue is the Americans' lack of willingness to
understand the other. In the first place, this is because the military and
political strategists in Washington have trusted the wrong sources. In
Iraq and Afghanistan, the individuals they have relied on to conduct
and justify their policy emigrated from their home countries more than

fifteen years ago to live in Great Britain or the United States. The strategists are therefore assured that these people will understand them.[3] That decision has only fed suspicion, since the local populations who remained in the country during the many successive wars (in Afghanistan) and the savage dictatorship (in Iraq) harbor deep resentment toward those who once had the opportunity to leave and who chose to come back riding along with the military power of the hour, the United States. Second, in the spring of 2003 the occupier made the mistake of declaring the Iraqi army illegal (in Afghanistan, the national army hasn't been in existence for long). As a result, hundreds of thousands of soldiers were deprived of their pay and work. It is not surprising that the first consequence of that blunder was that some of these malcontents turned to the resistance, led by, among others, supporters of the fallen regime. The disappearance of the regular army just as naturally favored the development of the militias, another major plague.

Another reason that the war on terrorism is far from won is that before the United States engaged militarily in the regions to be "liberated," no one tried to answer the question of why fundamentalism exists. According to Hubert Védrine, former French minister of foreign affairs, fundamentalism is the "final spasm"[4] of the Muslim world in the face of our modernity: "The logic of reestablishing the 'purity' of Islam, which the terrorists want, is unintelligible for our modern societies. We must try to understand it nonetheless." Unable to determine and treat the causes of terrorism, governments have confined themselves to a purely military-police strategy. But this limited strategy is inefficient. We are therefore justified in asking: Why should democracy as we understand it in the West be *the* response? How could what worked in Germany and Japan after World War II be adapted to Afghanistan and Iraq, where it is an open question whether a "Western-style" democracy is desirable in the end? We must acknowledge that the phrase "building democracy" does not mean the same thing at all on the U.S. side and on the side of the two "liberated" countries. When the Americans speak of human rights, the market economy, and the civic responsibility of self-governance, the people of these countries hear immediate reparation for war damages, employment, and a decent standard of living for everyone—in other words, a reflection of the prosperous existence they believe belongs to every citizen of Western countries, since that is what they see on the satellite television channels to which they now have access. My Afghan and Iraqi interlocutors were always astonished, even dismayed, when I informed them that thieves, criminals, and corrupt and privileged individuals also exist in the West. That tremendous misunderstanding marks the extent of the distrust and incomprehension existing between different cultures.

Finally, even conceding that no Afghan longs for the return of the Taliban and no Iraqi for that of Saddam, many openly regret the loss of the security that those two dictatorial systems imposed. The reconstruction that goes hand in hand with democratization is now and again interrupted by the reality of a pervasive lack of security. Since the August 2003 attack on the representative of the United Nations in Iraq, the activities of that international organization have clearly slowed, and the same happened in the southern part of Afghanistan after the murder of an expatriate on the High Commission for Refugees in November of the same year.

Lack of security, devastation, unkept promises of reconstruction: the people of Iraq and Afghanistan have difficulty understanding that such is the price of "liberation." And we in the West have difficulty admitting that they are not immediately as happy as we would like them to be. In both countries, moreover, the Americans are now negotiating with their former adversaries. In Iraq, after Al-Falluja spent weeks fighting U.S. troops in April 2004, the command of the city was assigned to a former member of Saddam's Republican Guard, despite the early de-Baathification decrees. In Afghanistan, when it appeared that President Karzai was incapable of enforcing the law outside the capital, negotiations were undertaken with "moderate" Taliban controlling the provinces to contain the influence of war chiefs. That inevitable realpolitik can only bewilder the residents.

The state of Afghan and Iraqi societies in the aftermath of the U.S. attacks reminds me of the state of Russian society after the Soviet empire was dismantled. I have lived in Russia for eight years and have witnessed that many Russians (those over fifty) at first were euphoric and frightened but gradually succumbed to nostalgia for a regime that, though certainly disgraced, was at least well known and guaranteed them a more or less secure future. In Iraq and Afghanistan, the euphoria of the population soon gave way to distrust and even open hostility. We in the West have to cope with this and be patient.

July 2005

Acknowledgments

I am infinitely grateful to Mona Khalidi for her thoughtful reading of the work and to the entire team at Beacon Press for wanting to bring it to an English-speaking audience as quickly as possible! I really enjoyed their enthusiasm.

Many thanks to my French editor, Claude Durand, for understanding the freedom I needed; to Hélène Guillaume for her efficient and flawless collaboration; and, more generally, to the Fayard team, which has supported me in the last five years.

Many journalist colleagues and specialists in the countries I refer to helped me to prepare for this trip. Although I cannot name them all, I would like to thank the following here: Alexandre Adler in Paris, Charlie Santos in Tashkent, and Marco Vigevani in Milan; Amr El-Bayoumi, Dr. Soheir Morsy, and Dr. Ashraf El-Bayoumi in Cairo, and Nyer Abdou, journalist at the weekly newspaper *Al-Ahram*; Bernard Bajolet, French ambassador to Baghdad, and François Blamont, former cultural adviser in Baghdad; Roland Besenval, director of the Délégation archéologique française en Afghanistan (DAFA; French Archaeological Delegation in Afghanistan) in Kabul; Anthony Borden and Tom de Wall in London; Maggy Zanger, Hiwa Osman, and the entire team of the Institute for War and Peace (IWPR) in Baghdad; Guy Causse and Joseph Dato of Médecins du monde (Doctors of the World); Jacques de Champchesnel, Éric de Lavarène, David Wahab, and the entire team of the NGO Aïna in Kabul; Hachémi Chekeba from the Afghan Embassy in Belgium and Aurore Juillard and Daoud Hachémi of the organization Afghanistan libre (Free Afghanistan) in Kabul; Pierre Chuvin, director of the Institut français d'études anatoliennes (IFEA; French Institute for Anatolian Studies) in Istanbul and his researchers; Jean-François Pérouse; Mark Franchetti, Moscow correspondent for the *Sunday Times*; Filippo Grandi, director of the United Nations High Commission for Refugees (UNHCR) in Kabul; Jean-Pierre Guinhut, French ambassador to Kabul; Peter Maas, reporter at large for the *New York Times Magazine*; Yves Manville of the French Embassy in Dushanbe, Tajikistan; Owen Matthews, Istanbul correspondent for *Newsweek*; Elisabetta Pique, Rome correspondent for the Argentine daily *La Nacion*; Frédéric Roussel, director of the Agence d'aide à la coopération technique et au développement (ACTED; Agency for Aid in Technical Cooperation and Development) and its remarkable local teams; Olivier Roy in Paris; Aram Saed, Baghdad correspondent for KURDsat; M. Sezgin, Turkish consul in France, and Nilgün Pirlot, head of press relations at the Turkish Embassy in France; Antoine de Tarlé, chief executive of *Ouest-France*; Murat Uyurkulak and Mavi in Diyarbakir; Claudine Vernier-Palliez, reporter at large at *Paris-Match*; Brian Williams, professor at the University of Massachusetts and contributor to *Terrorism Monitor*.

I would also particularly like to thank Pierre-Jean Luizard, whose *La question irakienne* (Paris: Fayard, 2002) was very valuable to me.

Notes

Introduction

1. The media have dubbed the territory located west of Baghdad the "Sunni triangle"; it is known for the authoritarianism of its conservative Sunni tribes. Under the old regime, the majority of officers in the Iraqi army and in the security organizations came from this region. Populated primarily by Sunnis and former collaborators of Saddam Hussein, it more or less forms a triangle marked out by Baghdad, Tikrīt, and Al-Fallujah.

2. En Route to Erbil

1. In 1992, thanks to a French initiative adopted by the UN and approved by the United States, the approximately four million Iraqi Kurds acquired their autonomy. Protected by U.S. and British planes in the "no-fly zones" of the Baghdad regime, autonomous Kurdistan of Iraq was able to evolve. After the first Gulf war, Baghdad completed its withdrawal of its civil administration from Kurdistan. The elections of May 1992 established the supremacy of Massoud Barzani's Kurdistan Democratic Party (KDP) and Jalal Talabani's Patriotic Union of Kurdistan (PUK), the two major Kurdish parties. The Kurdish "federal state" was proclaimed by the Kurdish parliament on October 4, 1992. Beginning in 1996, the UN Oil-for-Food Program also authorized the Kurds to receive 13 percent of Iraqi oil revenues.
2. Iraq is made up of four ethnic groups. The majority are Arabs living in the central and southern parts of the country. The Kurds comprise 16 to 18 percent of the population, and the Turkomans, 9 or 10 percent. The rest are Chaldeo-Assyrians, a group of Christians.

3. A Kurdish Family

1. Erbil, one of the oldest cities in the world, has been inhabited continously since the second millennium BCE. It was one of the important religious cities of Assyria, having been Christianized very early, and it served as an episcopal see until the ninth century. A large Assyrian Christian community still lives there.
2. From the name of an island where the prophet Muhammad is said to have gone. Based

in Qatar, where it was created in 1996, the private television channel Al-Jazeera became famous for covering almost exclusively the war in Afghanistan and broadcasting videos and sound recordings attributed to Osama bin Laden, head of the terrorist network Al-Qaeda. In mid-2004, the channel again came under fire from critics in the United States, who had already complained of its coverage of the war in Afghanistan.

3. This view would be seriously called into question in the wake of the double suicide attack that blew up the offices of the two main Kurdish parties on February 1, 2004, in Erbil, the day of the Feast of Sacrifice.

4. General Abdul Karim Kassem is one of the putschists who overthrew the Hashemite monarchy on July 14, 1958. He was in turn overthrown and executed on February 8, 1963, by officials in the Baath Party, the major party of Arab nationalism in Iraq.

5. Yet it was Kassem, who, in a show of Arab-Kurdish brotherhood, authorized the activities of the KDP. The 1958 constitution recognizes Kurdish as an official language, and it began to be taught in the schools at that time. Nevertheless, in 1961, after the bloody confrontations between Turkomans and Kurds in Kirkuk, the war resumed in Kurdistan. It lasted until 1968.

6. On March 6, 1975, the Algiers accords on the Shatt al Arab watershed between Iraq and Iran led the Shah to drop the Kurds. The Shah of Iran had supported the Kurdish leader Mustafa Barzani in his struggle against the central Iraqi government since 1974.

7. Ziveh is in the province of Iranian Kurdistan.

8. While participating actively in the actions of the U.S. Special Forces that liberated northern Iraq, thousands of *peshmerga* nursed the hope that their collaboration would later be repaid with clear support from the "liberators" for Kurdish demands for a federal state in Iraq. As least that is how the majority of the Kurdish population, now disappointed, understood it.

9. Mosul is located four hundred kilometers north of Baghdad, on the Tigris River. Christianity took root there in the second century. A convent built in the fifth century, which would be turned into a fort, was responsible for the city's development.

4. A YOUNG LEADER

1. The Iraqi Governing Council (IGC) met for the first time on July 13, 2003, in Baghdad. It was dissolved on June 30, 2004. The naming of its twenty-five "self-designated" members was subject to the approval of U.S. civil administrator Paul Bremer, who had right of veto over all their decisions. They could designate the ministers of a future cabinet, name Iraqi ambassadors abroad, approve the budget, and assemble a committee charged with writing the new constitution. Out of concern for "ethnic balance," the council comprised thirteen Shiites, five Sunnis, five Kurds, one Christian, and one Turkoman.

2. According to the PDK's Central Bureau of Research and Study—cited in Kharso Pirbal, *Kurdistan, a Regional Profile: An Economic Study about Iraqi Kurdistan* (Kurdistan, 2001)—in 1999 more than forty-five hundred Kurdish villages were destroyed by the central authorities in Baghdad.

3. The nongovernment organization is Counterpart, a U.S. organization that rebuilt the village south of the green line with the help of the Office of the United Nations High Commissioner for Refugees (UNHCR). After studying the possibility of doing the same in twenty-eight other villages in the Mahmour District, the organization finally gave up because of financing problems and now concentrates on projects in the northern part of the zone.

5. The Major Holidays

1. For just over a hundred dollars, the viewer can access more than eight hundred channels, including CNN, which is exclusively a pay channel, whereas BBC World News and Euronews—highly valued by the Iraqis—are available for free.
2. Launched in 2000, KURDsat is financed by Jalal Talabani's Patriotic Union of Kurdistan (PUK), and Kurdistan TV, launched in 1998, is financed by Massoud Barzani's Kurdistan Democratic Party (KDP).
3. A local cell phone network covers only the city of Sulaimaniya.
4. On February 1, 2004, the day of the Feast of Sacrifice, a double suicide attack perpetrated in the middle of Erbil, at the party headquarters of the KDP and of the PUK, killed more than fifty and wounded two hundred.
5. Mutanabi Street is in the old center of Baghdad, perpendicular to the Tigris. It was named after a major Arab poet (915–965). On Friday mornings, its sidewalks become a used-book market.
6. Mahdī is the twelfth imam in occultation, supposedly "hidden" since 874, whose return is expected by the Shiites.

6. A Turkoman Family

1. This is the name's spelling in Arabic transliteration, or Ersat Hūrmūzlū in Turkish transliteration. Arshad Al-Hirmizi is the author of *The Turkmen and Iraqi Homeland* (Istanbul: Kirkuk Foundation, 2003), an informative work designed to better explain the historical, economic, and social situation of the Turkomans in Iraq for the benefit of the Western media.
2. The "nationality" textbook, for example, devoted a dozen pages to the war between Iraq and Iran, which is called only "the Persian country." It showed Saddam in military dress haranguing his soldiers. The president was called "the Victorious," "the Great Commander," or "Allah's Faithful One."
3. Sherif Ali Ben Al-Hussein is one of three claimants to the Hashemite crown, along with Prince Raad Ben Zeid and Prince Hassan of Jordan. The monarchy was overthrown in 1958.
4. In keeping with the Baghdad regime's "Arabization" plan, members of the so-called ethnic minorities were invited to change "nationality" and become Arabs. If they declined what was modestly called a "correction of nationality," the Kurdish, Turkoman, and Assyrian individuals residing in Kirkuk, Khaniqin, Makhmour, Sinjar, and Tuz Khormatu, districts bordering autonomous Kurdistan, had tremendous difficulty finding work (even in agriculture), purchasing a house, or even having one built.

5. The Northern Oil Company, an Iraqi business, is part of the Iraq National Oil Company (INOC). When the petroleum industry was nationalized in 1972, the INOC replaced the Iraq Petroleum Company (IPC), which had been created in 1927.

6. Kirkuk became part of the Ottoman Empire in 1746, where it remained until after World War I. In 1924 it was given to Iraq by the Council of the League of Nations (CLN), despite Turkey's claims and against the will of the city's own population, which was loyal to the empire.

7. Ankara's interest in the stability of Kirkuk can also be interpreted as a way of preventing the Kurds in Iraq from declaring an independent Kurdish state or broadening their sphere of influence, which Turkey particularly fears. Istanbul has even accepted Washington's offer to send a "limited number" of military observers to the city.

8. Jalal Talabani, leader of the PUK, confirmed the gesture on Thursday, April 10, 2003, by speaking Turkish on CNN television. Talabani then promised that his soldiers would evacuate the city the next day.

9. In March 2003, the Turkish parliament refused to authorize access to U.S. troops and the opening of a northern front based in Turkey.

10. Nine days earlier, another demonstration, this one by Kurds, drew several thousand people but unfolded peacefully.

11. The treaty, signed by the new Turkish republic in 1926, ceded the former Ottoman *vilayet* of Mosul, which included Kirkuk. Quoted in Owen Matthews, "The Citadel of Kirkuk: City of Shadows," *Cornucopia* (May 2003): 54–66.

12. In fact, there are five tombs of the prophet Daniel scattered throughout the Near East.

8. BAGHDAD

1. The obsession with security in Baghdad dates from the attack against UN headquarters on August 19, 2003, which killed thirty-five people, including Sergio Vieira de Mello, the UN's special representative in Iraq. Most security agents are South Africans, usually former soldiers or police officers.

2. The Italian hostage Fabrizio Quattrocchi, murdered on April 14, 2004, was a former guard in the VIP corps who began a new career protecting businessmen in "high-risk" countries.

3. On that day the stage was amply set for the cameras of the Western media gathered at the Sheraton Hotel not far away. No more than a hundred Iraqis, just enough to be filmed, took part in what the chorus of world media called a "historic" scene.

4. See Awadh Al-Tae'e, "Baghdadis Resent Park Encampments," *IWPR's Iraqi Crisis Report,* no. 38 (December 4, 2003). The article can be found at www.iwpr.net.

5. According to the traffic bureau, more than a million cars have arrived in Baghdad since the fall of the old regime. Cited in *IWPR's Iraqi Press Monitor* 69 (May 4, 2004).

6. Under Saddam, billboards that included the names of foreign brands were banned, and advertising was therefore rare.

7. Mohammad Baqir al-Hakim had returned to Iraq in the spring of 2003 after twenty-three years of exile in Iran, where he had headed the Supreme Council for Islamic Revolution in Iraq (SCIRI) and the Badr militias since 1982. Since his death in an attack

on August 29, 2003, his younger brother, Abdel Aziz al-Hakim, a member of the ICG—established and later abolished by the coalition—has taken over the movement.

8. The last remaining younger son of the respected ayatollah is thirty-year-old Moqtada al-Sadr, a young cleric who stood up to the coalition in April 2004 and whose popular Friday sermons, delivered in Al-Kufa, are recorded on CDs and cassettes and sold throughout the country.

9. Ahmad Chalabi is head of the Iraqi National Congress (INC), a party opposing Saddam Hussein. He was able to draw U.S. support during his years in exile and on his return to Baghdad in April 2003, when he became a member of the Iraqi Governing Council. A year later, in April 2004, he was accused of colluding with Iran and was suspected of settling personal scores, abducting and torturing citizens on the pretext of de-Baathification, which he fervently defended. Finally, he was accused of widespread corruption. Chalabi, from a rich family of secular Shiite bankers, is extremely unpopular in Iraq.

10. The seventh and ninth imams are Moussa Al-Kazim and his grandson Mohammad Al-Taqi.

11. After several months of equivocation, the U.S. Army finally agreed to arm the fifty thousand police officers in the city, to whom it had transferred responsibility for maintaining law and order on June 30, 2004. Suspicion is still rampant, however.

9. A DOMINICAN FRIAR

1. According to Pierre-Jean Luizard, *La question irakienne* (Paris: Fayard, 2002), 42n1, the Assyrians are "one of the Christian communities of Iraq. Heirs to the old Eastern Syrian Church, also known as the Church of Persia, they represent what remains of the Nestorian heresy, one of the first major schisms of Christianity, which took place in the early fifth century . . . and separated the monophysites (Copts, Syriacs, Armenians) from Byzantine Christianity."

2. Again according to Luizard, *La question irakienne,* 42n1, the vernacular language of the Assyrians is Soureth, "a modern version of Syriac," itself derived from Aramaic. It belongs to the northern Semitic group (like Hebrew).

3. The library in the convent of Mosul contains forty thousand volumes.

4. Oriana Fallaci is a seventy-year-old Italian journalist and specialist in the Middle East, whose *Rage and the Pride* (New York: Rizzoli, 2002) sold more than a million copies in Italy. Written in the aftermath of the attacks of September 11, 2001, it presents itself as a declaration of war against Islamic fundamentalism. In France organizations such as the Ligue internationale contre le racisme et l'antisémitisme, or LICRA (International League against Racism and Anti-Semitism) and the Mouvement contre le racisme et pour l'amitié entre les peuples, or MRAP (Movement against Racism and for Friendship among Peoples of the World) took legal action against her for "inciting racial hatred" and "Islamophobia."

5. Samuel Huntington is known throughout the world for his *Clash of Civilizations and the Remaking of World Order* (New York: Simon and Schuster, 1996), in which he predicted that in the future conflicts would come from the interaction between Western

arrogance, Islamic intolerance, and Chinese assertiveness. Huntington is an American political scientist and the chairman of the Harvard Academy for International and Area Studies.

6. Daryush Shayegan, born in 1935, was professor of Indian studies and comparative philosophy at the University of Tehran. Former director of the Iranian Center for the Study of Civilizations, he now divides his time between Paris and Tehran. He is the author of *Qu'est-ce qu'une révolution religieuse* (Paris: Albin Michel, 1991); *La lumière vient de l'Occident* (Paris: Éditions de l'Aube, 2003); and *Cultural Schizophrenia: Islamic Societies Confronting the West* (Syracuse, NY: Syracuse University Press, 1997), among other works.

10. A RESISTANCE FIGHTER AND A FORMER FEDAYEE

1. Abdel Aziz al-Hakim is the younger brother of Ayatollah Mohammad Baqir al-Hakim, head of the Supreme Council for Islamic Revolution in Iraq (SCIRI). The ayatollah was murdered on August 29, 2003, as he was leaving Imam Ali's mausoleum in An Najaf. Abdel replaced his brother as the head of the SCIRI and runs the Badr militias composed of deserters and exiles living in Iran who fought beside the Iranians during the Iran-Iraq War. He was also a member of the Iraqi Governing Council. The ayatollah returned after twenty-three years of exile in Qom, Iran. He left Iraq a year after Saddam Hussein was named president and just after the return of Imam Khomeini in Iran. The Shiite Al-Dawa Party was founded by students of their father, the Grand Ayatollah, who was a leader in the *hawza* and died in 1970. During the Gulf War in 1991, Mohammad Baqir came back to Iraq, believing he would be aided by the United States in his rebellion against Saddam's central power. When he saw that was not the case, he returned to Iran.

2. Here Abu is alluding to the militias of the two Kurdish leaders, several thousand men attached to the security forces of the autonomous Kurdish region, a place whose status has not yet been fixed. But he is also referring to the Badr militias—between four and eight thousand men—which were officially dissolved but are still very present. These militias belong to Abdel Aziz al-Hakim, head of the Supreme Council for Islamic Revolution in Iraq (SCIRI), and to the "Army of the Mahdī," the militia of the young Islamic leader Moqtada Baqir al-Sadr.

3. Uday was the founder of Saddam's militia of fedayeen, whose sole mission was to sacrifice itself to defend the dictator.

4. Uday and Qusay, Saddam Hussein's younger son, were killed on July 22, 2003, by U.S. forces in Mosul after violent fighting.

5. Saddam Hussein was arrested on December 4, 2003, in an underground hiding place not far from his fief of Tikrit. He was imprisoned in Iraq in a place kept secret by the United States while awaiting his trial. The trial began in the summer of 2004.

11. IN THE "SUNNI TRIANGLE"

1. In April 2004 photos depicting the torture and degrading treatment of prisoners in Abu Ghraib, taken by their jailers, U.S. soldiers, caused a scandal in the United States

and in the rest of the world. The public wondered whether these were mere "incidents," as the legal proceedings instituted suggest, or whether the episode revealed "special" interrogation methods of the U.S. Army and intelligence service that were also used in Afghanistan. In a speech on May 24, 2004, President George W. Bush announced that the prison in Abu Ghraib would be demolished as soon as a new penitentiary had been built.

2. Following my stay in Al-Falluja in February 2004, the city was besieged by U.S. troops in April, after four U.S. civilians were murdered and their mutilated bodies exposed to the ire of the populace. The offensive began on April 5 and resulted in hundreds of dead civilians. The stranglehold was loosened after a former Iraqi division commander was placed at the head of a "protection army of Al-Falluja" (subordinate to the U.S. Marines), charged with restoring order in the insurgent Sunni bastion. In May the marines left Al-Falluja after "arrangements" were made to hand it over to the Iraqi Civil Defense Corps (ICDC), and after an evacuation lasting a month, families were allowed to return home.

3. During the siege of Al-Falluja in April 2004, several tons of food and medication were collected in the Shiite mosques of Baghdad and sent to the besieged Sunni city. Many faithful Sunni Muslims also prayed in the mosque of Ali's mausoleum in An Najaf, a bastion of Shiite Islam.

4. Brigadier Abd al-Salam Aref was involved in the putsch that overthrew Kassem on November 18, 1963. In 1966 he was killed in a helicopter accident that some considered an act perpetrated by the Baath Party.

5. The French law on secularism, passed on March 15, 2004, bans all items displaying "any religious affiliation openly."

12. EN ROUTE TO AN NAJAF

1. See Kamal Ali, "Children Held for Ransom," *IWPR's Iraqi Crisis Report,* no. 43 (January 9, 2004), available at www.iwpr.net. According to the author, a journalist, a special unit of the police was created in November 2003 to fight the rash of kidnappings. The unit focuses on cases targeted by central command and is not directly available to the public. About a hundred gangs were operating in Baghdad and in the neighboring provinces.

2. Ali, a cousin and son-in-law of the prophet Muhammad, converted to Islam as a child and became its fourth caliph. He was stabbed to death close to fifteen hundred years ago on the threshold of the Kufa Mosque, not far from An Najaf. He is revered by the 110 million Shiites in the world—out of 1 billion Muslims—as the Prophet's only true successor.

13. A SHIITE FAMILY

1. Since the clashes between U.S. soldiers and Moqtada al-Sadr's militiamen in April and the summer of 2004, the stream of pilgrims to An Najaf and Karbala has temporarily dropped off.

2. Concerned with the influx of illegal pilgrims (most of them Iranians) into Iraqi territory—notwithstanding the explosions of March 2, 2004, at the mausoleum in Karbala—Grand Ayatollah Sistani has issued a fatwa addressed especially to "our dear Iranian brothers," in which he declares *haram* (forbidden by religion) the crossing of the border without going through checkpoints. See Abdul Amir Al-Jubury and Emad Al-Sharee, "Pilgrim Influx, a Mixed Blessing," *IWPR's Iraqi Crisis Report*, no. 53 (March 15, 2004), available at www.iwpr.net.

3. Karbala is particularly revered by the Shiites for its mausoleum of Imam Hussein, who is considered a martyr. Five hundred yards away, one also finds that the mausoleum of his half-brother, Abbas, who fought beside him. Al-Kufa became the birthplace of Shiism after the death of Ali, who had made it his capital. An Najaf is the fourth largest holy city of Islam, after Mecca, Medina, and Jerusalem.

4. During a trip to Iran in September 1997, I entered the mausoleum of Imam Reza, the eighth imam, located in Mashhad in the northwestern part of the country, on the border with Afghanistan.

5. See the well-documented article by Usama Hashem Redha, "Competing Interests in Holy City," *IWPR's Iraqi Crisis Report*, no. 47 (February 9, 2004), available at www.iwpr.net.

6. In the wake of April 9, 2003, former prisoners created an organization, the Committee of Free Prisoners, to help the families of victims identify the bones of their loved ones in the many common graves discovered after the fall of the regime. They also obtained access to some of the archives of the former intelligence service, the Mukhabarat, and have undertaken to examine them and inform the families.

7. In March 1991, after the first Gulf war, the Shiite community in the south rose up against the central government. The repression undertaken by entire garrisons of Saddam's Republican Guard was bloody and brutal. According to the figures cited by Pierre-Jean Luizard in *La question irakienne*, there were "close to thirty thousand dead within a few days in the single city of Karbala, and more than one hundred thousand in the Shiite region."

8. The Army of Mehdi, the militia of Moqtada al-Sadr, was created in late August 2003, after the cleric Mohammad Baqir al-Hakim was murdered as he was leaving Ali's mausoleum in An Najaf. The army was also formed in reaction to the U.S. occupation, which it is fighting.

9. In the spring of 2004, a 5 percent tax was imposed, as in the other countries of the Persian Gulf.

10. Among Shiites, fatwas have the force of law.

11. In 2004 the average cost of the trip was on the rise. In the preceding years, under Saddam, fourteen thousand had been allowed to make the trip.

12. The first decree issued by Paul Bremer, temporary chief administrator in Iraq until the summer of 2004, banned former Baathists from playing a role in post-Saddam society. A year later, a few weeks before his departure, he partly rescinded his decision.

13. Under the former dictatorial regime, access to the Internet, unlike the possession of a satellite dish, was never completely banned, but it was severely restricted to about sixty

government-controlled centers. Today, given the prevailing legislative vacuum, many unlicensed cybercafes have opened. In-home connections, possible but not yet wide-spread, include the price of the cable and its installation, in addition to a subscription fee of fifty dollars a month. For more details, see Hisham Karim Alwan, "Internet Demand Spirals," *IWPR's Iraqi Crisis Report,* no. 44 (January 26, 2004), available at www.iwpr.net.

14. The vast majority of Baathists (close to two million people) were ordinary members of the party. Participation in the party assumed the form of a pyramidal structure: about thirty thousand in the next rank of *farqā,* two thousand in the next, then two hundred, and finally only twelve at the highest level. Bremer's decree barred ranking members, but not ordinary ones, from performing their duties.

14. A FORMER ADMIRAL

1. The world community as a whole considers the tragedy of Halabja a genocide perpe-trated against the Kurdish people. To this day, it has not been acknowledged by the Iraqi authorities. What Adnan relates is the official version. According to Pierre-Jean Luizard, *La question irakienne,* 198, "Halabja has thus come to be known as the Kurd-ish Oradour." [The residents of Oradour, France, were massacred by the Germans on June 10, 1944—trans.]

2. The British were preoccupied with turning Iraq into a "modern" state, by European stan-dards. Under the Hashemite monarchy they set in place, one of the first institutions es-tablished was the Iraqi army. The Anglo-Iraqi treaty of 1922 stipulated it would be overseen by the British. In 1921 the first ministry set in place was the Defense Ministry.

3. The six-lane highway connecting Safwan to An Nāsirīya was built in 1987. The high-way made it easier for the Iraqi army to invade Kuwait. In 1991 it was baptized the "road of death" after thousands of Iraqi soldiers fleeing the front were bombed by the U.S. Air Force. See Pierre Pinta, *L'Irak* (Paris: Karthala, 2003), 187.

4. See *Al Raey, Al Aam,* no. 1941 (September 15, 1968).

5. *Issa* in Arabic, considered a prophet and messenger of God and a precursor of Muham-mad.

6. See Yves Thoraval, *Dictionnaire de civilisation musulmane* (Paris: Larousse, 2001), 78.

15. A MAN OF THE THEATER

1. *Azzaman* is a daily Arabic-language newspaper published in London.

2. This happened before the Abu Ghraib Prison scandal erupted in May 2004.

16. EN ROUTE TO KUNDŪZ

1. By the terms of a ten-year accord signed by the heads of state of the Russian Federation and Tajikistan in 1993, a contingent of eleven thousand men under Russian command, including eight thousand Tajiks, ensures the protection of the border between Tajik-istan and Afghanistan, which is 837 miles long. This is the sole example of collabora-tion between a federal Russian structure and citizens of another country. The Russian

border guards of Tajikistan are 80 percent Tajik, the majority of them conscripts, whereas the officers' corps remains almost 100 percent Russian. In 2004 the responsibility for guarding the Tajik-Afghan border passed gradually from the Russians to the Tajiks. At the end of 2004, the Russians left, and now all guards on this border are Tajiks.

17. A TEACHER

1. A Tajik must pay sixty U.S. dollars for a one-month visa for Afghanistan.

2. Hamid Karzai, former vice minister of foreign affairs, is a Pashtun who was chosen as head of the interim government when Afghan leaders met in Bonn in December 2001 for what were known as the Bonn accords. He was elected president of that government at the Loya Jirga (Grand Council) of June 2002 and is running for the presidency in the general elections of September 2004, initially planned for June but delayed because voter registration was occurring at a snail's pace.

3. With the presidential elections of late 2004 and the parliamentary elections of 2005 in mind, the government planned to disarm and demobilize about forty thousand Afghan militiamen and collect all the heavy weapons circulating in the country. More than six thousand militiamen have already been disarmed through the Disarmament, Demobilization, and Reintegration (DDR) program, set in place jointly by the Afghan Ministry of Defense and the UN. In its experimental phase, implemented in five provinces since late 2003, this program was financed by the international community. Over the long term, its aim is to return one hundred thousand militiamen to civilian life.

4. In October 2003 NATO approved the principle of extending the ISAF's field of action beyond Kabul. That extension is supposed to be set in place by civilian military organizations known as provincial reconstruction teams (PRT), but NATO has struggled to find participating countries who will send troops. Only one PRT under the command of the ISAF, run by the German army and consisting of two hundred men, is operational in Kundūz. Twelve other PRTs are run by the U.S. Army, two of them assisted by British and New Zealand contingents.

5. In 1971 Burhanuddin Rabbani, a Tajik from a village in Bada, graduate of Al-Azhar University in Cairo, and professor of theology in Kabul before the war, founded the Jamiyat-i-Islami Party (to which Commander Massoud also belonged), which became one of the most powerful armed factions during the jihad against the Soviet occupation forces. He became president of the Islamic state of Afghanistan after the mujahideen took power in 1992, then the nonmilitary head of the Northern Alliance, the only government recognized by most Western countries while the Taliban were in power.

18. EN ROUTE TO BADAKHSHĀN

1. The Tajik commander Ahmed Shah Massoud, born in 1952, was the mythical "Lion of the Panshir," so named by the Western press after his native valley, the center of resistance to the Soviet invader and then to the Taliban. He was educated at the Istiqlal secondary school of Kabul, where he learned French. A member of the Jamiyat-i-Islami Party of Burhanuddin Rabbani, he took to fighting the Soviets when they invaded in

1979. His control of the valley, which remained inviolate until his death, earned him a reputation as a brilliant tactician in the field and a military strategist. He was minister of defense in the Rabbani government in 1992, before being forced to retire in 1996 when the Taliban arrived in Kabul, in the Panshir. He went to Europe, notably France, in the spring of 2001 in an attempt to gain the support of Western countries. He was assassinated on September 9, 2001, by two Arabs posing as journalists.

2. The vehicles arrive in Herāt via containers. They come from Dubai, in the United Arab Emirates, a true hub for trafficking in many goods, including automobiles for the Southeast Asian and Persian Gulf markets.

19. AN ENGINEER

1. There is also Tajik Badakhshān, more commonly known as the Pamirs, located just on the other side of the Panj River, which becomes Amu Dar'ya and marks the border between Tajikistan, Uzbekistan, and Afghanistan.

2. The Loya Jirga dates from the monarchical period. It is the Grand Council assembling different representatives of the population and charged with debating key questions on the country's political future. Since the fall of the Taliban regime in the autumn of 2001, the coalition forces have convoked two Loya Jirga, the first—called an "emergency" session—in June 2002, and the second in December 2003.

3. The new Afghan army (NAA), which came into being in May 2002 within the context of the reconstruction of the Afghan government, has the mission of "guaranteeing the country's stability." The multiethnic army, whose creation was stipulated by the interAfghan accords in Bonn in late 2001, answers to the transitional government and is supposed to allow the state to establish its authority in the provinces. The NAA is about ten thousand men strong, having encountered major problems with recruitment and desertion. By the summer of 2004, in time for the September presidential election, the NAA had almost twelve thousand soldiers. Its training is supervised by the U.S. Army, with the help of Great Britain and France. In the long run, the objective of the government and the international community is to train nearly seventy thousand soldiers. Two years after its creation, the NAA is deployed in the south, southeast, and east of the country, where it contributes on a modest scale, alongside the U.S. Army, to the struggle against the Taliban and their Al-Qaeda allies.

4. The Northern Alliance, or United Front, under the leadership of Commander Massoud, was made up of military forces opposed to the Taliban. In October 2002 they joined with those of Uzbek general Rashid Dostum (under the indirect command of the U.S. Special Forces units) to evacuate the Taliban from the north of the country.

5. Mohammad Qasim Fahim was Massoud's right-hand man for many years. As vice commander of the Northern Alliance, he later became minister of defense in the Karzai government.

6. Najibullah, an Afghani politician, was trained as a doctor—which explains why the Afghans called him Dr. Najib—and was former head of the secret service (Khad). He seized power in a coup d'état in 1986, deposing the third Marxist president, Babrak Karmal. He resigned in 1992 when the mujahideen came to power, tried unsuccess-

fully to flee, and took refuge in the United Nations building of Kabul, where he lived for four years until the Taliban flushed him out in 1996, tortured him to death along with his brother, and hanged both bodies from lampposts in a square in the center of the city.

7. Gulbuddin Hekmatyar is a notorious anti-Western Islamist. In May 2004 members of his party, the Hezb-i-Islami, are said to have rallied behind Karzai's government, though he himself is still on the run. Originally allied with Burhanuddin Rabbani and hence close to Commander Massoud, he distanced himself from them and created his own party, which became the favorite of the Pakistani secret service. Through the Pakistanis, the American CIA secretly financed the Hezb-i-Islami during the jihad against the Soviets. After refusing the position of prime minister in the Rabbani government, Hekmatyar fought his former allies the Northern Alliance. For the Afghans, this was civil war. Under the Taliban regime, he took refuge in Iran, returning in early 2002, only to disappear again.

8. I heard that questioning of motives many times from other Afghans, who were always quick to criticize the United Nations staff, which is considered extremely corrupt and seems to the people of Afghanistan to be more preoccupied with its personal comfort and safety than with efficient action in the field. Although these criticisms seem to be exaggerated, a certain insular way of life on the part of employees and behavior that is sometimes considered provocative in Muslim countries, are certainly regrettable.

9. Zahir Shah, the last king of Afghanistan, assumed the throne in 1933 at the age of nineteen, after his father was assassinated. He reigned until his cousin Mohammad Daud Khan dethroned him in 1973. Daud Khan abolished the monarchy and proclaimed a republic. Zahir Shah went into exile in Italy, where he lived for twenty-nine years; in April 2002 he returned to Kabul, where his political role is symbolic.

10. On December 27, 1979, the Soviets entered Kabul. They executed Hafizullah Amin, who had been in power since March, and imposed Babrak Karmal, who had returned with them from the USSR, as head of the government.

11. The television station stopped showing women's faces during the civil war of the mujahideen (1992–1996) and was quite simply banned under the fundamentalist regime of the Taliban (1996 to late 2001). In early 2002, when the moderate government of Hamid Karzai came to power, its broadcasts resumed. Women have participated presenting news programs on national television (broadcast only in Kabul) and on provincial television stations. Their presence on-screen usually remains unobtrusive, however, even though the new Afghan constitution, adopted on January 4, 2004, officially recognizes equality between men and women.

20. A GYNECOLOGIST

1. Despite the April 2004 appeal by Afghan president Hamid Karzai for a jihad against drug trafficking, which, according to him, jeopardizes the stability of institutions, Afghanistan remains the foremost producer of opium, from which morphine and heroin are derived. Nearly 90 percent of the heroin consumed in Europe comes from Afghanistan. The production of opium in 2003, estimated at 6.5 million pounds and

almost two hundred thousand acres, represents an increase from the already elevated 2002 figures. It is said to have generated a revenue of $2.3 billion, equivalent to half the gross domestic product of Afghanistan, according to the UN. In an attempt to change that situation, in April 2004 the Afghan government launched a national campaign to eradicate the poppy fields in three provinces—Nangarhār, Kandahār, and Helmand—with the aim of destroying nearly 10 percent of the next poppy crop. But that campaign remained ineffective: the eradication, conducted by progovernment militias whose leaders were often themselves involved in that lucrative business, was conducted in already harvested fields, or the peasants managed to pay off the leaders to spare their poppy fields.

22. A WAR CHIEF

1. Dostum was an ally of the Soviets before changing camps in 1992, when he joined with Commander Massoud to participate in the fall of Najibullah, the last Communist president, and in the taking of Kabul by the mujahideen. After fighting beside Massoud and Rabbani against their rival Gulbuddin Hekmatyar, he formed an alliance with the latter in 1994. Two years later, when the Taliban were marching on Kabul, he again went over to Massoud's side. Under the Taliban, he fled to Turkey twice, in 1997 and 1998. In 2001 he agreed to fight against the Taliban alongside the Northern Alliance, assisted by U.S. special commandos, who managed to retake the city of Mazār in November.

2. The Jamiyat-i-Islami Party was run by Professor Burhanuddin Rabbani, former president of the republic following the fall of Najibullah in 1992 and nonmilitary head of the Northern Alliance, the only Afghan government recognized by many foreign powers during the Taliban period. The Jamiyat was one of the seven mujahideen parties based in Peshawar, Pakistan, in the 1980s. Composed primarily of Tajik minorities in the north, it was the party of the famous war commander Ahmed Shah Massoud and of Ismail Khan, the strongman from Herāt in the west of the country. The Jamiyat battled other mujahideen groups for control of Kabul between 1992 and 1995. Since 1996, it has fought the Taliban under various names (United Front, Northern Alliance).

3. It was under President Najibullah that certain large border cities such as Mazār and Herāt were authorized to house subsidiaries of the Ministry of Foreign Affairs in order to develop diplomatic relations with neighboring countries.

4. See the excellent report by Brian Glyn Williams, "Rachid Dostom: America's Secular Ally in the War on Terror," *Terrorism Monitor* 1, no. 5 (November 20, 2003), available from the Jamestown Foundation, www.jamestown.org.

5. A trained engineer who became an Islamist, Gulbuddin Hekmatyar was prime minister under the mujahideen. Currently on the run, he is a former protégé of Burhanuddin Rabbani. He left Afghanistan after Daud Khan's coup d'état in 1973 and in the 1980s formed his mujahideen party, the Hezb-i-Islami (Islamic Party), based in Pakistan. During the jihad against the Soviets, the party received financial support from

the Pakistani government via its secret service (ISI); beginning in 1994, however, Pakistan began to lend more support to the Taliban. Under that regime, Hekmatyar observed the changes in his country from Iran, where he had taken refuge. He is now being sought as a "terrorist" by U.S. authorities.

23. EN ROUTE TO KABUL

1. The Salang Tunnel's reconstruction, begun in early 2003, was financed primarily by the World Bank at a cost of six million dollars and was carried out by the Turkish business Cukurova. The tunnel was inaugurated by President Karzai on December 28, 2003.

24. KABUL

1. Ahmad Shāh Durrāni reigned between 1747 and 1773. After the battle of Panipat in 1759, his empire extended to the Indus River. His son Tīmūr Shāh, also known as Timur the Lame, succeeded him.
2. King Amānollāh reigned from 1919 to 1929.
3. Abulhaq is talking about the Communist coup d'état. Daud Khan and those close to him were killed and replaced by Taraki, with Babrak Karmal as vice president and prime minister. Both were under Moscow's orders.

25. EN ROUTE TO KANDAHĀR

1. The road from Kabul to Kandahār was finally inaugurated with great pomp and ceremony on December 16, 2003, by President Karzai, just before the opening session of the Loya Jirga.
2. One dollar equals fifty afghanis.

26. A FORMER TALIBAN

1. Bābur (1483–1530) was the first ruler and founder of the Mogul dynasty of India, a descendant of Timur through his father and of Genghis Khan through his mother. As a very young man, this warrior fought to secure his legacy as prince of the Fergana, but he was also a writer and mystic poet, the author, notably, of an autobiography, written in Turkish and titled *Bāburnāma*.
2. Nevertheless, in April 2004, the Afghan government and the U.S. Army would develop a plan allowing the return to the political stage of the Taliban and members of the fundamentalist Hezb-i-Islami Party. To that end, they would divide these people into three categories: a blacklist of criminals (between 100 and 150 people, including the spiritual leader of the fundamentalist militia, Mullah Mohammad Omar, and the head of the Hezb-i-Islami, Gulbuddin Hekmatyar), who would be denied amnesty; a "gray" list of about 200 people, who would be granted conditional amnesty after they had served a prison term; and finally the rest—ordinary fighters, militants, and leaders not involved in acts of terrorism or criminal activities—who would receive unconditional amnesty.

3. Abdul Rasul Sayyaf was one of the most extremist Muslim fundamentalists in Afghanistan and the founder of the Ittihad-i-Islami (Islamic Alliance) Party in 1981, which was financed by Saudi Arabia and various other conservative Arab groups. In 1992, when the mujahideen took power in Kabul, he accepted the post of vice president in the coalition government. He is one of the people who were most destructive to the city, which he fled in 1996. He has now returned to Kabul and is in his fief of Paghman.

4. Mullah Muttawakil is the Taliban's former minister of foreign affairs.

5. Sherzai asked Khan Mohammad, one of his former assistants who came from the same tribe, to fill the post.

6. As I observed everywhere in central Asia and the Caucasus, male dancers use their arms a great deal. In Chechnya, where men's dances are highly valued, the movements are almost jerky.

27. En Route to Khost

1. Under the Taliban regime, any visual representation of a human being was forbidden, and photographers could no longer practice their profession.

28. A Governor and Former Commander

1. The two economies are so closely connected that in March 2004 the shopkeepers of the city of Khost observed a general three-day strike, refusing to open their stores to protest the rise in taxes on goods imported from Pakistan. The authorities, on a broadcast on local public radio, demanded the immediate reopening of all shops and threatened the strikers with fines and prison terms. They even accused "the Taliban and the Al-Qaeda organization" of being behind the strike.

2. He was removed in April 2004 to become minister of mines and industry.

3. Finally arrested in April 2004, Pasha Khan would be pardoned by President Karzai and liberated the same month.

4. The road from Gardez to Khost is no longer occupied by Pasha Khan Zadran's fighters, but he has not stopped getting himself talked about. When Hakim Taniwal was named minister of mines and industry, his position became vacant. Accompanied by six thousand Pashtuns, members of the Zadran tribe, Pasha Khan headed a demonstration demanding that the Karzai government "keep its promises" and name his brother, Amanullah Khan, governor of the province.

29. The Minor Holidays

1. This New Testament was translated from Greek into Pashto and published in Pakistan in 1991.

2. Since mid-2002, ten girls' schools have opened in the district.

3. The only mujahideen who authorized opening schools for girls were Rashid Dostum in the Uzbek north and Ahmed Shah Massoud in the Panshir Valley.

4. [My translation from the French—JMT.]
5. Among Pashtuns, a boy begins to go to the mosque to pray when he is six or seven.
6. On average, there are three families in each house.
7. The destruction of the Buddhist statues took place in March 2001 and was strongly condemned by the international community, which was unable to prevent it.

30. Detour through Peshawar

1. The "Durand line" was established to mark the boundary between the British Empire and Afghanistan in 1893, officially for the duration of a hundred years.
2. The Afghan Pashtun tribes never legally recognized the "Durand line."
3. According to an Afghan custom, it's possible for an engagement party to be held without the fiancée's presence. The important thing is that it happen in the fiancé's family, who organizes everything.

Conclusion

1. National Commission on Terrorism Attacks, *The 9/11 Commission Report: Final Report of the National Commission on Terrorism Attacks upon the United States* (New York: W. W. Norton, 2004).
2. See Mark Danner, "Torture and Truth," *New York Review of Books,* 51, no. 10 (June 10, 2004).
3. Zalmay Khalilzad, for example, current U.S. ambassador to Iraq, ex-ambassador to Afghanistan, and President Bush's representative in Kabul, is an Afghan American. Ahmad Chalabi, a banker whom the Iraqis consider "shady," was until mid-2004 an important partner of the United States in Iraq, a member of the defunct Iraqi Governing Council.
4. See "Horizons," *Le Monde,* interview, March 27, 2004, 16.

Select Bibliography

IRAQ

Luizard, Pierre-Jean. *La question irakienne*. Paris: Fayard, 2002.

Mackey, Sandra. *The Reckoning: Iraq and the Legacy of Saddam Hussein*. New York: W. W. Norton, 2002.

AFGHANISTAN

Barry, Michael. *Le royaume de l'insolence: L'Afghanistan, 1504–2001*. Paris: Flammarion, 2002.

Centlivres, Pierre. *Chroniques afghanes, 1965–1993*. Lausanne: Éditions des Archives contemporaines, 1998.

Delloye, Isabelle. *Des femmes d'Afghanistan*. Paris: Des Femmes, 1980.

Dorronsoro, Gilles. *La révolution afghane*. Paris: Karthala, 2000.

Dupaigne, Bernard. *Afghanistan, rêve de paix*. Paris: Buchet-Chastel, 2002.

Dupaigne, Bernard, and Gilles Rossignol. *Le carrefour afghan*. Paris: Gallimard, 2002.

Dupree, Louis. *Afghanistan*. Princeton, NJ: Princeton University Press, 1973.

Dupree, Nancy Hatch. *An Historical Guide to Afghanistan*. Kabul: Afghan Tourist Organization, 1977.

Zikria, Habib, and François Missen. *Pour mieux comprendre l'Afghanistan*. Paris: Édisud, 2002.